Modern & Contemporary Art at the Virginia Museum of Fine Arts

by John B. Ravenal

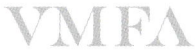

Virginia Museum of Fine Arts, Richmond

Distributed by the University of Virginia Press,
Charlottesville and London

Modern and Contemporary Art at the Virginia Museum of Fine Arts

Library of Congress Cataloging-in-Publication Data available upon request

ISBN 978-0-917046-80-3

Printed in Italy by Mondadori

Produced by the Virginia Museum of Fine Arts, 200 N. Boulevard, Richmond, VA 23220

Edited by Deirdra H. McAfee and Lucy Keshishian Grey
Book design by Jean Kane
Project management by Sara Johnson-Ward
New photography by Katherine Wetzel, Chief Collections Photographer, and Travis Fullerton
Composed by the designer in QuarkXpress. Type set in Futura
Printed on Gardamatte Demi Matt

Front cover: detail of **Number 15, 1948** by Jackson Pollock, see pages 2–3
Back cover: detail of **Jessie #34** by Sally Mann, see pages 232–33

Table of Contents

Funding Credits

Ann and Robert Burrus

The Council of VMFA

Kay and Philip Davidson

Virginia and Birch Douglass

Mary Ann and William Frable

Margaret Freeman

Friends of Art

Agnes Gund and Daniel Shapiro

Deborah and Alan Kirshner

Charlotte and Gil Minor

Sally and Bob Mooney

The Julia Louise Reynolds Fund

Anne and Dick Riley

Carolyn and John Snow

Director's Foreword

This is an exciting time for the Virginia Museum of Fine Arts! Our building expansion, culminating in 2009, will give us fifty percent more exhibition space. During this dynamic period, we are continuing to acquire artworks in every area of our collection, including work by up-and-coming contemporary artists.

This book, by John Ravenal, The Sydney and Frances Lewis Family Curator of Modern and Contemporary Art, not only presents a comprehensive view of the museum's outstanding collection of modern and contemporary art, but also offers a generous taste of the new art and beautiful installations to come.

Modern and Contemporary Art at the Virginia Museum of Fine Arts succeeds the last catalogues of the Modern and Contemporary collection, namely Fred Brandt and Susan Butler's *Late Twentieth-Century Art from the Sydney and Frances Lewis Foundation* (1981), and Fred Brandt's best-selling *Late 20th Century Art: Selections from the Sydney and Frances Lewis Collection in the Virginia Museum of Fine Arts* (1985). Building on those resources, this book highlights new acquisitions and connects them to the collection as a whole, while putting our impressive holdings in the context of worldwide developments in twentieth- and twenty-first-century art.

The most prominent and generous figures in the story of modern and contemporary art collecting at the Virginia Museum of Fine Arts are, of course, Sydney and Frances Lewis. As this book shows, however, the museum has been fortunate in having a community of benefactors as well.

The succession of enterprising Directors of the Virginia Museum of Fine Arts who proceeded me were instrumental in beginning and continuing the growth of the collection featured in this book. We owe thanks to Tom Colt, Leslie Cheek, James M. Brown, Peter Mooz, Paul Perrot and Katharine Lee Reid for their dedication to this extraordinary collection. My immediate predecessors, Michael Brand and Tom Allen, also kept sight of the museum's goal in this area—to acquire significant works of twentieth- and twenty-first-century art. Their leadership during the creation of this book is greatly appreciated.

The benefactors, the curators, and the galleries themselves, like this book, aim to connect art with audience. John Ravenal's discussion of the works and the accompanying images are a wonderful introduction to this rich and intriguing collection. They are also your invitation to visit and revisit the modern and contemporary collection—on every occasion, you will discover something new and understand more about the art of our time.

Alex Nyerges
Director
Virginia Museum of Fine Arts

Acknowledgements

For their support of this book, I am grateful to the Director's Office at the Virginia Museum of Fine Arts, including Michael Brand, former Director; Tom Allen, former Trustee Executive for Administration; Alex Nyerges, Director; and Lee Anne Hurt, Assistant to the Director. I also appreciate the support of Joseph Dye, Chief Curator; Carol Amato, Chief Operating Officer; Suzanne Hall, Acting Associate Director of Marketing and Communications and am grateful to the Publications Department, namely Suzanne Freeman, Publications Manager and Head Librarian; Rosalie West, Editor in Chief; Sarah Lavicka, Assistant Publications Manager and Chief Graphic Designer; Lucy Keshishian Grey, former Editor and freelance proofreader; and especially Jean Kane, Senior Graphic Designer, who created the beautiful object you hold, and Sara Johnson-Ward, Project Manager, who shepherded the book to completion. The majority of editing was placed in the very capable hands of freelancer Deirdra McAfee.

Katherine Wetzel and Travis Fullerton, assisted by Susie Rock, produced extensive new photography, with the help of registrars Mary Sullivan and Susan Turbeville, and art handlers Roy Thompson, Randy Wilkinson, and Geoff Strong. Howell Perkins, Head of Photographic Resources, and assistant Margaret Richardson, deserve recognition for their considerable efforts. Research assistance was ably provided by Lee Viverette, Reference Librarian; Jon Stuhlman, former Research Assistant; Caryl Burtner, Administrative Coordinator; Lisa Ashe, University of Virginia; and Maxwell Perry, Virginia Commonwealth University. In addition, I am grateful for assistance from the Lewis private collection curator Jay Barrows.

I would also like to acknowledge my predecessor, Fred Brandt, and current and former staff in the Modern and Contemporary Department—Julie Boyd, Margo Crutchfield, Tosha Grantham, and Ashley Kistler—for their roles in building the collection, about which I have had the privilege to write.

For their fundraising efforts on behalf of this project, sincere thanks are due to Pete Wagner, Director of Development, assisted by Anne Barriault and Sharon Casale, and with the special effort of Robert L. Burrus, Jr., a great friend of the museum. For their tremendous generosity in helping make this book a reality, I am deeply grateful to our funders, who are recognized on page v.

As ever, my love and gratitude go to Virginia Pye, Eva, and Daniel.

John B. Ravenal
The Sydney and Frances Lewis Family Curator
of Modern and Contemporary Art
Virginia Museum of Fine Arts

Introduction

Although Modern and Contemporary art spans just 100 of the 6,000 years of world culture represented in the Virginia Museum of Fine Arts' holdings, the collection looms large and is nationally recognized as outstanding.

This book focuses on postwar art, the Modern and Contemporary collection's strength. The 114 works in these pages range from Jackson Pollock's dynamic 1948 drip painting to Kehinde Wiley's 2006 hip-hop-meets-Old-Master portrait.

Here is a portable visit to this part of the museum—a chance to recall old favorites and to discover hidden treasures and new acquisitions. Works appear chronologically within the book's three sections—paintings; sculpture and video art; and prints, drawings, photographs, and collage.

The Forties and Fifties | AbEx, Action, Color Field

The postwar period that begins this book was particularly fertile for American art. Abstract Expressionism, or New York School art, reflected New York's rise in the 1950s as the art world's new center. The New York School's high-minded embrace of the unconscious, of myth, and of aspects of European Modernism resulted in a uniquely American style.

Some of these artists were called Action painters; their broad slashing strokes were outward signs of strong emotion and of the struggle to create. Other New

York School artists immersed viewers in large fields of saturated color, while still others combined elements of both gestural and Color-Field approaches to make their emotionally expressive work.

Their successors in the late fifties and early sixties built on this uniquely American abstraction. Sculptors extended the Action painters' bold gestures into three dimensions by fusing cast-off materials, while some painters took the merger of gestural and Color-Field painting a step further by pouring paint onto unprimed canvases and letting it soak into the fabric. Other painters, however, united the painterly side of Abstract Expressionism with found materials and imagery from everyday life. This approach, called Proto-Pop, connected Abstract Expressionism with the Pop Art to come.

The Sixties | **Pop, Minimalism, Process Art, Conceptual Art**

By the early sixties, the once avant-garde New York School had become the Establishment. The new generation of artists treated everyday objects and images with a cool detachment whose irony and humor were just the opposite of the seriousness of fifties art.

Pop artists, as they came to be called, embraced American popular culture from the glamorous to the mundane. An almost gestureless style reflected their work's sources in mass reproduction, the media, and consumer society. Pop Art offered multiples of movie stars, as well as picture-postcard and funny-paper images, billboard motifs, and monumental household objects.

The Pop sensibility varied regionally. The meticulous, idiosyncratic work of Chicago Imagists merged popular culture, folk art, Surrealism, and non-Western art, while West Coast Funk artists in the San Francisco area pursued an equally irreverent but more expressionistic path, often embracing the "low-art" medium of ceramics.

By the mid-sixties, the art world began shifting toward a cooler style of geometric abstraction called Minimalism. This movement developed around the same time as Pop but emerged a few years later as a dominant form. Minimalism shared East Coast Pop Art's rejection of Abstract Expressionist gesture and subjective expression. But it also revolutionized content by banishing illusion, imagery, and, usually, any reference outside the work's own formal properties.

Although Minimalism was primarily about sculpture, certain painters also took Minimalist approaches. However, these painters' pared-down abstractions also drew on the Old Masters, ancient history, early-twentieth-century Modernism, and direct observation from nature.

Almost the moment that Minimalism arose, artists began building on its practice but diverging from its "pure" formalism and closed forms. In Process Art, for example, the physical properties of unconventional materials, simple actions like cutting and hanging, and chance determine the work's nature and appearance.

Conceptual Art, on the other hand, which in the late sixties became a truly international movement, often downplayed material properties, emphasizing instead linguistic and mathematical systems for making art. Unlike Minimalism, Conceptual Art valued the idea over the object; sometimes the object was a mere by-product that could be executed from instructions.

The Seventies | **Post-Minimalism, Photorealism, New Image**

By the early to mid-seventies, a new generation of Post-Minimalist sculptors built on Minimalism and Process Art. They used simplified forms and unconventional methods and materials, but they combined this vocabulary with a renewed interest in the artist's touch, and with references to things outside the work itself. Their interest in the figure, in nature, and in personal experience reintroduced much that an earlier generation of sculptors had rigorously excluded.

At this time, too, new Realist movements appeared. These challenged Minimalist and Conceptual practices, reclaiming representation, illusion, and the human figure. Some artists produced figurative paintings from observation; others cast figurative sculpture directly from live models, and still others, the Photorealists, used photographs as their source.

Some representational painters from the early and mid-seventies avoided what they considered realism's literalist tendency, developing a deliberately crude style originally dubbed "bad" painting. Influenced by Pop Art's sensibility, these New Image painters used bright artificial colors, subjects derived from mass media or the everyday, and simplified forms. Unlike Pop artists, however, they employed a renewed painterliness and even added a Conceptual twist.

The eighties confirmed the return of the figure, of painterly gesture, and of personal expression, as Neo-Expressionism came in from Europe, especially from Germany and Italy. The Neo-Expressionists' ambitious, emotion-laden paintings and sculptures looked toward early twentieth-century Expressionist painting, mythology, and history, and dovetailed with some New Image concerns.

In the nineties, photography and video art achieved new levels of recognition. Large-scale photographs rivaled paintings, and video installations filled entire rooms. At the same time, contemporary art grew increasingly global, reflecting contemporary society at large. Today's cutting edge art is as likely to come from Tehran, Beijing, or Johannesburg as one of the traditional Western art centers.

The Collection and Its History

Sydney and Frances Lewis donated more than half of the works in this book. They first gave art to the museum in 1969, contributing three Andy Warhol *Marilyn* prints. Their collecting began modestly in the early sixties, when they visited museums and galleries for relaxation from the demands of their business, Best Products, Inc.

They collected much more actively once they met Andy Warhol in 1965; his multiple portrait of Frances, sometimes known as *Sydney's Harem,* was the first Warhol in their collection.

Their friendship with Warhol confirmed the Lewises' desire to buy the art of their time, especially American art, and to befriend the artists whose work they collected.

By the end of the sixties, the Lewises were part of the top tier of those collecting American contemporary art. In the early seventies, after Best Products went public—expanding nationwide from four Virginia stores—the Lewises began an active barter program with emerging and under-recognized artists.

Over the next twenty years, many struggling artists received their first washer, dryer, television, or dishwasher from Best Products in payment for their artwork. The corporate collection ultimately grew to nearly 1600 works, thirty-three of which the company gave to VMFA in 1978 and 1990.

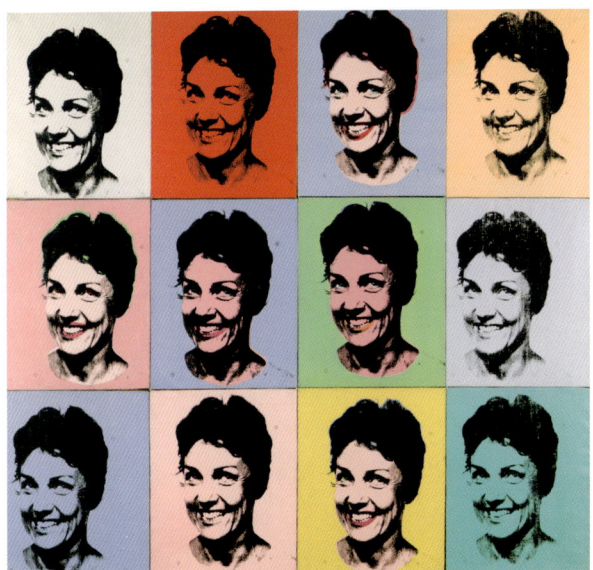

Andy Warhol
American, 1928–1987
**Frances Lewis
("Sydney's Harem"),**
1962, acrylic and
silkscreen ink on linen,
twelve canvases,
20 x 16 inches each,
Collection of Sydney
and Frances Lewis

In 1971, the Lewises offered VMFA a five-year grant of $100,000 (around $500,000 today) to support emerging artists by buying artworks that cost $1500 to $3500. The Lewis Contemporary Art Fund, administered by New York art dealer Ivan Karp, added forty-seven paintings, sculptures, and drawings to VMFA's holdings.

Eight years later, the Lewises announced that they would give the best of their private collection, now more than 1,000 objects, to VMFA. They continued collecting, meanwhile, and the museum received their gift of more than 230 works in 1985.

Since that time, key acquisitions—many using funds from the endowment the Lewises provided—have brought VMFA's holdings through the end of the twentieth century and up to the present.

The Museum and Its Community

Our collection, and this book, also reflects many other donors' generosity. We are a state museum; our entire collection belongs to the citizens of Virginia, but we use no public funds for purchases, with the occasional exception of interest from a National Endowment for the Arts purchase grant.

Gifts and funds from individuals, groups, corporations, and foundations build our collections. The important and generous donors preceding the Lewises include: Judge John Barton Payne, the museum's first president, who established a general purchase fund that includes contemporary art; the Arthur and Margaret Glasgow Fund, which helped bring in Henry Moore's reclining figure; and other VMFA endowments, including The Kathleen Boone Samuels Memorial Fund and The

Adolph D. and Wilkins C. Williams Fund. Such museum support groups as the Fabergé Society have also contributed substantially.

Great public art collections testify to their communities' generosity, vision, and civic spirit. The breadth and depth of the museum's holdings, especially its rich collection of Modern and Contemporary Art, offer eloquent testimony to our community. We are fortunate in and grateful for the help and support that continue to sustain us as an institution and a cultural resource.

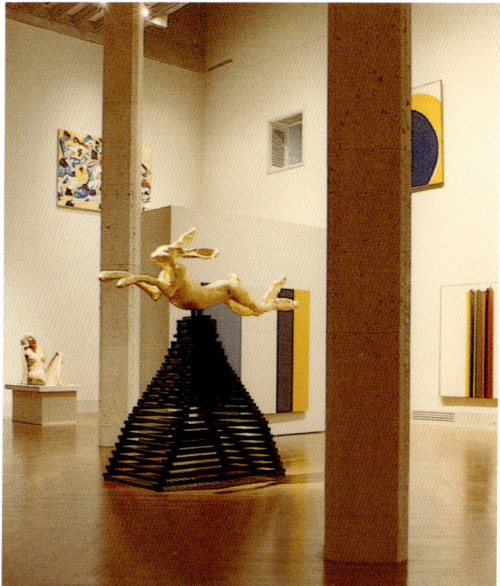

First installation of the Lewis Collection in VMFA's West Wing, 1985.

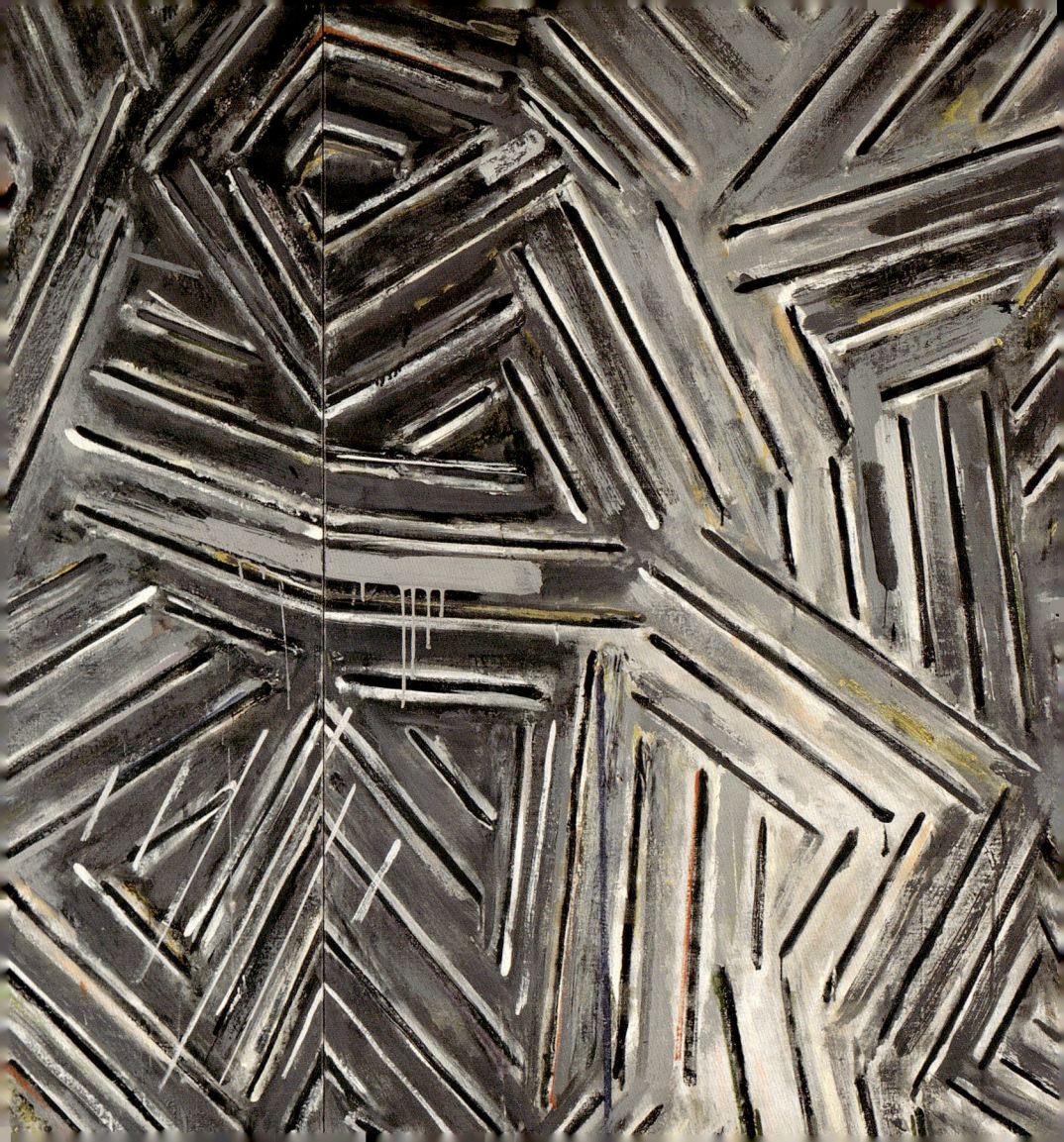

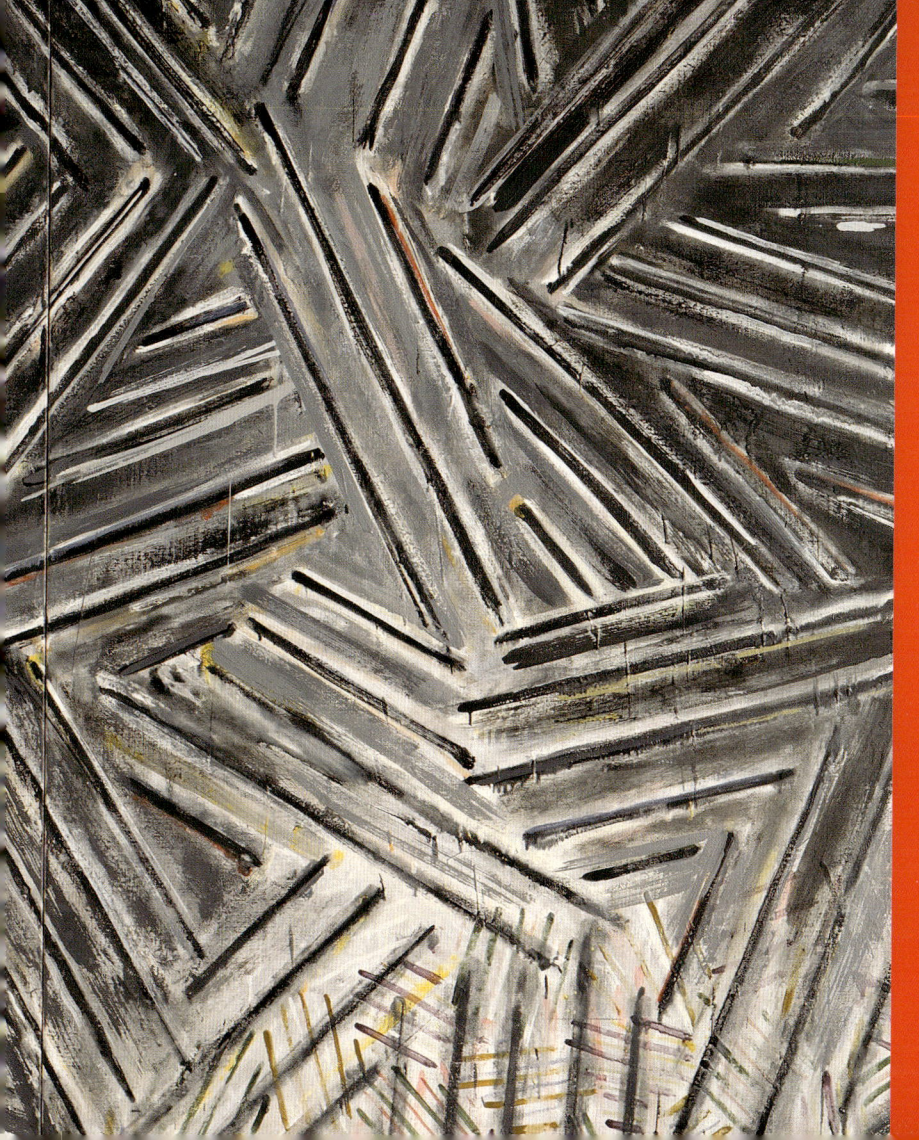

When I am in my painting, I'm not aware of what I'm doing. It is only after a sort of get-acquainted period that I see what I have been about. I have no fears of making changes, destroying the image, etc., because the painting has a life of its own. I try to let it come through. — Jackson Pollock

Jackson Pollock | American, 1912–1956 | **Number 15, 1948** | 1948 | Enamel on paper | 22 ¼ x 30 ½ inches
Gift of Mr. and Mrs. Arthur S. Brinkley, Jr., 78.2

In late 1947, rather than using brushes and an easel, Pollock began pouring and dripping paint onto canvases placed on the floor. This was his artistic breakthrough. For *Number 15, 1948,* he laid down a black ground; while it was still wet, he poured white paint onto it, which feathered and spread into the black. After establishing this rhythmic pattern, Pollock added accents of color. *Number 15, 1948,* like all of Pollock's drip paintings, is full of energy and freedom, qualities that inspired the labels Abstract Expressionism and Action painting.

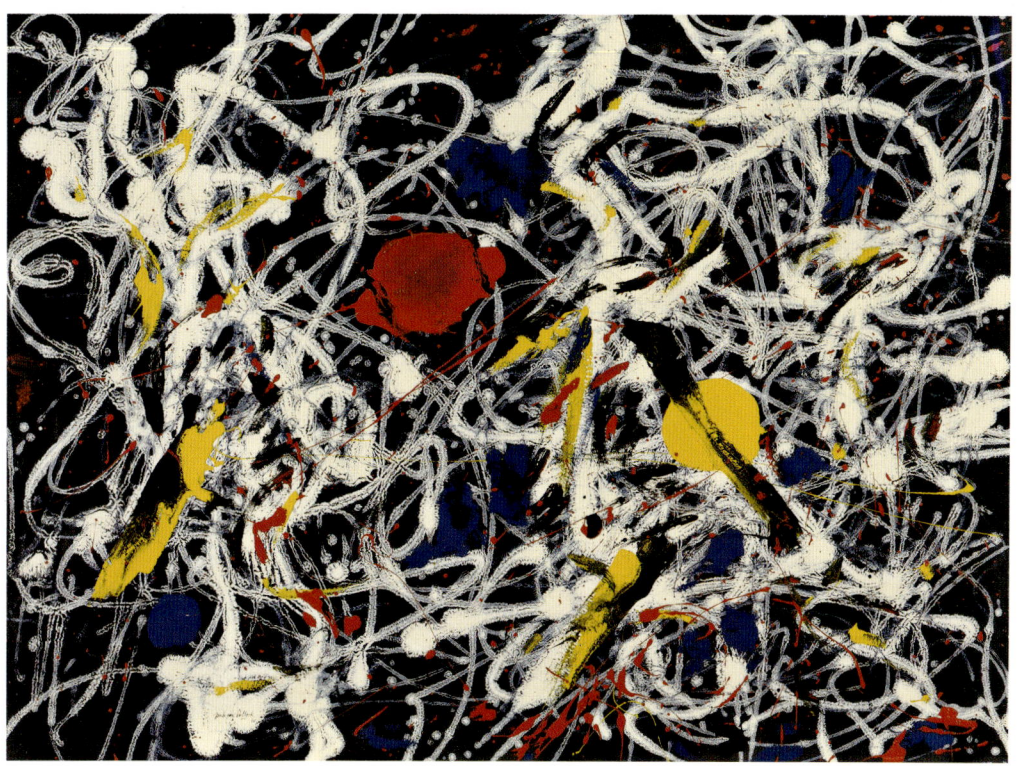

There is no such thing as a good painting about nothing. —Adolph Gottlieb and Mark Rothko

There is no such thing as a good painting about something. —Ad Reinhardt

Ad Reinhardt ⏐ American, 1913–1967 ⏐ **Red Painting** ⏐ 1952 ⏐ Oil on canvas ⏐ 60 x 82 inches ⏐ Gift of Sydney and Frances Lewis, 85.434

As Jackson Pollock and Willem de Kooning became recognized for their painterly, action-oriented style of abstraction, Ad Reinhardt was developing his own much more reductive style. The difference between these approaches suggests the wide range of Abstract painting at midcentury.

Red Painting is one of the first in which Reinhardt made geometry and color the focus, eliminating all traces of brushwork. Emotion and narrative have no place in this work; its subject is chromatic relationships. Reinhardt's spare, nearly monochromatic works paved the way for both the Color-Field painters later in the decade and the Minimalists of the 1960s.

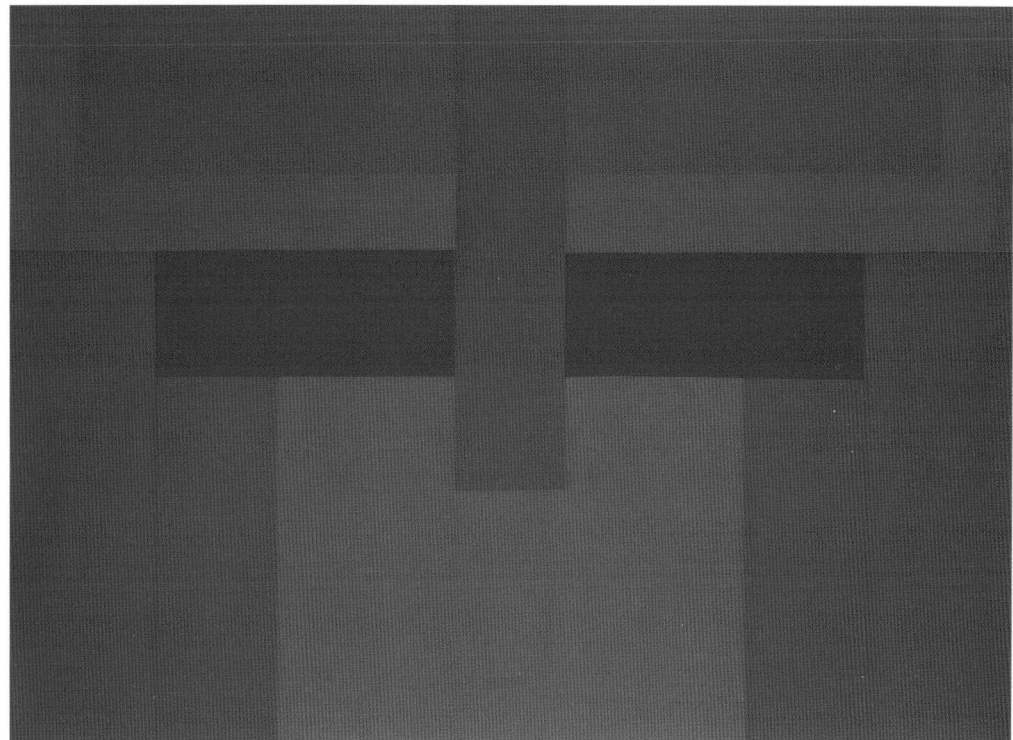

People sometimes think I take a white canvas and paint a black sign on it, but this is not true. I paint the white as well as the black, and the white is just as important. — Franz Kline

Franz Kline | American, 1910–1962 | **Untitled** | 1955 | Commercial oil-based paint on canvas | 67 ½ x 83 inches
Gift of Sydney and Frances Lewis, 85.415

In the early 1950s, Kline used commercial paint and housepainters' brushes to make a series of large canvases. His bold black brushstrokes created an impression of spontaneous movement and energy, which is why Kline became known as an Action painter, as did fellow artists Willem de Kooning and Jackson Pollock. Although Kline's paintings look as if he dashed them off, he usually made preliminary sketches in which he took care to balance opposites, including dark and light, energy and restraint, volume and line, and flatness and depth.

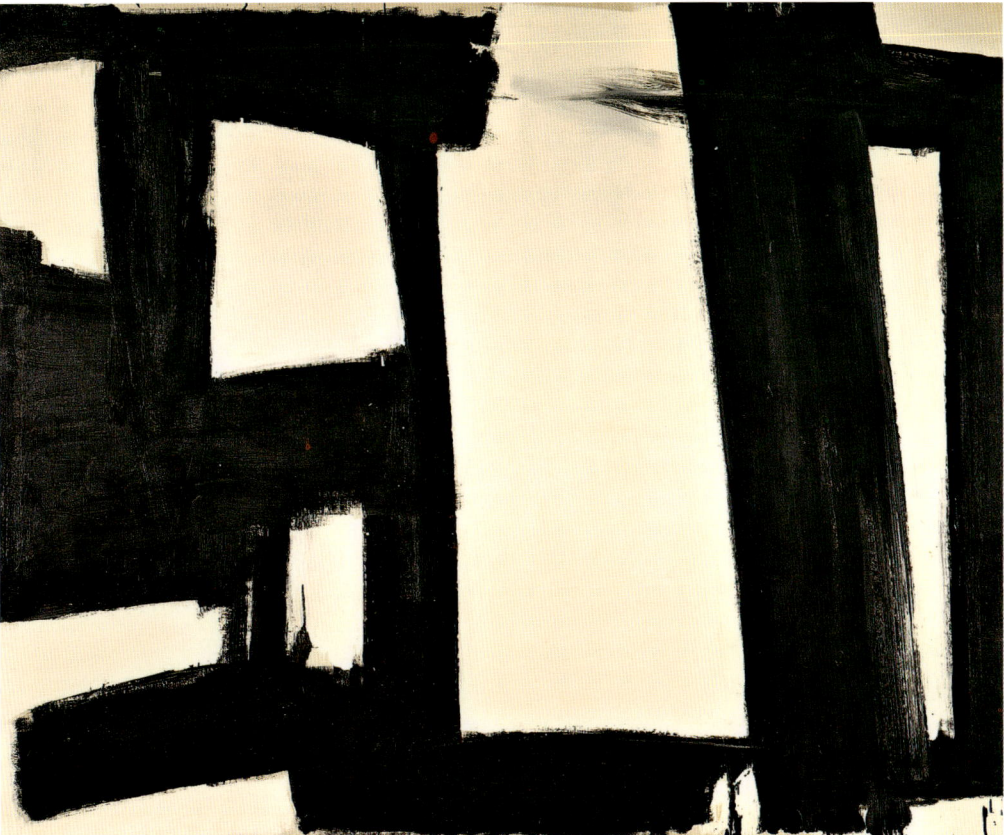

Art is an adventure into an unknown world, which can be explored only by those willing to take the risk. This world of the imagination is fancy-free and violently opposed to common sense. It is our function as artists to make the spectator see our way, not his way.   — Adolph Gottlieb and Mark Rothko

Adolph Gottlieb | American, 1903–1974 | **Blue at Night** | 1957 | Oil on canvas | 42 x 60 inches | Museum Purchase, The John Barton Payne Fund, 58.13.4 | © The Adolph and Esther Gottlieb Foundation/Licensed by VAGA, New York, NY

Gottlieb sought to express deep, subconscious levels of thought and emotion through abstract shapes and colors. *Blue at Night* belongs to a series that he called "imaginary landscapes." In each, a horizon line divides the canvas. The jostling shapes filling the upper section exemplify Abstract Expressionism's emphasis on dynamic brushwork, while the expanse of blue signals the movement's focus on fields of pure color.

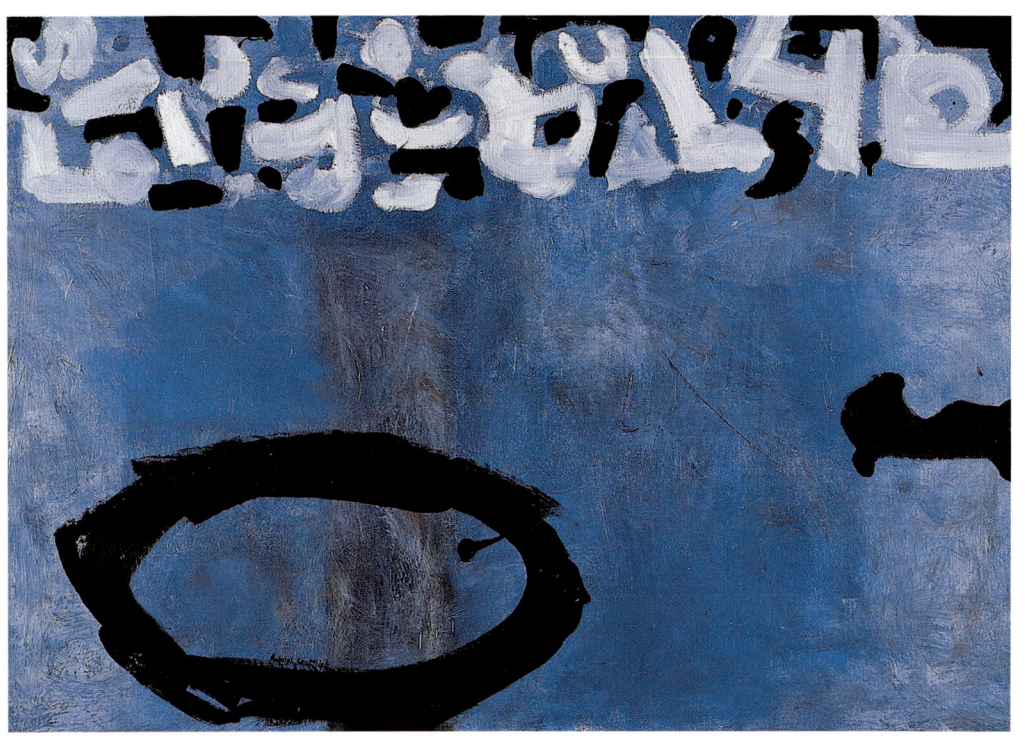

I don't paint with ideas of art in my mind. I see
something that excites me. It becomes my content.

— Willem de Kooning

Willem de Kooning | American, born in the Netherlands, 1904–1997 | **Lisbeth's Painting** | 1958 | Oil on canvas
49 ¾ x 63 ¾ inches | Gift of Sydney and Frances Lewis, 85.379

The bold, energetic brushstrokes in this work are characteristic of de Kooning's
Abstract Expressionist style. Abstract Expressionists took as their subject the artist's
inner life, as captured by spontaneous gestures.

De Kooning recalled returning to his studio the morning after completing this
painting to find that his two-year-old daughter had pressed her paint-covered
hands onto the canvas. De Kooning left Lisbeth's handprints and titled the painting
in her honor. Like the Surrealists, who explored the unconscious using chance and
randomness, de Kooning and his contemporaries embraced the importance of the
accidental as a source of creative expression.

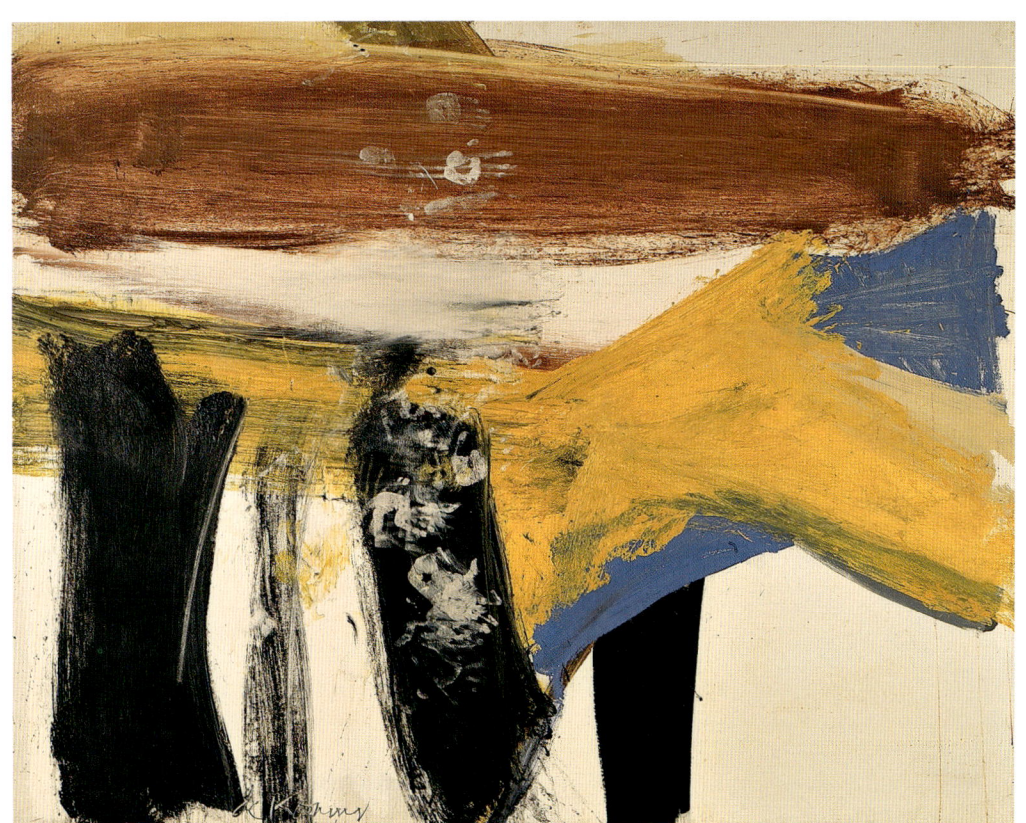

The painter makes something magical, spatial, and alive on a surface that is flat and with materials that are inert. That magic is what makes a painting unique and necessary. Painting, in many ways, is a glorious illusion. —Helen Frankenthaler

Helen Frankenthaler | American, born 1928 | **Mother Goose Melody** | 1959 | Oil on canvas | 82 x 104 inches
Gift of Sydney and Frances Lewis, 85.387

In *Mother Goose Melody,* Frankenthaler combines the gestural splashes and drips of Abstract Expressionist painting with the innovative stained-canvas technique she helped pioneer in 1952. The array of colors, shapes, and lines makes this composition rhythmic and dynamic. The spiraling red form on the right counters the dense area of color on the left, while the broad yellow band stretching across the bottom unites both. The artist noted that the three brown shapes could refer to herself and her two sisters, and that the red and black lines "made a sort of stork figure—the whole thing had a nursery-rhyme feeling."

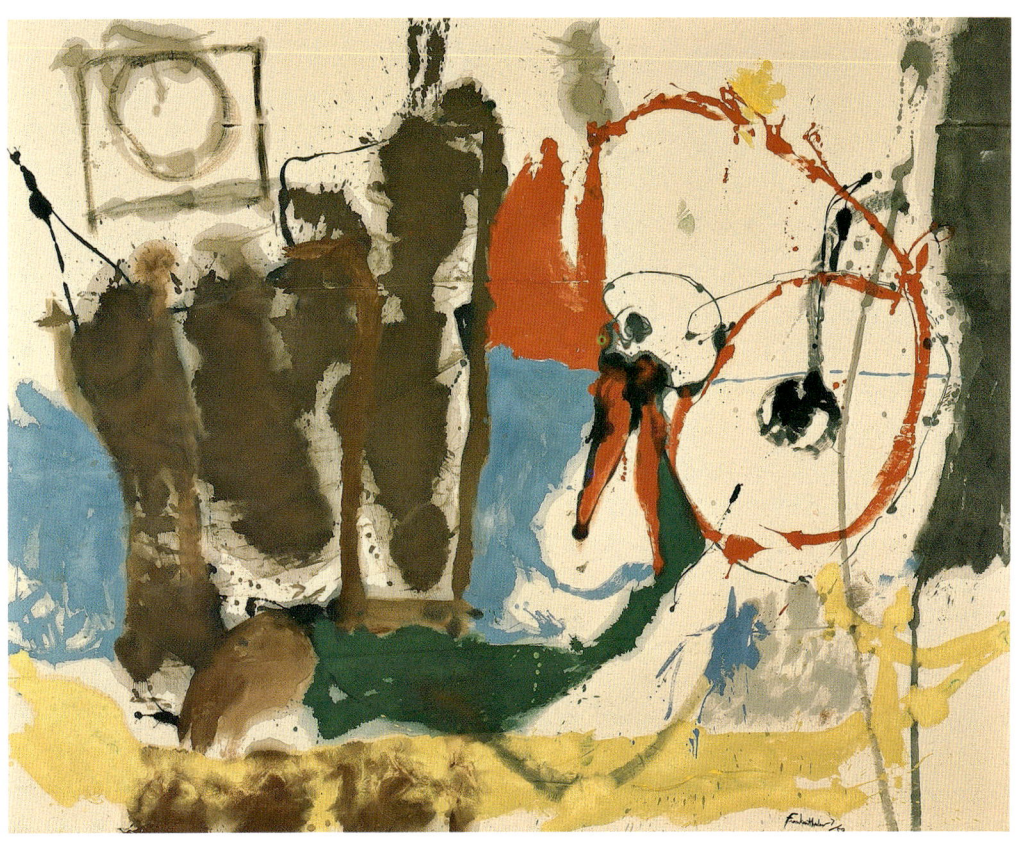

A painting is not a picture of an experience; it is an experience. —Mark Rothko

Mark Rothko | American, born in Russia, 1903–1970 | **Untitled** | 1960 | Oil on canvas | 79 $\frac{1}{2}$ x 69 $\frac{1}{4}$ inches
Gift of Sydney and Frances Lewis, 85.438

Rothko used abstraction and the expressive power of color to evoke a range of human emotions. His paintings vary from smaller works to monumental canvases that envelop the viewer with expansive fields of luminous color.

By 1949, Rothko had eliminated recognizable objects from his work and had developed his signature composition: soft-edged rectangular shapes hovering above one another. These self-imposed limitations freed him to explore rich colors that produced remarkable effects ranging from the spectacular and ecstatic to the somber and austere.

In a 1958 lecture, Rothko listed seven ingredients essential to his paintings, among them "a clear preoccupation with death." During the 1960s, when he painted *Untitled,* Rothko's work became increasingly dark. Some have seen his comments and the changes in his work as reflecting his deepening depression, while others view them as exploring the mystery and subtlety of light and darkness.

My concern is to build things that express our relationship to this country—to other countries—to this world—to other worlds . . . to glimpse some of the fear, hope, ugliness, beauty, and mystery that exist in us all. —Lee Bontecou

Lee Bontecou ⫶ American, born 1931 ⫶ **Untitled (No. 25)** ⫶ 1960 ⫶ Welded steel, canvas, copper wire ⫶ 72 x 56 x 20 inches ⫶ Gift of Sydney and Frances Lewis, 85.364

Between 1959 and 1967, Bontecou made work using canvas wired to a welded-steel framework. These wall-mounted constructions questioned the boundary between painting and sculpture, an issue the artist explored further by using raw canvas as a sculptural material. Bontecou meant her works to defy easy interpretation. Their gaping voids, backed with black, simultaneously invite and repel.

The canvases call to mind army fatigues, laundry bags, or tarps; the wire that attaches them suggests sutures closing a wound. Bontecou's use of common materials allies her with the Assemblage approach of artists like Robert Rauschenberg, and her pared-down materials and interest in geometry hint at Minimalism. But her work's strong emotions and political and cosmic allusions set her apart from both these movements.

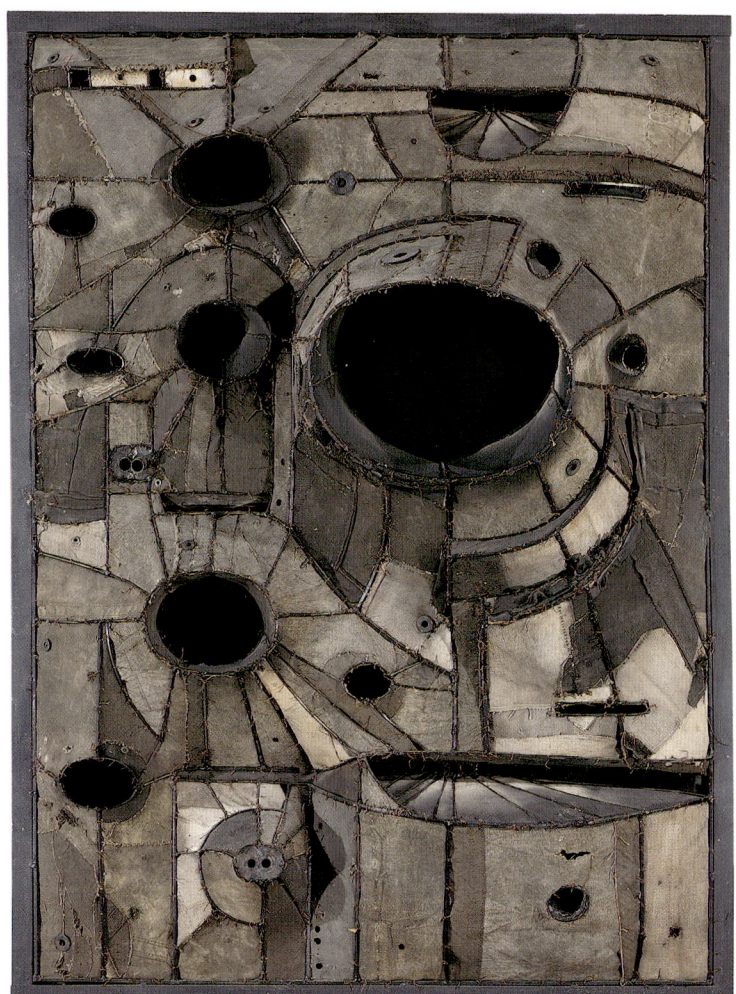

Painting relates to both art and life. . . . (I try to act in that gap between the two.) —Robert Rauschenberg

Robert Rauschenberg ⏐ American, born 1925 ⏐ **Coexistence** ⏐ 1961 ⏐ Oil, fabric, metal, wood, and other found materials on canvas ⏐ 60 x 42 x 13 ¾ inches ⏐ Gift of The Sydney and Frances Lewis Foundation, 85.433 ⏐ © Robert Rauschenberg/Licensed by VAGA, New York, NY

In the mid-1950s, Rauschenberg began using found objects, attaching some to his canvases and using others as supports for paintings. Rauschenberg called these works "combines," hybrids of painting and sculpture.

His palette here is an assortment of materials salvaged from the street— a rusty baton, a medallion displaying a human tooth, fragments of a police barricade, and other items that evoke a human presence in an urban environment. Rauschenberg's work fuses gestural painting and the flotsam of everyday life; some have called it a bridge between Abstract Expressionism and Pop Art.

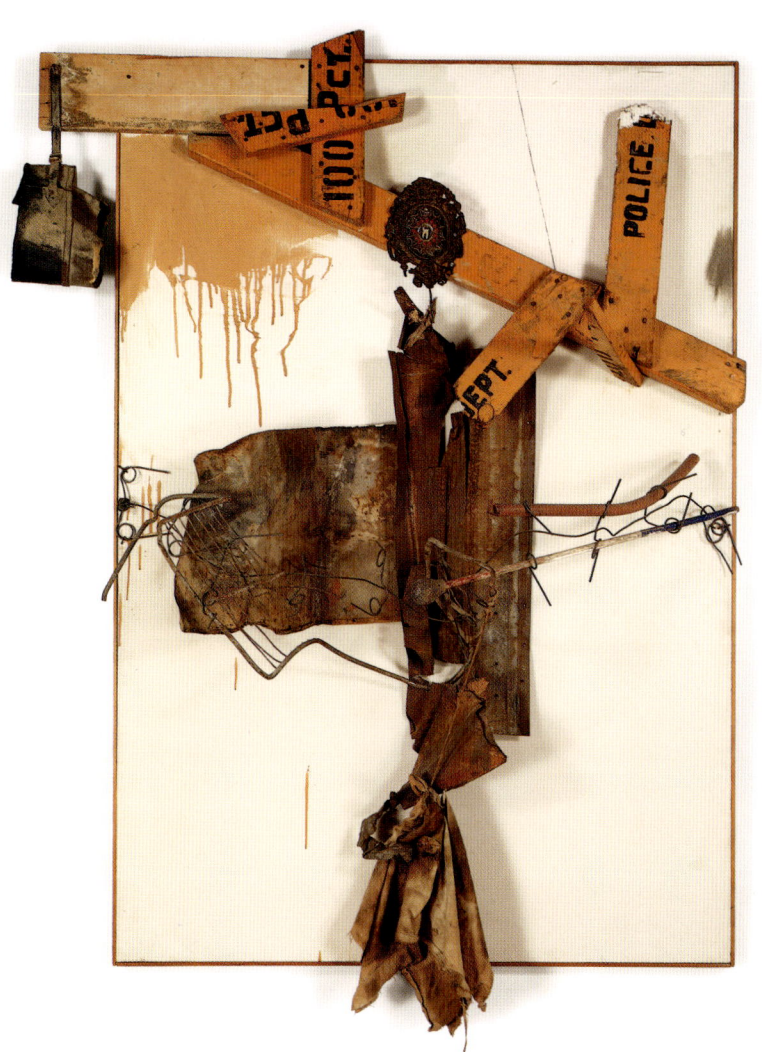

Tradition for a painter is an intolerable burden. To hold in one's mind those great paintings of the past will inevitably cut off the spontaneous flow of creative ideas. —Morris Louis

Morris Louis ┊ American, 1912–1962 ┊ **Claustral** ┊ 1961 ┊ Oil on canvas ┊ 85 x 64 ½ inches ┊ Gift of Sydney and Frances Lewis, 85.421

Louis explored pure color in his mature paintings, pouring paint onto unstretched, unprimed canvas. Here, he left the ends of the drips visible but situated them at the top rather than the bottom of the finished work. Louis cropped his canvases to create subtle asymmetries: this painting's stripes fall slightly to the right of center, as do the stronger hues, creating a delicate tension and giving the sense that the painting expands to the left.

"Claustral" means "related to a cloister," and "cloister" derives from bar, bolt, or confining space. The title refers to the painting's vertical structure and perhaps to its feeling as well.

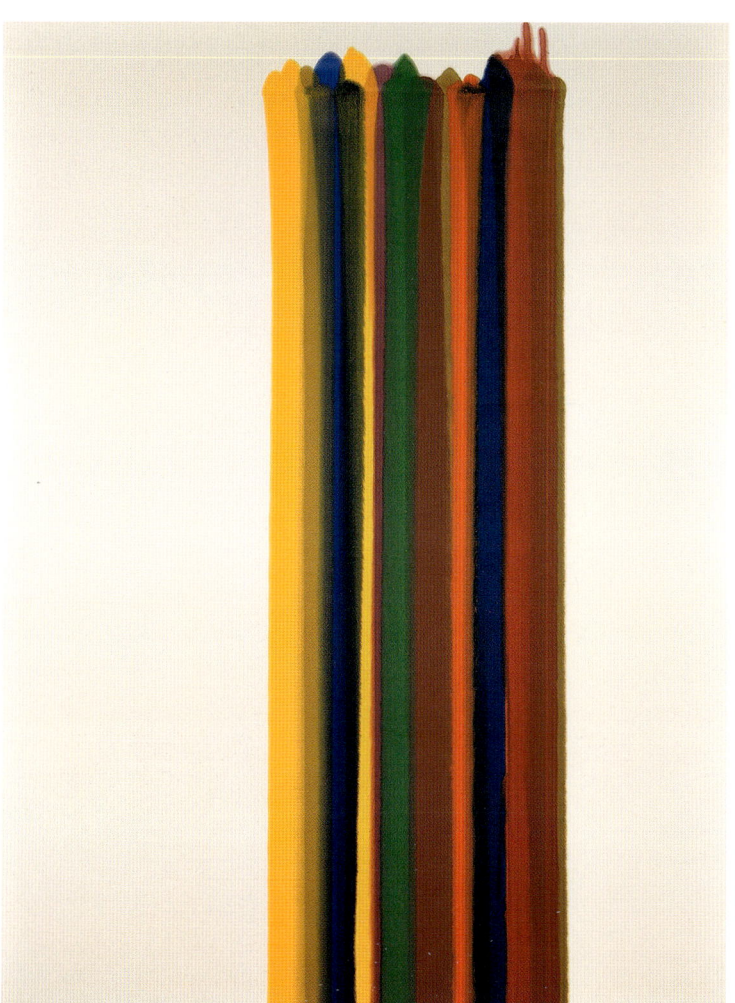

I was a Pop artist to the extent that I deliberately
chose American imagery. . . . I used what was
around me, so my culture was what I used.

—Tom Wesselmann

Tom Wesselmann | American, 1931–2004 | **Great American Nude #35** | 1962 | Enamel, polymer, and found
materials on board | 48 x 60 inches | Gift of Sydney and Frances Lewis, 85.454 | © Estate of Tom Wesselmann/
Licensed by VAGA, New York, NY

Great American Nude, the title Wesselmann gave to an extended series of related
works, humorously evokes the clichéd notion of the Great American Novel.
Wesselmann used images and objects that surrounded him in his daily life, including a pair of windows found in the gutter in Greenwich Village, in this, his first
female nude to incorporate a found element. Wesselmann's evocative combination
of actual objects, collage, and paint makes *Great American Nude #35* an unmis-
takably American update of a classic theme.

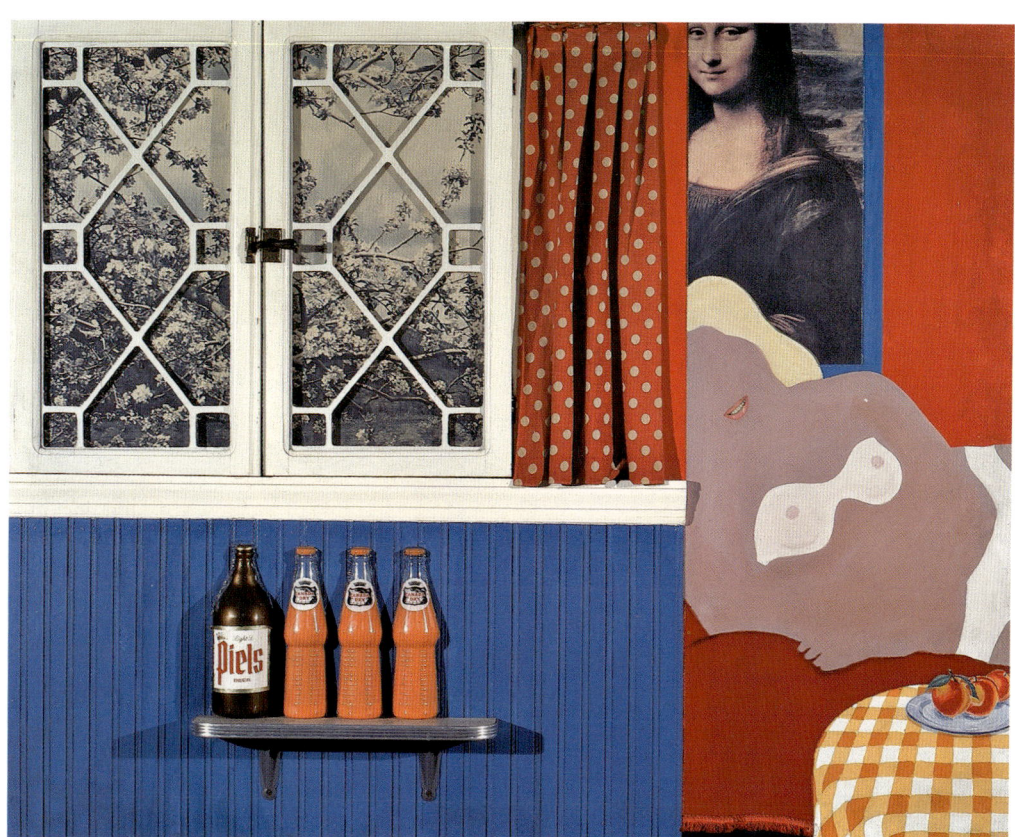

I wanted to shorten the distance between meaning and metaphor. I looked for a visual language that would be broadly communicable, direct and clear, and that was intimately part of my experience.

—Allan D'Arcangelo

The American landscape is D'Arcangelo's subject matter here, as though glimpsed from a speeding car. Two monumental, isolated signs loom against the background as the highway recedes sharply into the distance. D'Arcangelo first exhibited this series in New York in the early 1960s, at the same time his fellow artists took other icons of everyday life as their subjects and used the clean lines and flat colors of commercial printing to make their images both familiar and new—a trend soon called Pop Art.

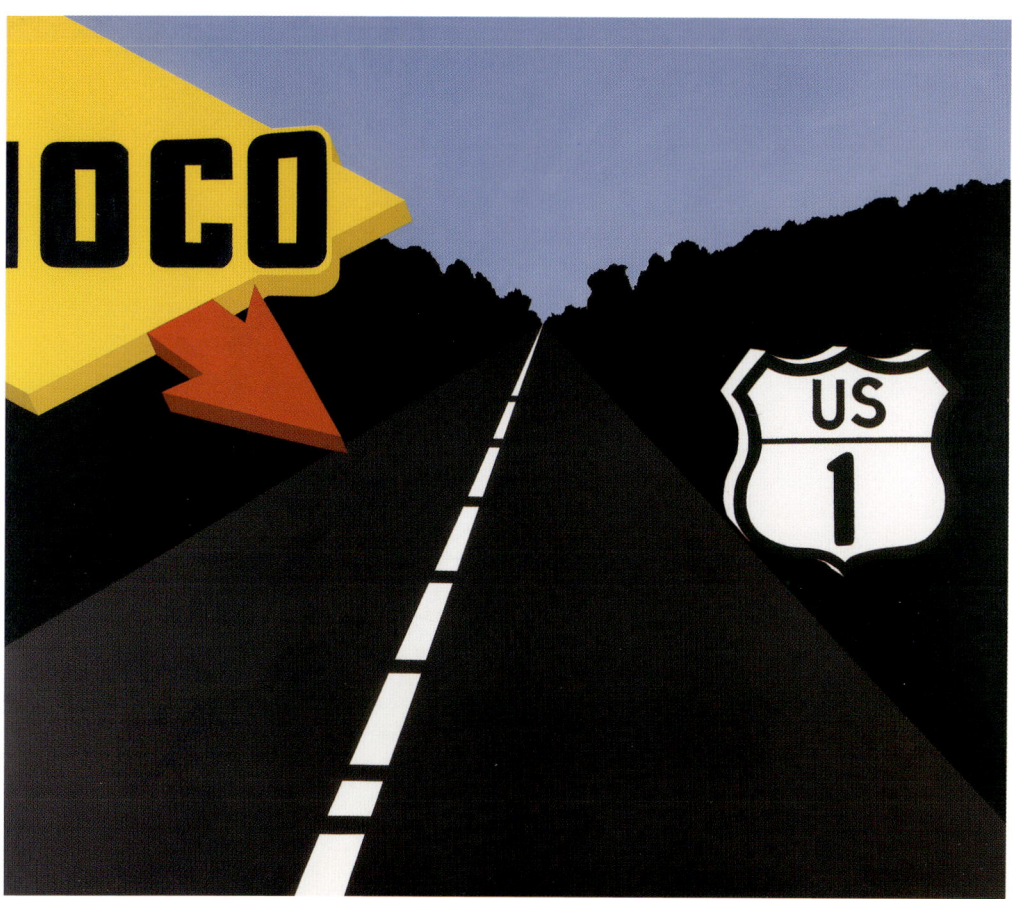

I see everything that way, the surface of things,
a kind of mental braille, I just pass my hands over
the surface of things. —Andy Warhol

Andy Warhol | American, 1928–1987 | **Triple Elvis** | 1963 | Silkscreen ink, silver paint, and spray paint on linen
81 x 71 inches | Gift of Sydney and Frances Lewis, 85.453

Warhol based this macho, singer-turned-gunslinger portrait of Elvis Presley on
a publicity photograph for the 1960 Western *Flaming Star.* This public persona,
as carefully packaged as Campbell's Soup, was ideally suited to Warhol's aims
and to his focus on surface appearance rather than psychological interpretation.
Warhol's repetition of identical images and his silk-screen technique often allude
to the pervasiveness of consumer culture. The overlapping multiple figures here
also suggest individual film frames and cinematic motion, while the work's metallic
background evokes Hollywood's silver screen.

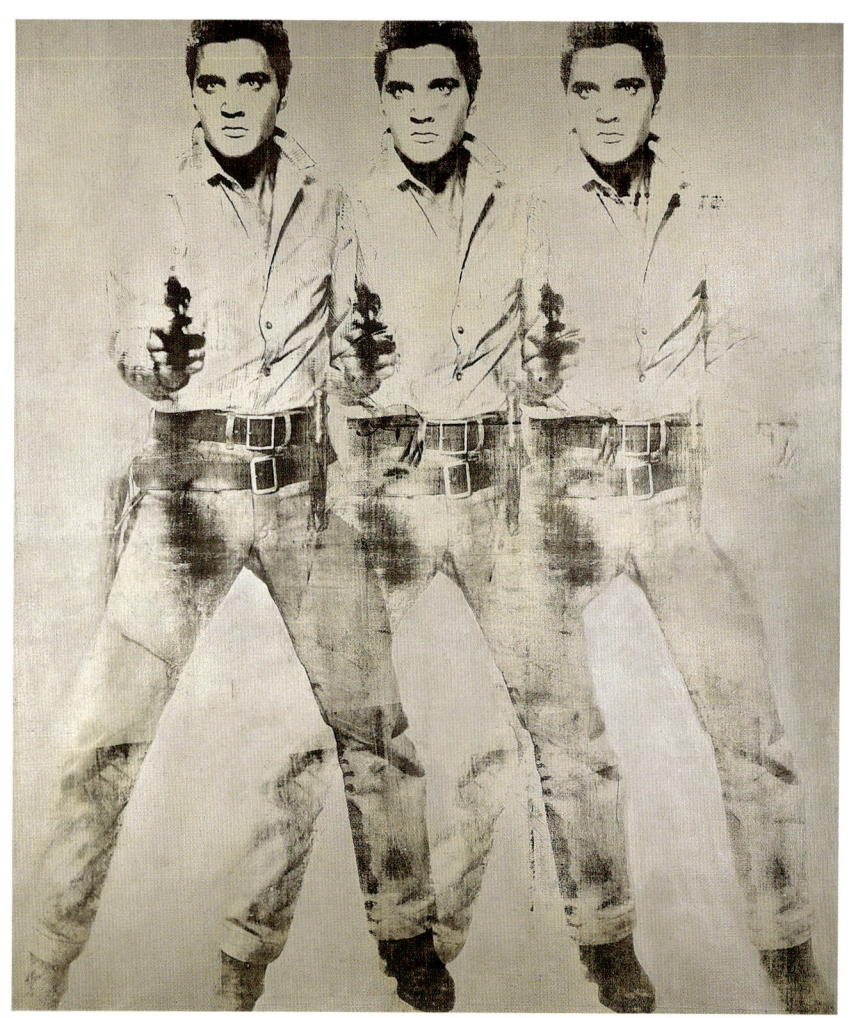

I don't think of my work ever as a complete thing. I think of it as a tool to get someone off into their own vision. —James Rosenquist

James Rosenquist | American, born 1933 | **Early in the Morning** | 1963 | Oil on canvas, plastic | 95 x 56 inches
Gift of Sydney and Frances Lewis, 85.436.1–2

Rosenquist's early experience as a billboard painter in Times Square shaped his approach to art. In his paintings, Rosenquist adopts ready-made images from magazines, packaging, ads, movies, and television. He fragments, enlarges, and rearranges them in unexpected, and unexpectedly thought-provoking, combinations. Each element of this composition—cloudy sky, sliced orange, pocket comb, and striding legs—evokes innumerable associations, yet the painting's meaning remains elusive. Like a dream or a memory, Rosenquist's work challenges us to leave logic behind and enter into an odd and hallucinatory world.

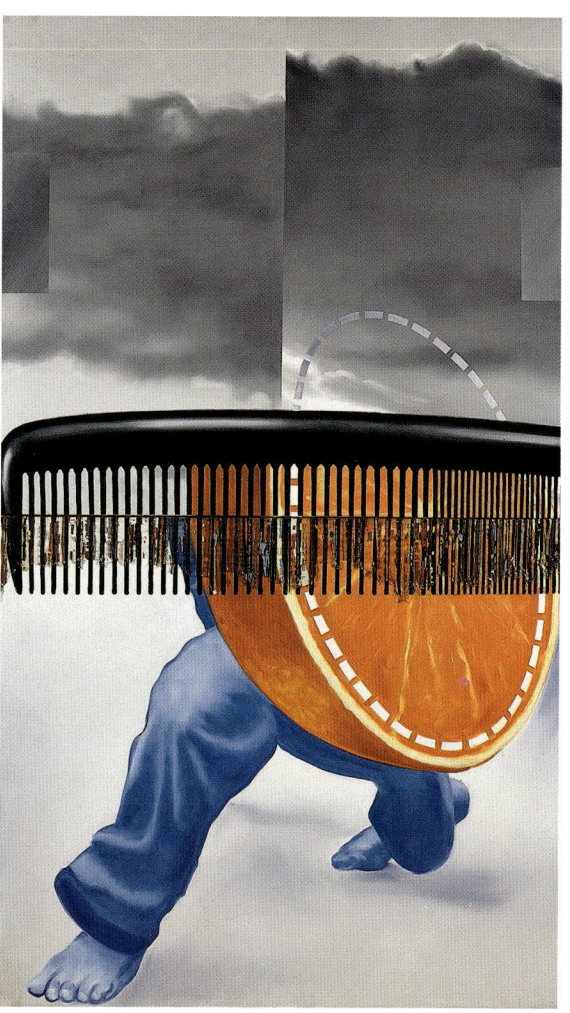

I wish I'd kept some of my better-known works. I weep over that. . . . I consider [this painting] my best one. . . . It embodies the aesthetics of all my work. —Ed Ruscha

Ed Ruscha ┆ American, born 1937 ┆ **Noise, Pencil, Broken Pencil, Cheap Western** ┆ 1963 ┆ Oil and wax on canvas 71 1/4 x 67 inches ┆ Gift of Sydney and Frances Lewis, 85.439

Ruscha's training in commercial art—layout, lettering, and design—is often cited as an influence on his work. Its clean lines, clear colors, and subjects borrowed from commerce and popular culture resemble much in Pop Art. But Ruscha's work stands between Pop Art and Conceptual Art because of the important role words play and the way the image involves the viewer in interpreting an open-ended narrative.

Here, a visual element anchors each edge of the painting, but this careful tension has been "broken" by the snapped pencil on the right. The word "noise" expands toward the center, as if increasing in volume, and suggests the sound of the pencil breaking.

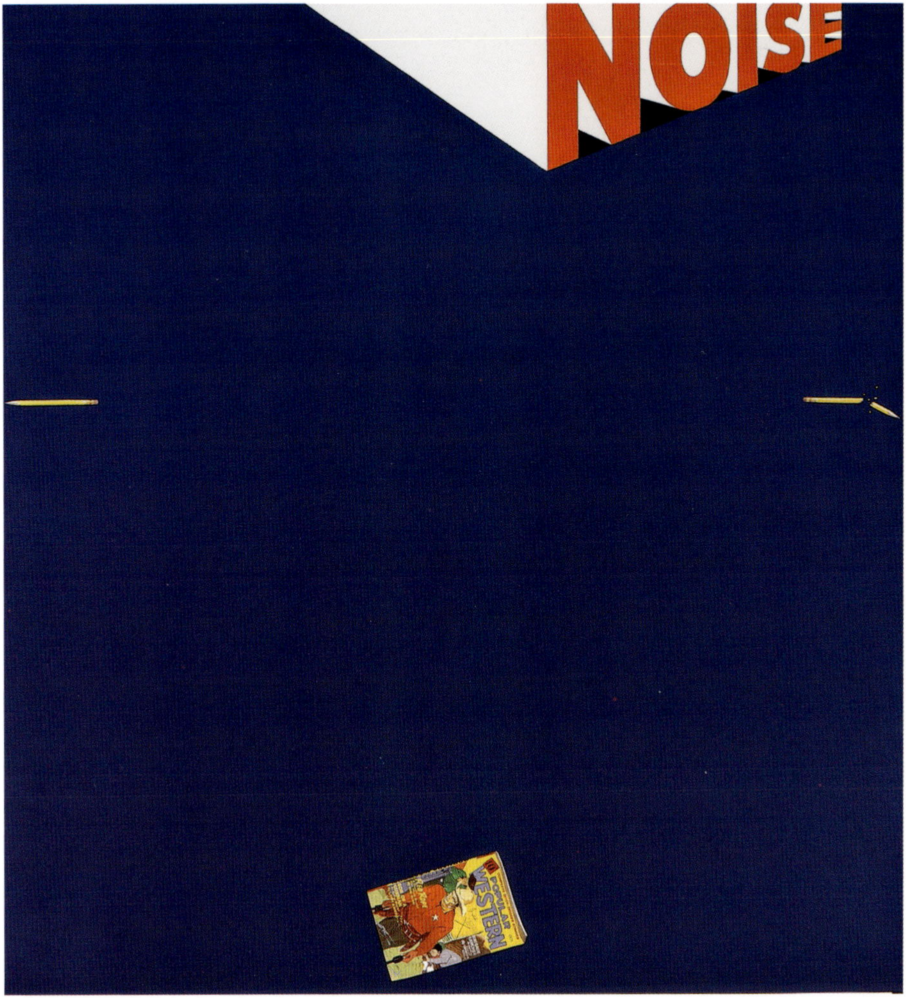

NOISE

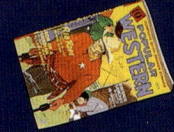

[Art] seeks to find hitherto ignored or unknown combinations of forms, colors, and textures, and even psychological phenomena, and perhaps to cause new types of experience in the artist as well as the viewer. —Norman Lewis

Norman Lewis | American, 1909–1979 | **Post Mortem** | 1964 | Oil on canvas | 64 x 50 inches | Gift of the Fabergé Society of the Virginia Museum of Fine Arts, 2001.9

Like many of his peers, Lewis turned to abstraction in the mid-1940s. Active in the New York School of Abstract painters, Lewis was close to many, especially Ad Reinhardt (see page 4). Lewis was also an important teacher and mentor in the Harlem arts community. In addition, he was highly political and active in the Civil Rights movement. Lewis helped found the black artists' collective known as Spiral in the early 1960s.

Post Mortem, from Lewis's *Civil Rights* series in the early 1960s, reflects his lifelong interest in the expressive potential of the color black. Here, Lewis used abstract forms and gestures to allude to interracial conflict. White forms evoke hooded and mounted figures, bringing a chilling association to what remains a nonrepresentational image.

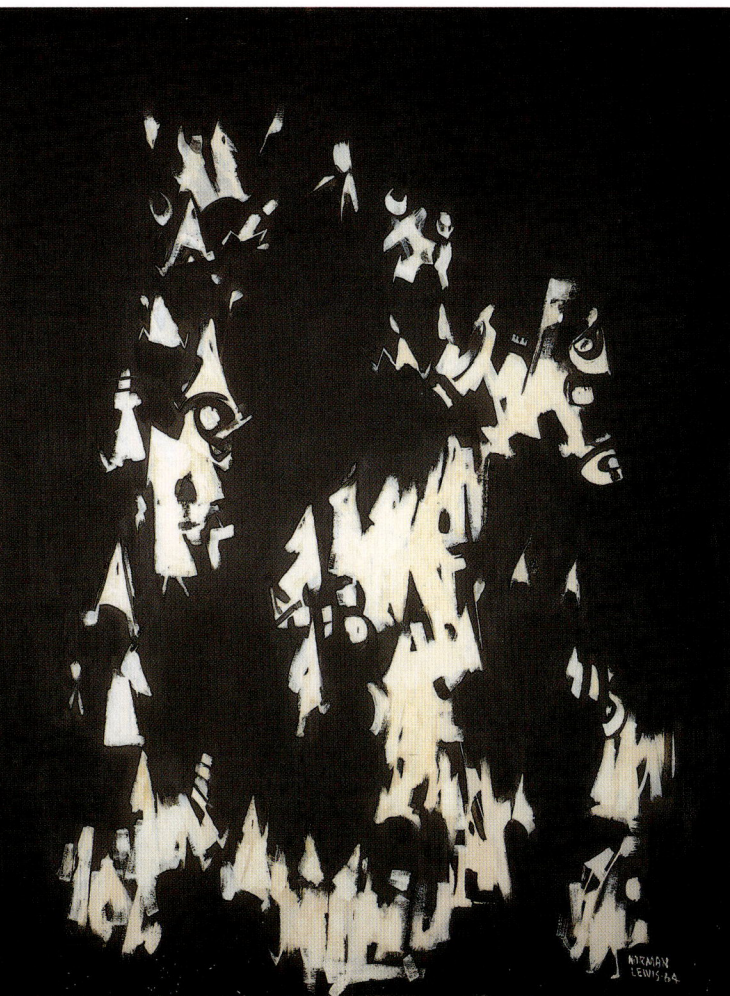

There is something humorous about doing a landscape in a solidified way, especially the rays, because a sunset has little or no specific form.

—Roy Lichtenstein

Roy Lichtenstein ¦ American, 1923–1997 ¦ **Gullscape** ¦ 1964 ¦ Oil and acrylic on canvas ¦ 68 x 80 inches ¦ Gift of Sydney and Frances Lewis, 85.418

An originator of Pop Art, Lichtenstein borrowed images from American popular culture, especially comic strips, advertising, and art reproductions. His signature vocabulary of black outlines, primary colors, and Benday dots derived from commercial printing, emphasizes his subjects' everyday origins. In this painting, Lichtenstein reinterprets and monumentalizes the kind of conventional and familiar image usually found on picture postcards, raising questions about what distinguishes art from illustration or advertising.

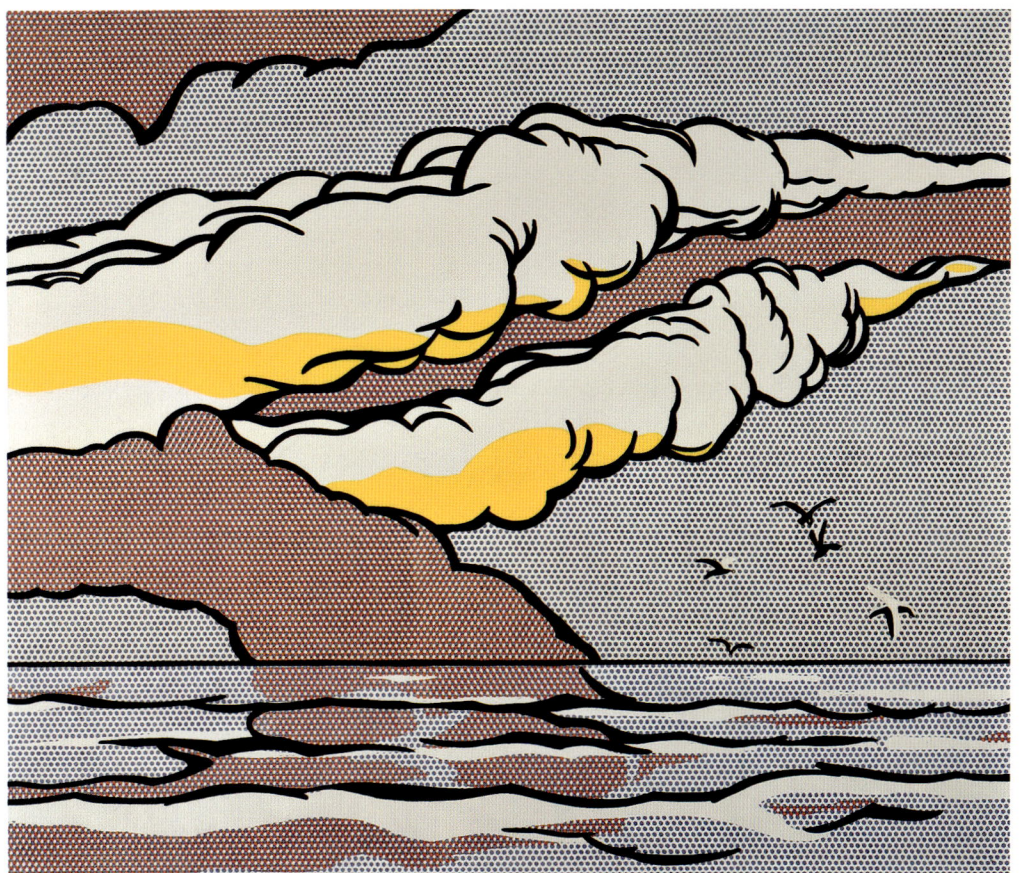

The ad shows a robe with the man airbrushed out of it. There was nobody in the bathrobe, but when I saw it, it looked like me. —Jim Dine

Jim Dine | American, born 1935 | **Red Robe with Hatchet (Self-Portrait)** | 1964 | Oil on canvas, metal, wood, hatchet | 87 x 60 x 24 inches | Gift of Sydney and Frances Lewis, 85.381a–c

In the early 1960s, Dine's paint-filled canvases with attached clothing, tools, and other store-bought items brought him critical acclaim as a Pop artist, an identity he never accepted. Although his imagery makes reference to popular culture, Dine drew inspiration from his own personal history and from art history. He cited the European tradition, from Dada and Surrealism back to classical antiquity, as his source.

In 1964, inspired by an advertisement in the *New York Times Magazine,* Dine began using the image of an empty bathrobe as a form of self-portraiture. In this early version, Dine's colorful, precisely painted image of the robe stands behind a hatchet embedded in a log, linking not only Dine's bathrobe and tools series, but also painting and sculpture.

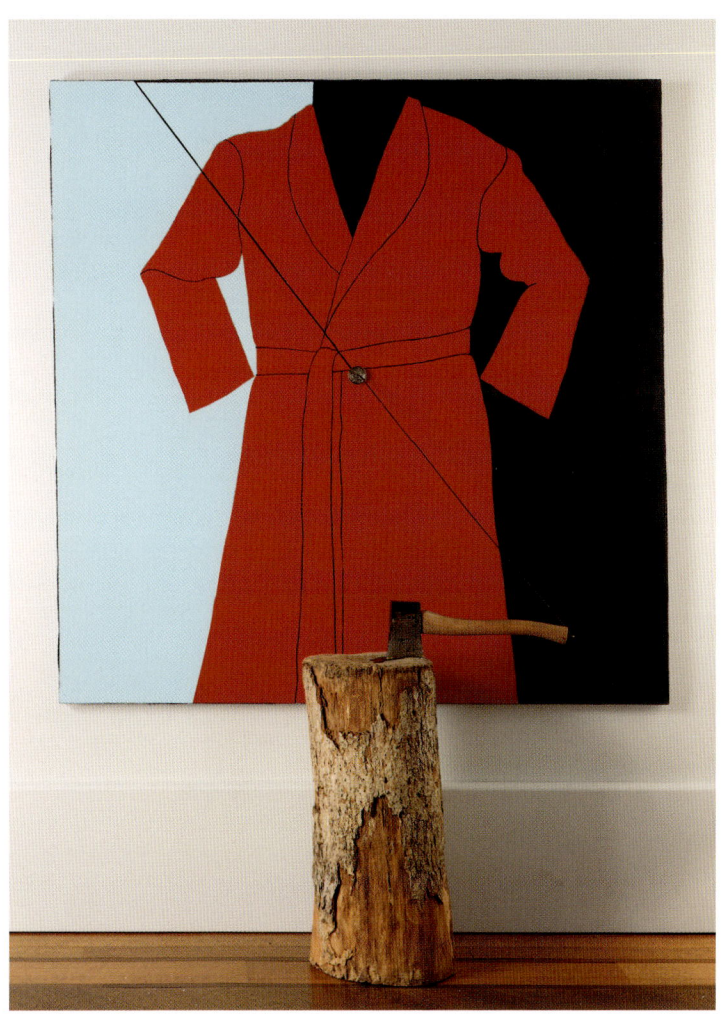

I am less interested in marks on the panels than in the presence of the panels themselves. —Ellsworth Kelly

Ellsworth Kelly | American, born 1923 | **Four Panels: Green Black Red Blue** | 1966 | Acrylic on canvas | 53 x 104 inches | Gift of Sydney and Frances Lewis, 85.413.1–4

Kelly's work often originates in his fascination with the patterns of the urban landscape. Shadows, architectural fragments such as a building's windows, or even the spaces between a tree's branches, become for Kelly abstract shapes and colors. In the hard-edged geometric paintings that are his hallmark, Kelly explores these shapes and relationships.

In *Four Panels: Green Black Red Blue,* each canvas's shape, size, and color, and the spaces between the panels contribute to the composition's harmony and balance. Strong, saturated colors evoke the stained canvases of Color-Field painting, while the panels' spare simplicity strikes a Minimalist note.

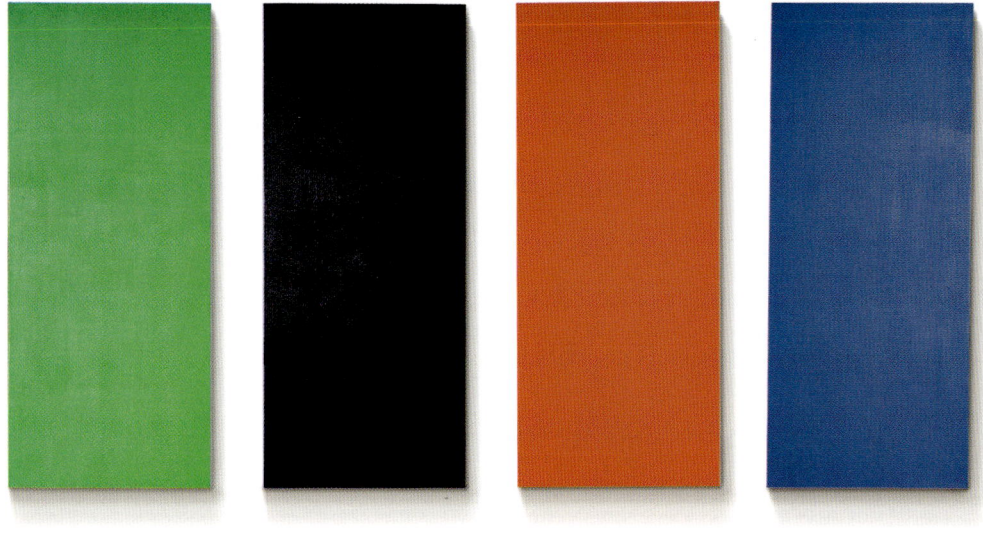

What I am trying to establish is that Modern Art isn't dislocated, but something with roots, tradition and continuity. For myself the past is the source (for all art is vitally contemporary).

—Cy Twombly (from 1952 fellowship application to Virginia Museum of Fine Arts)

Cy Twombly | American, born 1928 | **Synopsis of a Battle** | 1968 | Commercial oil-based paint and wax crayon on canvas | 79 x 103 1/8 inches | Gift of Sydney and Frances Lewis, 85.451

The vibrant, freewheeling compositions of Virginia-born Cy Twombly often allude to historical and mythological subjects. In *Synopsis of a Battle,* what appear to be random, chalklike scrawls on a slate gray blackboard are actually drawn and painted signs and symbols that refer to a specific event—the Battle of Issus (333 B.C.E.), in which Alexander the Great defeated Darius of Persia's much larger army.

Among the many cryptic, graffiti-like markings in the work, the words "Issus" (upper left) and "flank" (left and right) provide clues to the painting's military subject. The radiating, or flanking, form suggests military diagrams of troop movements.

Twombly combines the energy of Abstract Expressionist gesture with the simplifying urges of Minimalism. The painting also reflects the inquiring attitude of Conceptual Art. Twombly is interested in language as both a visual form and a mental construct, here capable of bringing the past vitally into the present.

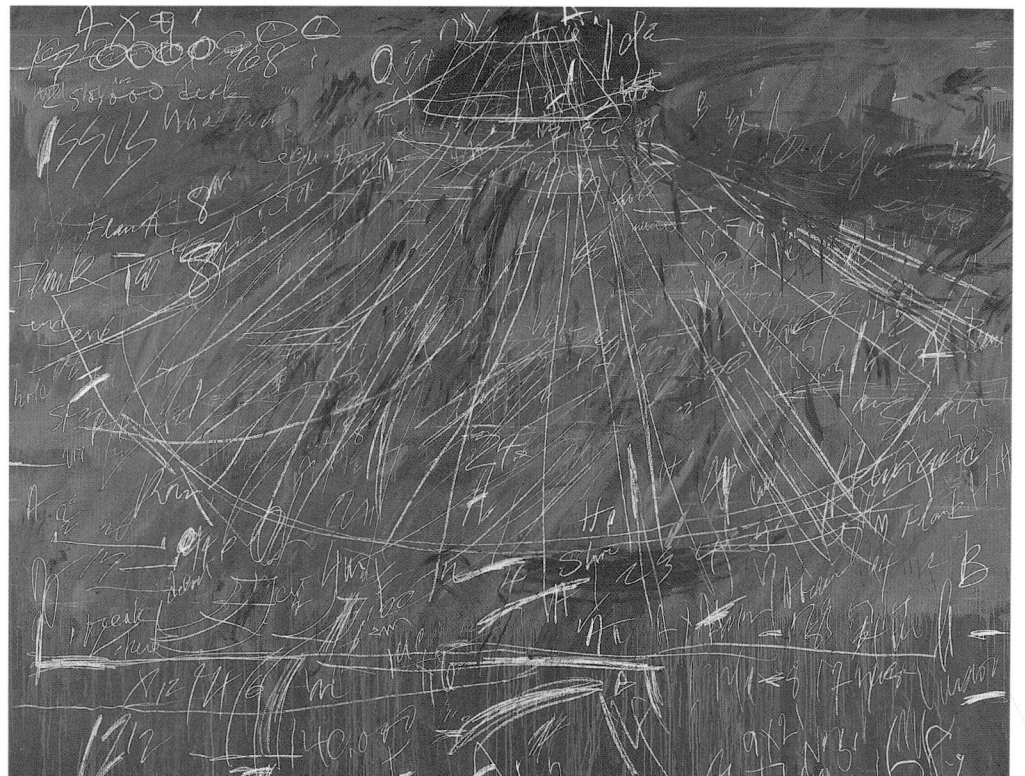

Temperamentally, I have always been a landscape painter. —Richard Diebenkorn

Richard Diebenkorn | American, 1922–1993 | **Ocean Park No. 22** | 1969 | Oil on canvas | 93 x 81 inches | Gift of Sydney and Frances Lewis, 85.380

Shortly after moving to southern California in 1966, Diebenkorn abandoned representation for abstraction, focusing on the monumental, sequentially numbered *Ocean Park* series. Titled after the seaside Santa Monica neighborhood where Diebenkorn lived and worked, these paintings embody his response to his new environment. Their gentle luminosity and geometric structure evoke that locale's coastal light. *Ocean Park No. 22* takes notice of Minimalism by emphasizing simplified colors and basic structures, but it also looks to the work of earlier twentieth-century artists, including Henri Matisse and Pablo Picasso.

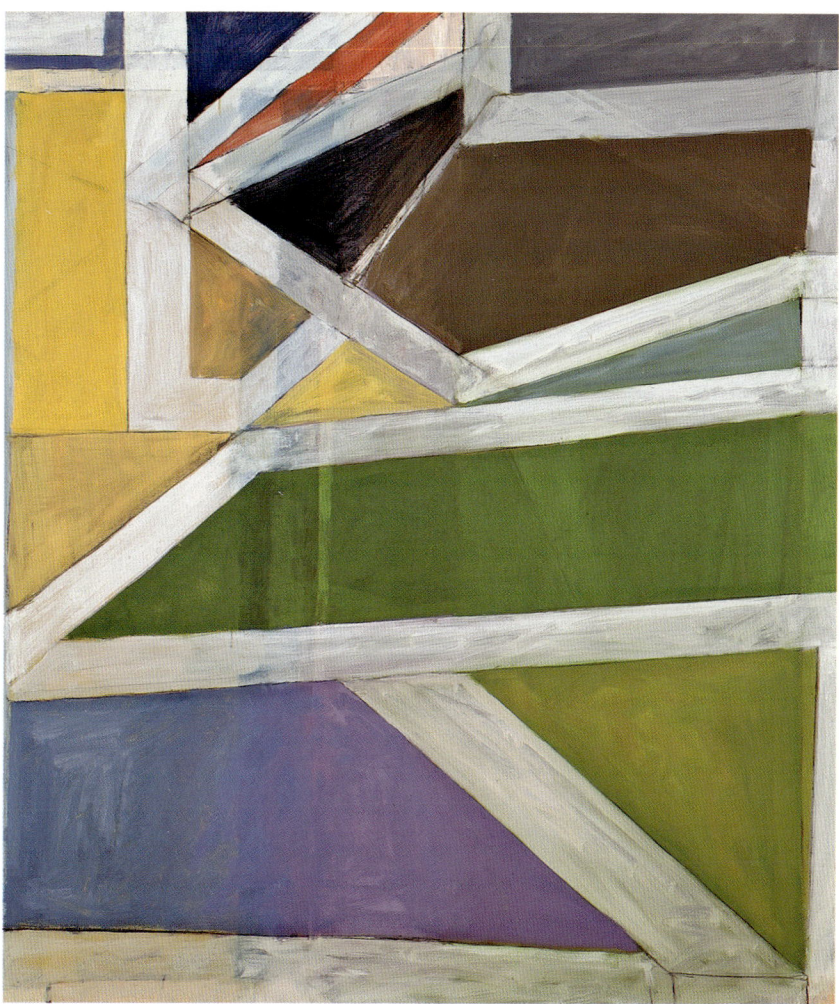

Style and appearance are the things I'm more concerned about than what something means. I'd like to
have style take the place of content, or the style be
the content. —Alex Katz

Alex Katz ┊ American, born 1927 ┊ **Self-Portrait with Sunglasses** ┊ 1969 ┊ Oil on canvas ┊ 96 x 68 inches ┊
Gift of Sydney and Frances Lewis, 85.412 ┊ © Alex Katz/Licensed by VAGA, New York, NY

Katz was one of the first artists to return to figurative painting following Abstract
art's dominance at midcentury. Katz's simplification of forms and elimination of
detail relates to hard-edged Color-Field painting and to Pop Art's emulation of
commercial graphics—two early 1960s styles that influenced him.

Katz began concentrating on casual portraiture of family and friends in the late
1950s. Self-portraits appear periodically throughout his career. Here he extends
his familiar methods of drastic cropping and sharp juxtapositions of scale to create
a particularly imposing image. Never one to dwell on inner psychology, Katz further denies access to his interior here with sporty dark glasses, which, along with
long sideburns, link the image to its time. The changing quality of light—strong
contrasts of sun and shade across the face and reflections in the lenses—further
shows Katz's interest in the specific moment.

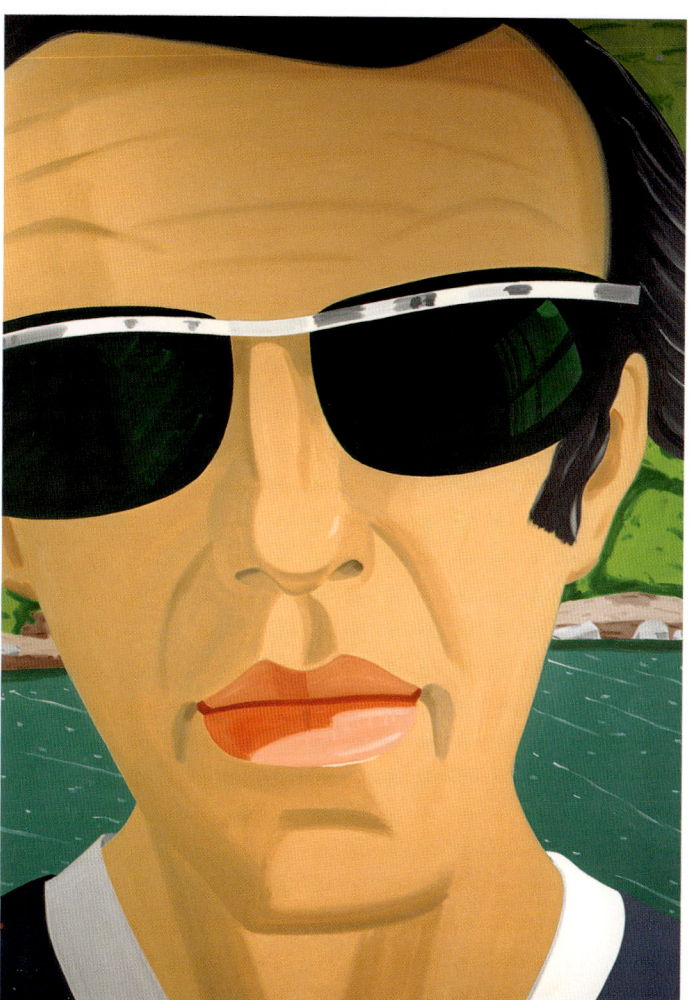

> These [works] sort of kick at you constantly. They won't let go of you. I want them to do that.
>
> —Nicholas Krushenick

Nicholas Krushenick | American, 1929–1999 | **Jungle Jim Lieberman** | 1969 | Acrylic on canvas | 82 x 72 inches
Gift of Sydney and Frances Lewis, 85.416

Although Krushenick's bright colors, clean edges, and simplified forms seem to resemble those of such Pop artists as Roy Lichtenstein, his art is not figurative and has its roots in earlier works by Mondrian, Matisse, and midcentury Abstractionists. Krushenick's interest in the optical effects of strong colors and hard-edged forms anticipated the Op artists of the 1970s.

In this painting named for famous stock-car racer Jungle Jim Lieberman, Krushenick captures the excitement of the races. Krushenick paints what has been called "caricatured pictorial space," using an abstract, somewhat comic manner to create tensions among shapes, patterns, and colors.

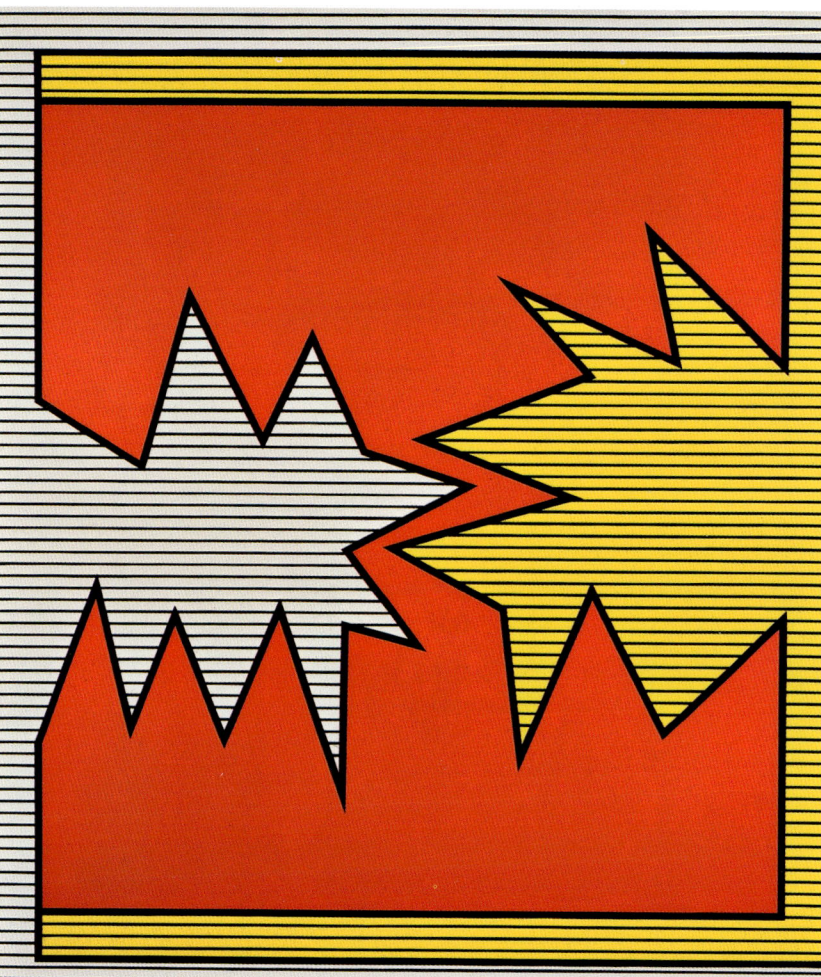

I am not trying to duplicate something that I see in nature because you must always compromise—it is always going to be paint, you cannot outpaint the paint. —Neil Jenney

Neil Jenney | American, born 1945 | **Swimmer and Reflection** | 1970 | Acrylic on canvas | 73 ½ x 52 ½ inches
Gift of Sydney and Frances Lewis, 85.409

As a young painter in the late 1960s and early 1970s, Jenney shared with Pop artists an interest in concrete, recognizable subject matter. In works from this period, he explored how simple, familiar images like a swimmer and the swimmer's reflection exist in relation to each other.

This painting's gestural quality, however, with its loose brushstrokes, drips, and scratches, makes it very different from the sleek styles of Pop Art. In giving equal importance to realistic subject matter and to expressive effects, Jenney's work challenges Pop Art's detached irony.

Jenney's characteristic inclusion of the title, here added in bold letters to the large black frame, emphasizes the subject while resisting explanation. This approach characterized a new generation of artists loosely grouped as New Image painters.

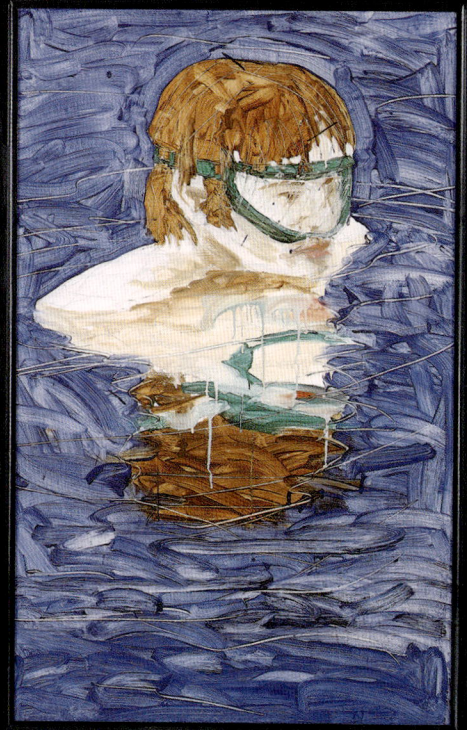

SWIMMER REFLECTION

It's all a lie. I always like to think that the paintings look very realistic, but the subjects don't actually exist in this way. . . . It's a selection, taking a few elements of reality, of the visual elements—never mind the noise, the smell, the actual dimensions.

— Richard Estes

Richard Estes | American, born 1932 | **Paris Street Scene** | 1972 | Oil on canvas | 40 x 60 inches | Gift of Sydney and Frances Lewis, 85.382

In the late 1960s, Estes became known for his dazzling re-creations of such mundane urban subjects as the reflections of cars in storefront windows on deserted city streets, all apparently rendered with photographic precision. About the time he painted *Paris Street Scene,* Estes had begun to use multiple photographs from several perspectives as sources for the same image.

Estes set almost all of these scenes in New York City; in *Paris Street Scene,* a rare exception, the row of buildings on the right thrusts deep into the background—a daring compositional strategy. Reflections in the plate-glass window alternate with more solid architectural details to enliven this Paris street. Estes has signed the work on the license plate of the car closest to the painting's center.

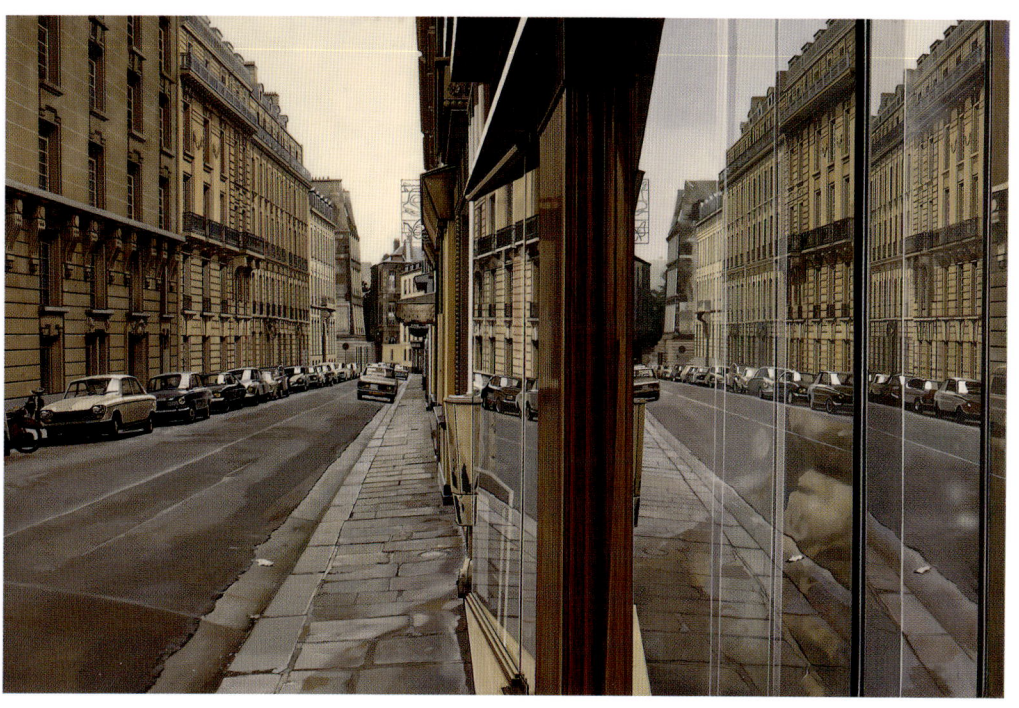

I find man-made things always intriguing, from sophisticated design to cruder street or shop signs. . . . I've always liked urban imagery as opposed to landscape or "nature." —Patrick Caulfield

Patrick Caulfield | English, 1936–2005 | **In My Room** | 1974 | Acrylic on canvas | 108 x 108 inches | Gift of Th Sydney and Frances Lewis Foundation, 85.529

Caulfield's paintings apply Pop Art's simplification of color and line to all kinds of subjects, including the interior scenes that he began painting in the early 1960s. By simplifying, carefully cropping, and applying broad areas of vibrant color to ordinary rooms, Caulfield transforms them into disorienting spaces. Here, the artist's extensive use of hot pink flattens the space, while clever complementary touches of cool green and blue, paradoxically, represent light and warmth.

The title comes from the Beach Boys song, "In My Room." This space is not, however, Caulfield's own room; he describes it as "a made-up interior that seems alien, and not intimate, in contrast to the title."

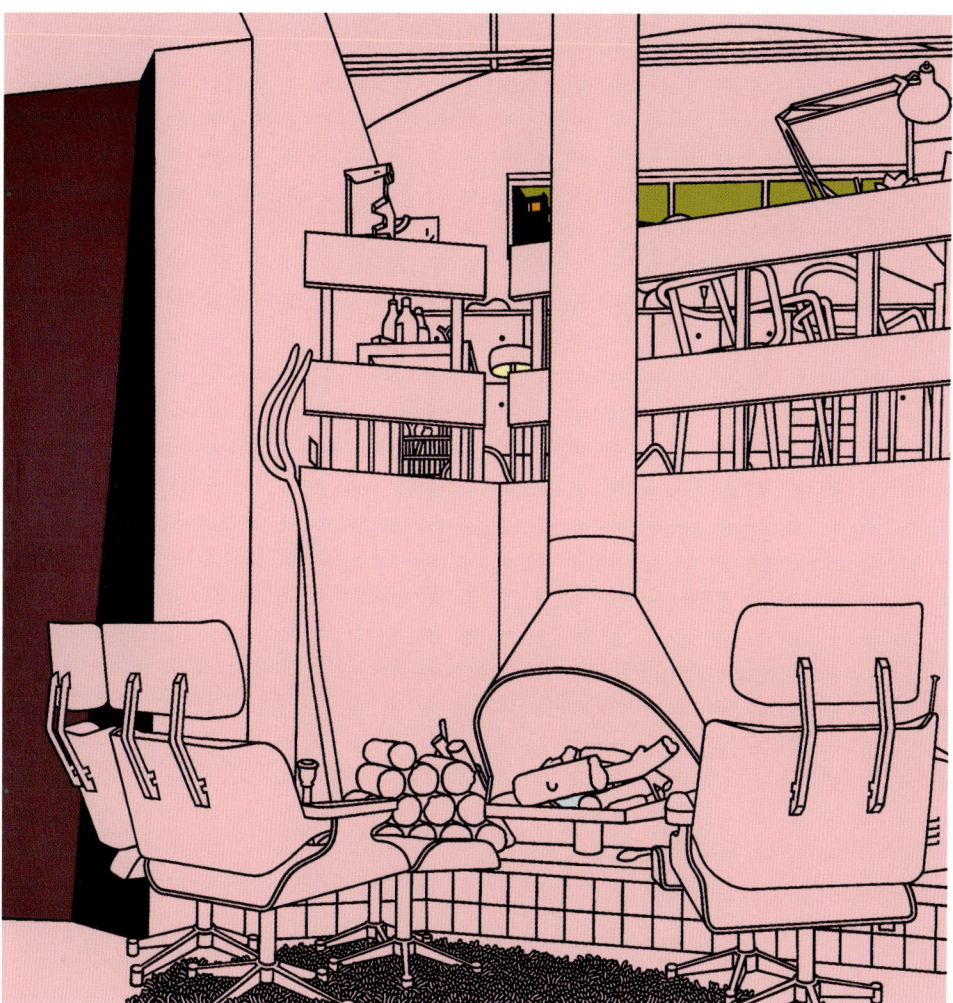

I hope to paint the body as it continues to wrinkle and sag and bulge and slide towards its own death. . . . Painting self-portraits is, no doubt, my way of dealing with the whole process. —Gregory Gillespie

Gregory Gillespie ⏐ American, 1936–2000 ⏐ **Self-Portrait (Torso)** ⏐ 1975 ⏐ Oil and acrylic on canvas ⏐ 30 ¼ x 24 ¾ inches ⏐ Gift of Sydney and Frances Lewis, 85.391

Gillespie's career as a painter can be seen as an homage to self-absorption. He stares out of many self-portraits, recording his aging body and its physical flaws with brutal honesty. His exacting realism is perfectly suited to representing flesh as well as a need to be "real" with oneself, no matter how painful.

In *Self-Portrait (Torso),* Gillespie places himself within the tradition of Christ as the "Man of Sorrows": devotional images painted for prayer or meditation that generally show the resurrected Christ as a half-length figure with bleeding wounds. Gillespie casts the artist as martyr—although his wounds are more psychological than physical.

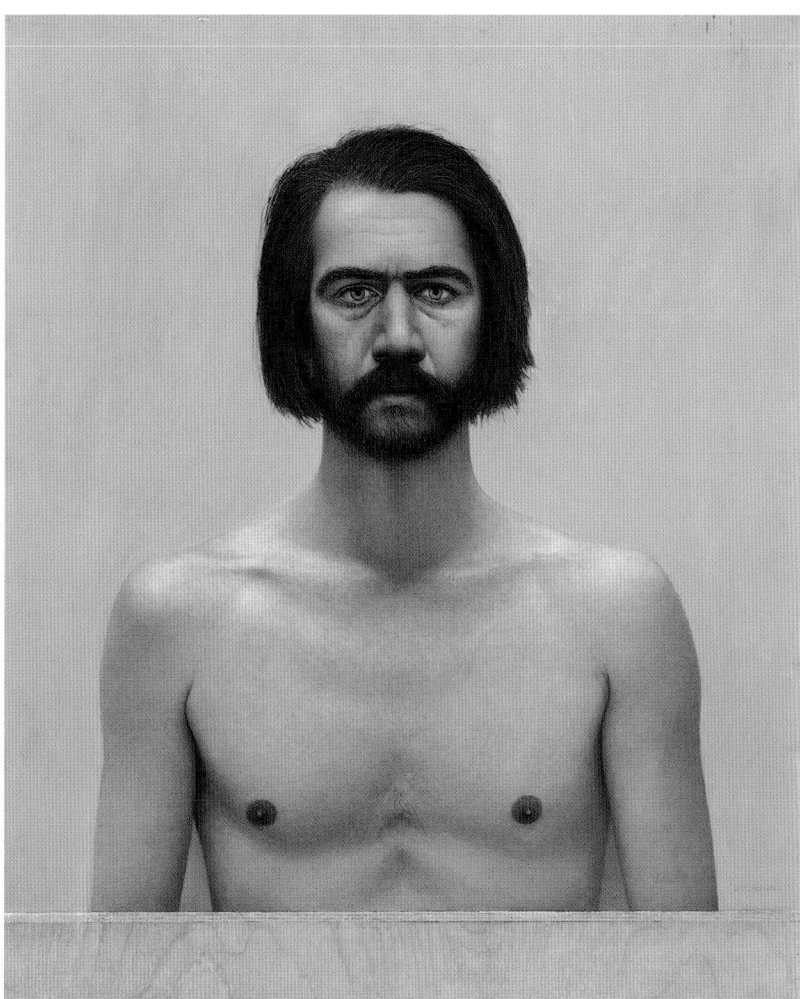

There is nothing to do now but paint my life. . . .
My dreams, surroundings, predicament, desperation,
[my wife] Musa—love, need. Keep destroying any
attempt to paint pictures or think about art. If someone bursts out laughing in front of my paintings, that
is exactly what I want and expect.   —Philip Guston

Philip Guston ⫶ American, born in Canada, 1913–1980 ⫶ **The Desert** ⫶ 1974 ⫶ Oil on canvas ⫶ 72 1/2 x 115 inches ⫶ Gift of Sydney and Frances Lewis, 85.400

In the last decade of his career, Guston returned to figurative subjects—recalling his early work as a social realist painter in the 1930s and 1940s—while maintaining the loose brushwork and rich palette of his midcareer Abstract Expressionism. The bare lightbulb, the heap of shoes, and the cigarette-puffing head with its bulging, bloodshot eye, which the artist considered a self-portrait, are recurrent motifs in his late paintings.

Guston employed such cartoonlike images to address momentous and difficult themes, including the creative capacity of a Jewish artist after the Holocaust. This depiction of self-flagellation expresses Guston's struggle to persevere as an artist in the face of self-doubt and self-criticism.

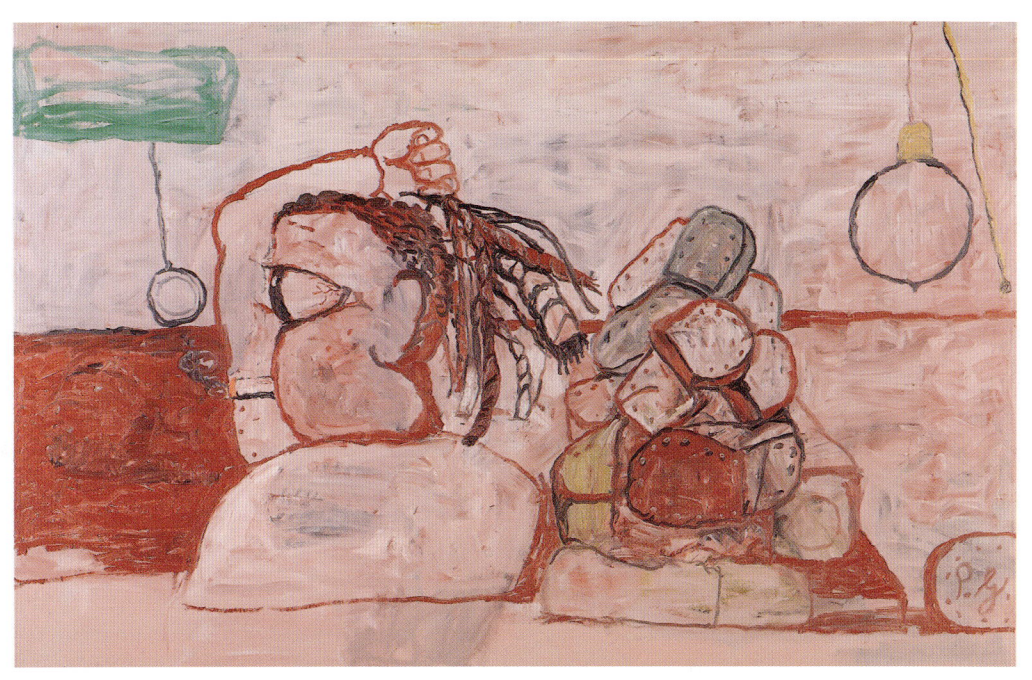

All I'm trying to do is see things as they are at a particular moment. — Philip Pearlstein

Philip Pearlstein ┊ American, born 1924 ┊ **Two Female Models Reclining on a Cast-Iron Bed** ┊ 1976 ┊ Oil on canvas 72 x 72 inches ┊ Gift of Sydney and Frances Lewis, 85.432

In the early 1960s, Pearlstein became a leader in the return to realism. Using the human figure as his subject, Pearlstein rejected the prevailing emphasis in painting and sculpture on abstraction. Yet his focus on surface and contour and his radical cropping of models' heads and limbs at the edge of the canvas treat the human figure more as an object than as a sentient being.

Working directly from live models in the studio, Pearlstein was very matter-of-fact in his approach to the nude. He described the human body as a "constellation of still-life forms," to be analyzed in terms of solids and voids and volumes and edges and the way these relationships worked in the compressed space of the picture. Pearlstein's dispassionate assessments of his subjects downplay psychological interpretation and erotic content.

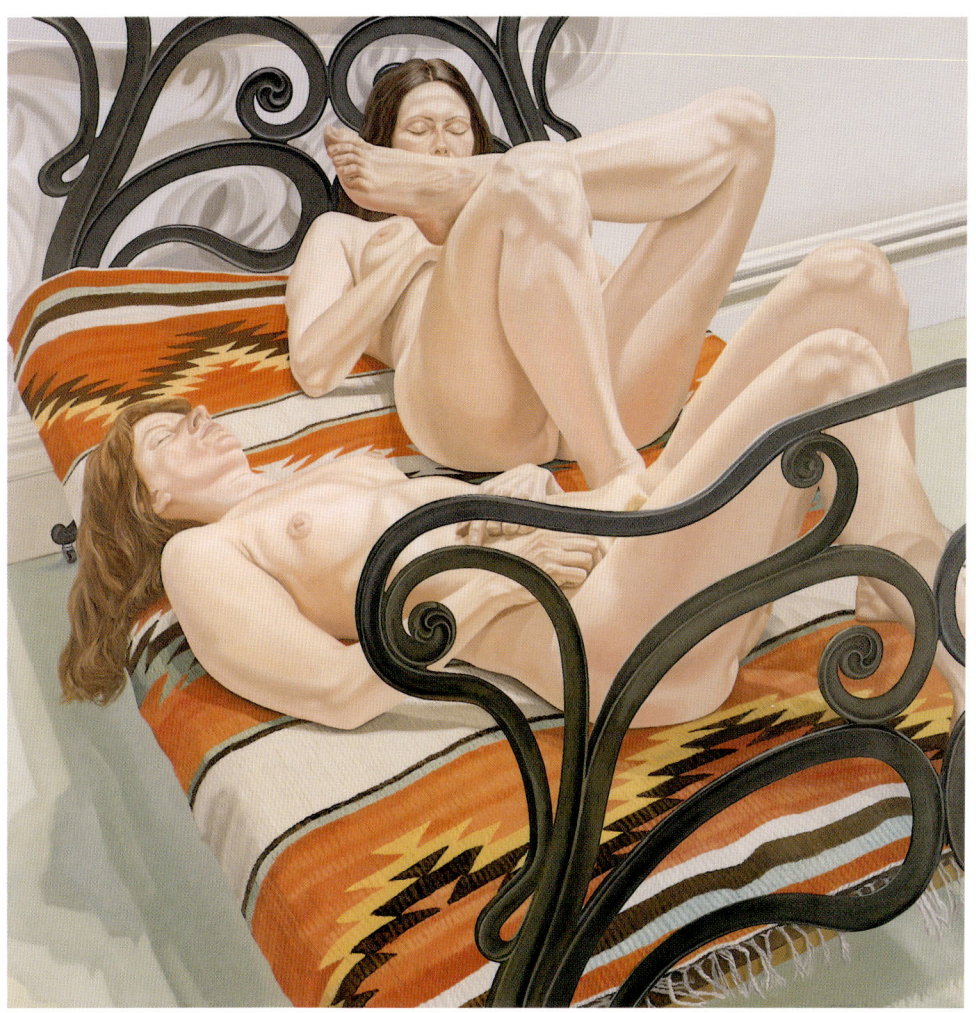

Some people keep talking about the grotesque,
as though I think of these figures as grotesque, and
I don't. . . . The work is grotesque only in terms of
a norm. — Jim Nutt

Jim Nutt ⏐ American, born 1938 ⏐ **"Please! this is important."** ⏐ 1977 ⏐ Acrylic on watercolor paper with hand-painted papier-mâché over wood frame ⏐ 27 ½ x 25 ½ inches ⏐ Gift of Sydney and Frances Lewis, 85.428

During the 1960s, when he took part in a midwestern alternative to Pop Art called Chicago Imagism, Nutt found inspiration in comics, wrestling magazines, and advertising, along with Surrealist, Expressionist, and outsider art. By the mid-1970s, his colors had mellowed and his debt to lowbrow culture was less overt. Nutt retained his meticulous style, but he now turned inward, letting imagination provide a cast of hybrid characters enacting stiff dramas of courtship and denial.

"Please! this is important." belongs to this period, when the metaphor of theater dominated Nutt's work. Nutt modeled his dense narratives on early Renaissance art, presenting his figures in an ambiguous space where scale distortions under-score their roles. Here, the central nude flees a menacing male profile, while lesser figures watch or perform their own microdramas. The apparently humorous scene quickly reveals edgy elements of discipline, punishment, and voyeurism, as well as gender and racial conflict. A fanciful frame of painted papier-mâché over wood gives the whole a feeling of quattrocento religiosity.

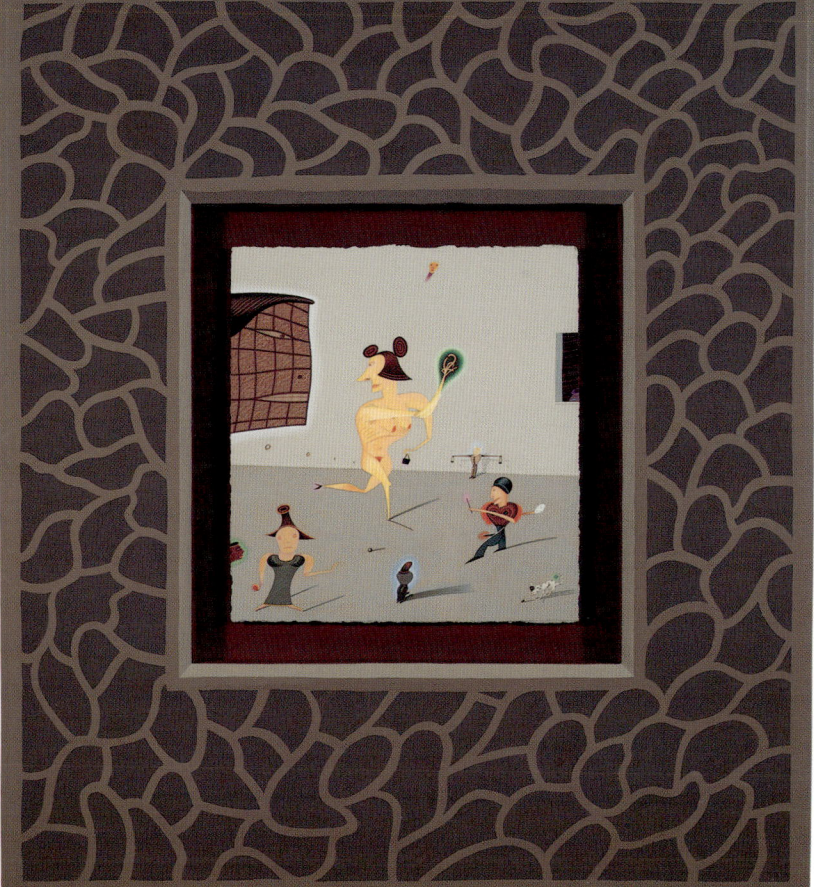

I wanted my paintings to change. I felt if I could restrict all the physical decisions about the work, maybe something would happen with the content. I decided to work on the plates for five years, no matter what I felt was coming out on them.

— Jennifer Bartlett

Jennifer Bartlett ⏐ American, born 1941 ⏐ **237 Lafayette Street** ⏐ 1978 ⏐ Enamel and silkscreen on baked enamel on steel ⏐ Twenty-seven plates, each 12 x 12 inches; 38 x 142 inches overall ⏐ Gift of Sydney and Frances Lewis, 85.360.1–27

Bartlett's impersonal, analytical approach to a limited repertoire of shapes, colors, lines, and marks resulted in brightly painted multi-part works. Labor-intensive and process-driven, they make reference to Expressionism as well as to Impressionism.

237 Lafayette Street, Bartlett's address in downtown Manhattan at the time, belongs to a series incorporating a rudimentary house form as the primary image. The foot-square steel plates coated with baked enamel were inspired by signs in New York City subway stations. Bartlett shifted the center panel of each image here, altering the composition's rhythm while preserving its orderly, mosaic-like pattern.

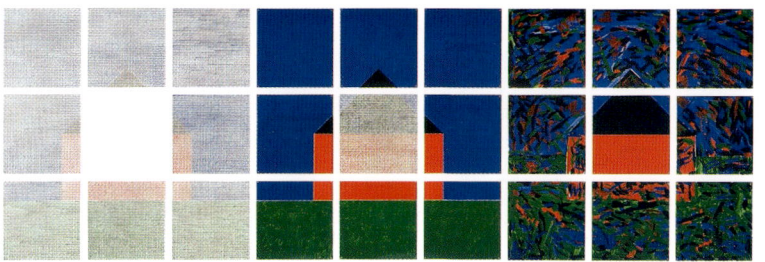

> In my mind, the small panels are the light and the darkness . . . the idea of Christ as light. —Brice Marden

Brice Marden | American, born 1938 | **Meritatio** | 1978 | Oil paint and wax on canvas | 84 x 96 inches | Gift of The Sydney and Frances Lewis Foundation, 85.423

Meritatio is one of a sequence of five multi-panel paintings, collectively titled *Annunciation.* The series interprets a fifteenth-century Italian priest's commentary on Mary's response to the news that she would give birth to a savior: disquiet; reflection; inquiry; submission; and—in this painting—merit. The panels' varying widths and colors reflect thoughts about light and darkness and good and evil.

Like other artists associated with Minimalism, Marden communicates through abstract means, emphasizing smooth surfaces, carefully mixed colors, and simple geometric units. The paintings' titles, and Marden's comments on his inspiration, however, allow—even encourage—the kind of symbolic content more often associated with representation than with abstraction.

There is an unconsciousness in society that comes out in its toys. . . . I discover that there is actually an archetypal activity going on in these figures, because it is the underbelly of society of which it is not aware. —Malcolm Morley

Malcolm Morley | American, born in England, 1931 | **The Grand Bayonet Charge of the French Legionnaires in the Sahara** | 1979 | Oil on canvas | 72 x 108 inches | Gift of The Sydney and Frances Lewis Foundation, 85.424

During the 1970s, Morley's work veered away from realistic paintings based on postcards and advertising and toward vigorously brushed images of collisions, disasters, and tropical animals. His earlier work pointed toward Photorealism; the later work looked toward Neo-Expressionism.

In addition to shifting style and subject, Morley began painting from actual objects rather than found images. *The Grand Bayonet Charge* shows a single lead toy repeated over and over across the flat "desert" plane in the same position but at different heights and scales. Reproducing the toy's crude style and elevating it to monumental scale brings out something of its latent ferocity, reflecting Morley's fascination with it as an icon of gender for teaching aggression to boys.

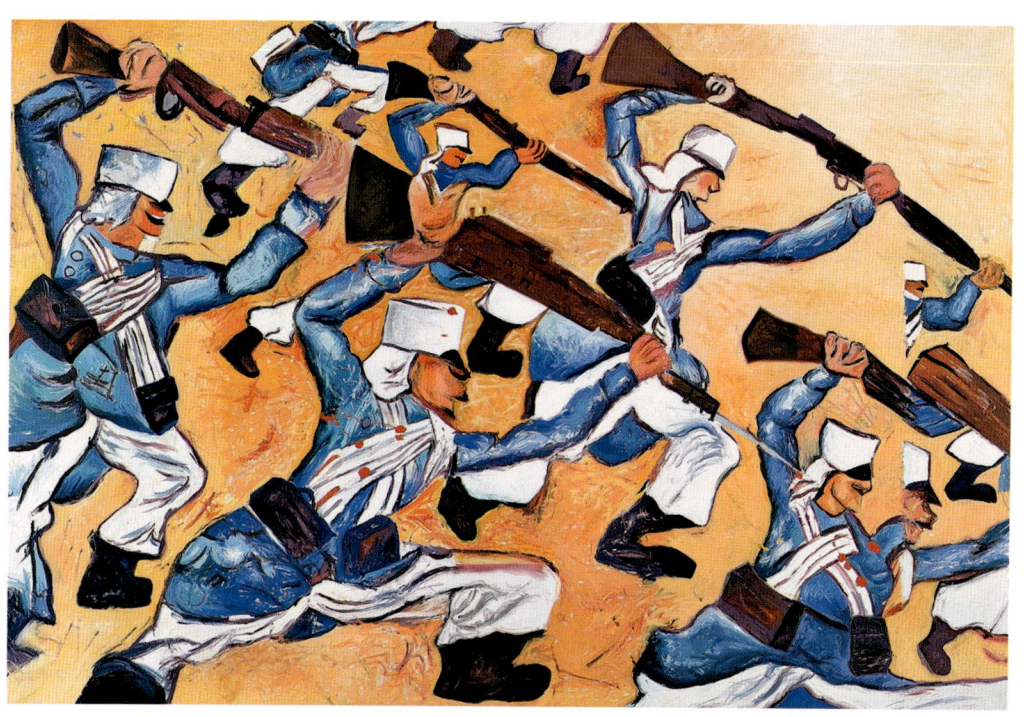

I was searching for an image and all I had to find it with was my head and my hand. . . . That's what a painter is—a hand and a head. —Susan Rothenberg

Susan Rothenberg | American, born 1945 | **Blue Head** | 1980–81 | Acrylic and vinyl-based paint on canvas | 114 x 114 inches | Gift of The Sydney and Frances Lewis Foundation, 85.437

Rothenberg's paintings exemplified the return to representation and personal symbolism apparent in many younger American artists' work beginning in the mid-1970s. This development was, in part, a reaction to the previous generation's exploration of abstract, often geometric, forms. Rothenberg's potent, highly simplified images resist explanation, but her emphasis here on the painter's two essential assets—the head and the hand—suggests the interdependence of concept and craft.

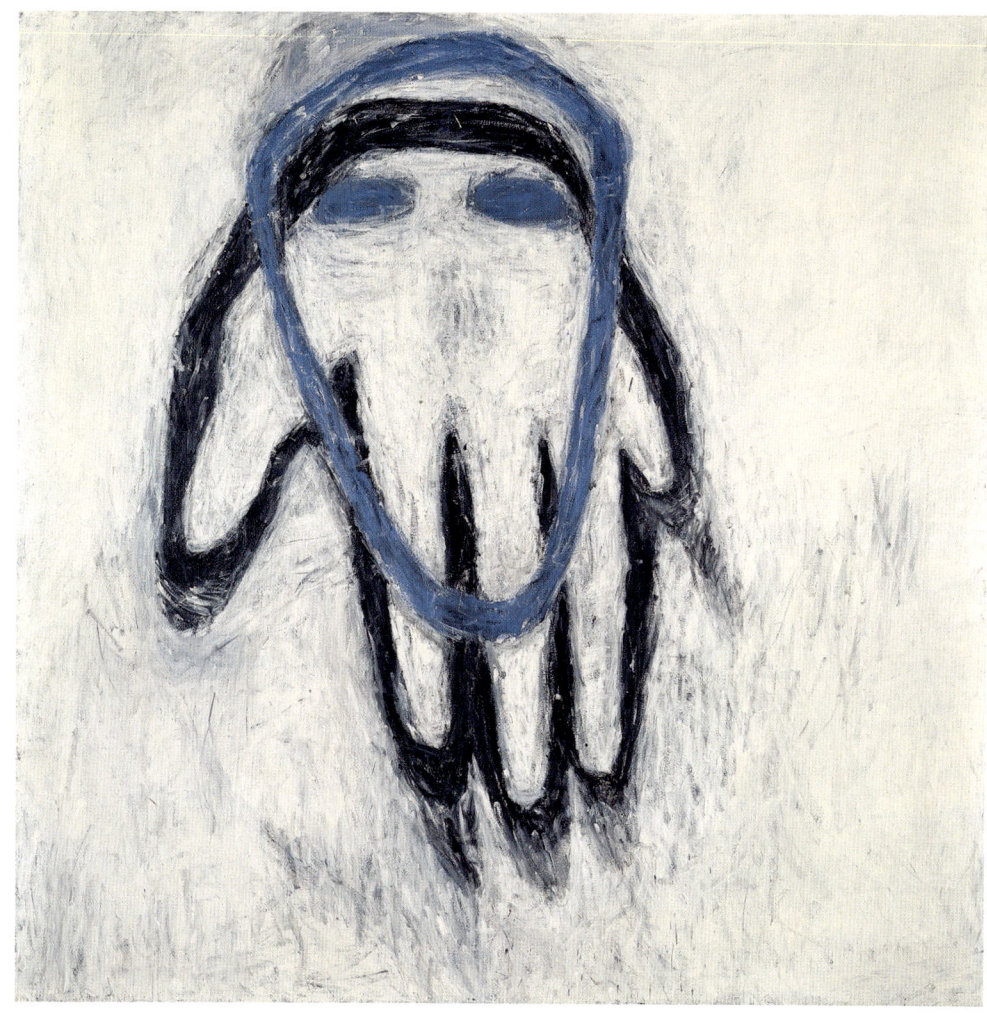

In India I never go to the museums, I go to the streets and look at all the things I like. The most beautiful things you see in India are the ones that only last for a day. — Francesco Clemente

Francesco Clemente | Italian, born 1952 | Detail of **Francesco Clemente Pinxit** | 1981 | Natural pigment on paper
Twenty-four parts, each 8 ¾ x 6 inches | Gift of Sydney and Frances Lewis, 85.373.1–24

Clemente made these works on hand-made rag pages taken from a 200-year-old Indian book that was considered of no particular value, a common practice in India, where the artist has lived. Clemente wiped off the written text but preserved the border, within which he painted his own "Indian" miniatures.

His highly personal subject matter includes figures (often missing limbs) engaged in such common or fanciful activities as dancing, swimming, looking through a telescope, and laying an egg. Clemente combines these figures with symbolic objects like trees, fish, eggs, and the sun. The artist uses ambiguous and fantastic acts to communicate a range of human emotions from agony to joy.

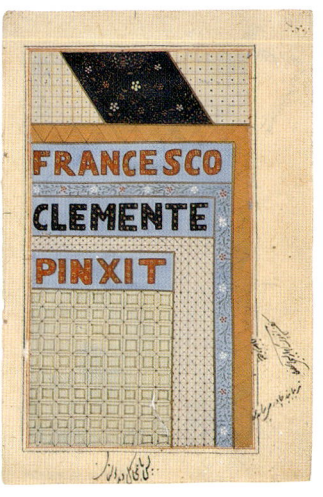

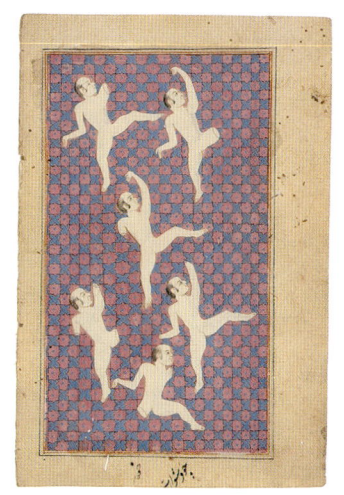

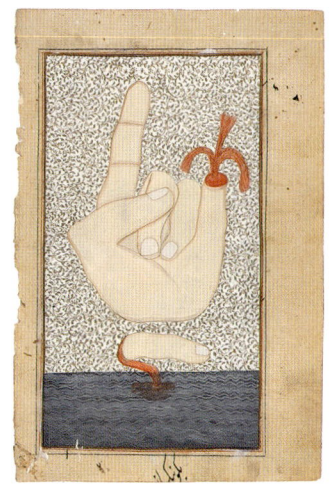

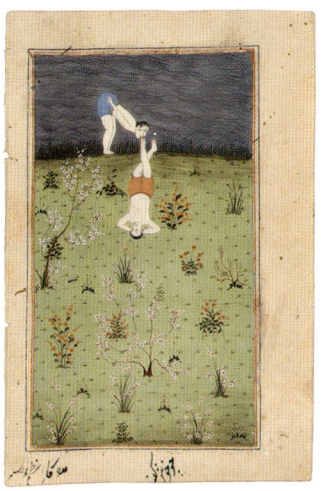

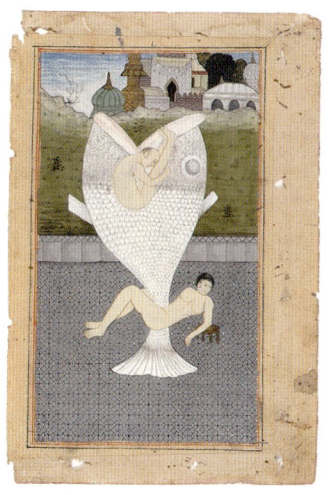

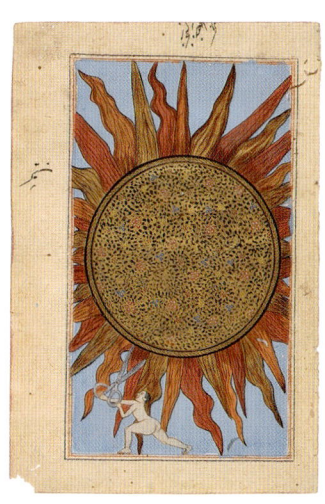

I work with symbols that link our consciousness with the past. The symbols create a kind of simultaneous continuity, and we recollect our origins. — Anselm Kiefer

Anselm Kiefer | German, born 1945 | **Landscape with Wing** | 1981 | Oil, straw, lead on canvas | 130 x 218 inches
Gift of The Sydney and Frances Lewis Foundation, 85.414

Kiefer's paintings use historical and mythological themes to explore his country's past, aligning him with the Neo-Expressionists—a group of artists, particularly some from Germany and Italy, active during the 1980s, whose works referenced culture and history.

Kiefer's immense desolate landscapes, made from such unorthodox materials as tar and straw, allude to centuries of conflict and devastation on German soil. The large object dominating this canvas refers to the Icelandic myth of Wayland, a crippled and imprisoned metalsmith who escaped on wings he made himself. Although this version is made of lead, such wings often symbolize redemption in Kiefer's art.

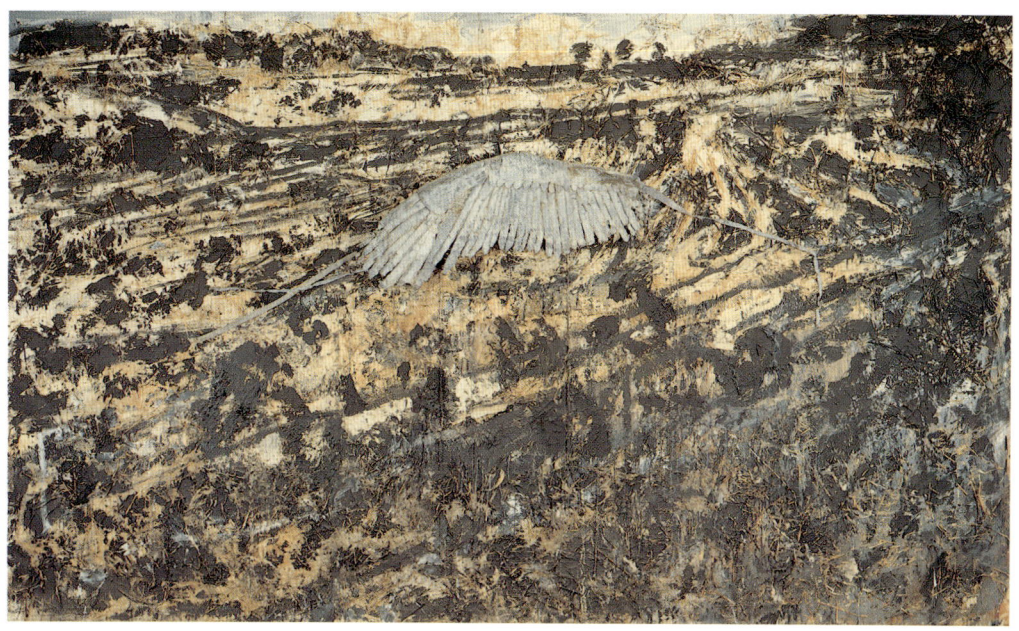

It was Formica which touched it off. Formica, the great ugly material, the horror of the age, which I came to like suddenly because I was sick of looking at all this beautiful wood. —Richard Artschwager

Richard Artschwager | American, born 1923 | **Williamsburg Pagoda** | 1981 | Acrylic and charcoal on textured fiberboard, Formica, painted wood | 87 x 73 ¾ x 8 inches | Gift of The Sydney and Frances Lewis Foundation, 85.358

Artschwager's work, like that of his Pop Art peers, focuses on American domestic culture and its icons. *Williamsburg Pagoda,* which features an image of the arsenal in Colonial Williamsburg framed by panels of Formica, raises ironic questions about conventional notions of old and new, reality and illusion.

The arsenal dates from 1715 and stands in an otherwise mostly reconstructed environment. Rows of bushes in the foreground recede in classical single-point perspective, culminating at the pagoda's peak. The painting's beveled edges push the image toward the viewer, yet the Formica panels above and below help set it back in space: the brown panel, like wainscoting in a period room, suggests that the image appears out a window, and the white panel seems to form a ceiling. Artschwager's play with spatial illusion and his unlikely combination of banal, modern materials with an eighteenth-century subject is meant, the artist says, "to make you stop, reconsider, look."

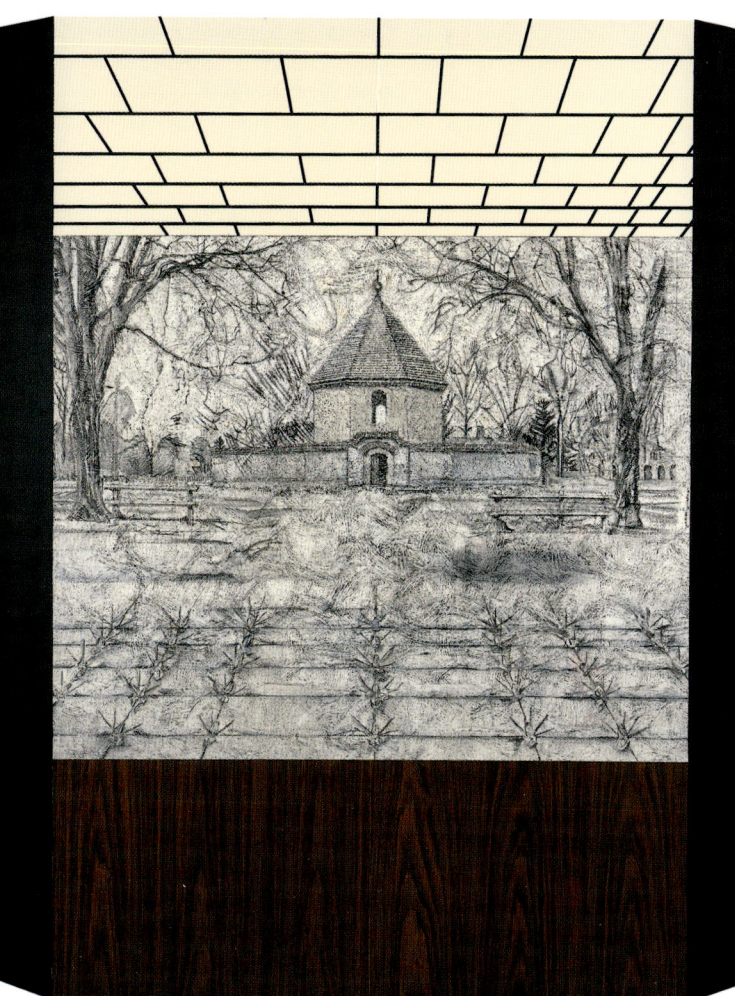

If you do work that is honest and committed, then the notion of beauty overlaps with the notion of truth. . . . I try to reach people who are looking for truth, for identity. Even though these notions are incredibly hackneyed, we must try to get back to these simple ideas. —Jörg Immendorf

Jörg Immendorf ┊ German, born 1945 ┊ **Kaltmut (Cold Courage),** from the series **Café Deutschland** ┊ 1982 ┊ Oil on canvas ┊ 98 ½ x 122 inches ┊ Gift of Sydney and Frances Lewis, 85.408

Immendorf's *Café Deutschland* series, painted before the Berlin Wall fell, takes place in an imaginary café symbolizing post–World War II Germany. The artist places himself in the foreground, drawing on a snow-covered table. The snow and chunks of ice evoke the atmosphere of the Cold War.

Other denizens of the crowded café include figures suggesting Adolf Hitler (at left, with red armband) and Chinese leader Mao Tse-tung (at right, with flashlight), symbolizing the totalitarian regimes—Nazism and Communism—that dominated modern German history. Other potent symbols include barbed wire, dying horses (from the Brandenburg Gate), an icy swastika, and a hammer and sickle. These symbols, part of Immendorf's vigorous style and satirical tone, are his pointed commentary on the arrogance of power and the pressure of living in a divided country.

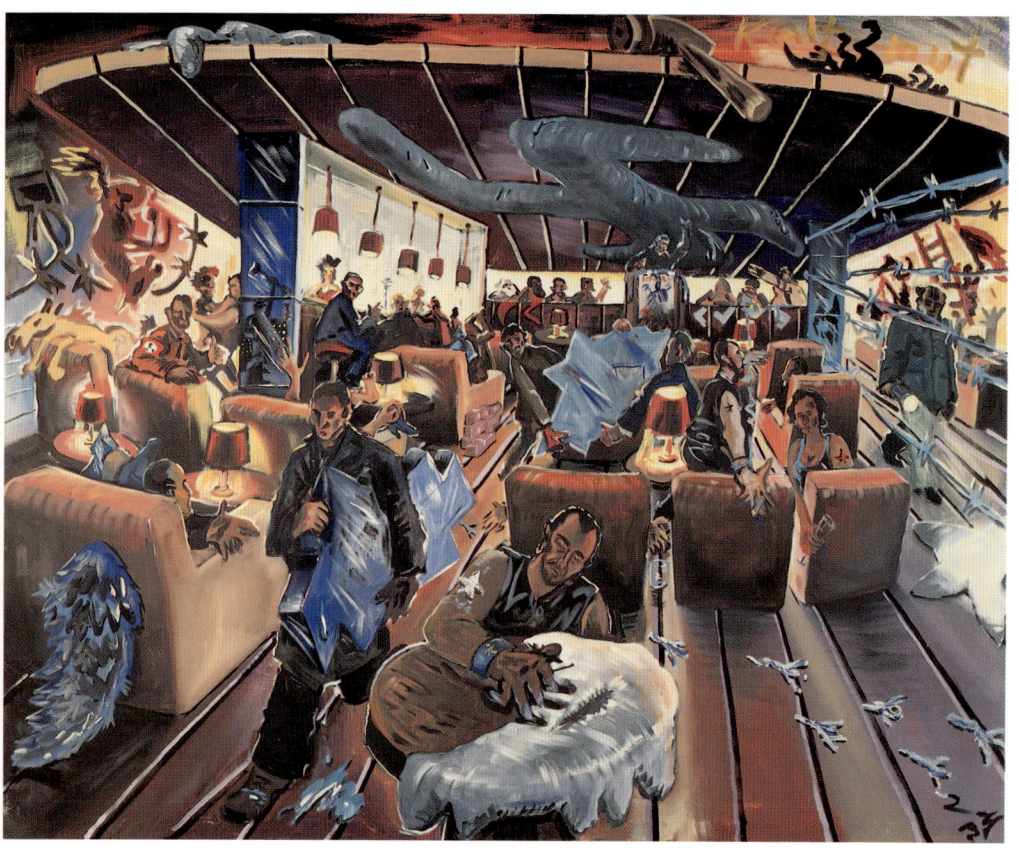

If you do your job right, if you do it one bit at a time, one piece of information at a time, you end up with something that has emotional impact without having to resort to emotional gestures. —Chuck Close

Chuck Close | American, born 1940 | **Jud** | 1982 | Pulp paper collage mounted on canvas | 96 x 72 inches
Gift of The Sydney and Frances Lewis Foundation, 85.374

In Close's work, photographs of friends and family members—his "mug shots," as he calls them—are the basis for seemingly endless variations in paintings, drawings, collages, and prints. A typical Close portrait is a virtual landscape of the face. This one, of sculptor Jud Nelson, consists of countless fragments of tinted, hand-made paper that compose a mosaic. At close range, the image dissolves into abstract patterns; only from a distance does it come into focus.

Although this is not always apparent in his finished works, Close has developed a rigorous method to guide the placement of individual marks or bits of paper that make up the whole. This approach links his work to Conceptual Art and to Process Art—movements of the sixties and seventies that emphasized systematic methods and properties of materials. However, the realism in Close's works and his practice of carefully transforming photographic images into other media have also aligned him with Photorealist artists.

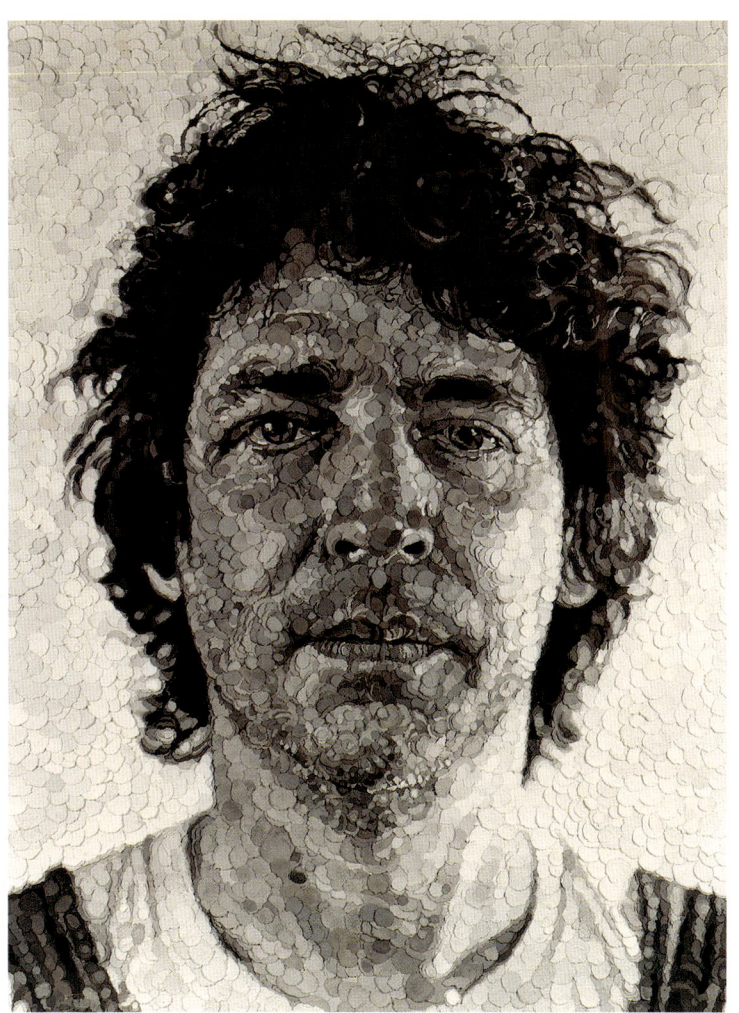

I was riding in a car, going out to the Hamptons for the weekend, when a car came in the opposite direction. It was covered with these marks, but I only saw it for a moment—then it was gone—just a brief glimpse. But I immediately thought that I would use it for my next painting. —Jasper Johns

Hatch marks appear as details or as an overall pattern in many of Johns's paintings and prints, beginning in the early 1970s. In *Between the Clock and the Bed,* what at first seem to be random marks are, in fact, a carefully structured system of repeated and reversed patterns. The left- and right-hand sections of the three-part painting mirror each other exactly.

Johns's paintings are often densely layered visual puzzles that explore the paradoxes inherent in the twin poles of painting, abstraction and representation. This piece's title, *Between the Clock and the Bed,* comes from a late self-portrait by Norwegian artist Edvard Munch (1863–1944), after Johns noticed the resemblance between his own hatch-mark pattern and the pattern of Munch's bedspread.

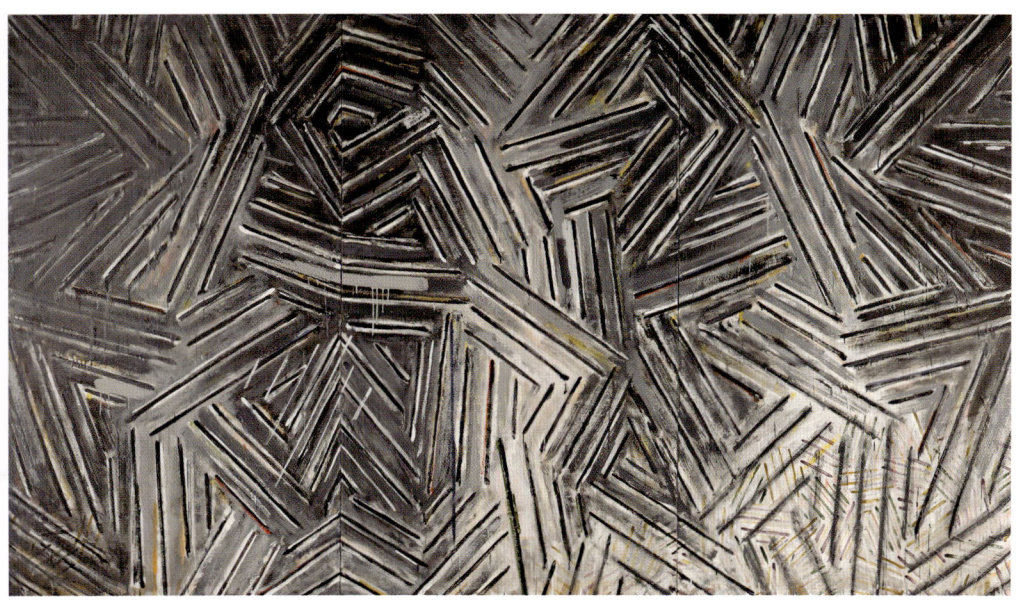

My work is a blending of process and imagery. . . . There's a lot to question: Is this shape solid? Is it space? What is it really about? There's a filling in of sexuality and there's also trying to make the image very real. —Donald Sultan

Donald Sultan | American, born 1951 | **Lemons** | 1984 | Latex paint and butyl rubber on vinyl tile over wood | 97 x 97 ½ inches | Gift of The Sydney and Frances Lewis Foundation, 85.583

Sultan's paintings contrast the delicacy of nature with an extremely physical process and materials. Strong outlines and bright colors characterize his images—primarily fruits and flowers, although initially also industrial landscapes and accident scenes. He began painting lemons in 1983, inspired by painters Zurburán, Velázquez, and Manet. Here the yellow forms merge into a pyramid of sensually swelling ovals with nippled ends. The faint trace of a plate locates them against the dark ground.

Sultan made this massive still life in four separate sections, covering each plywood sheet with Masonite, vinyl tile, and butyl rubber, a roofing material. He drew the image over this built-up surface, then removed the positive shapes, refilled the space with plaster, and, finally, painted. The balance Sultan strikes between abstraction and representation and figure and ground makes simple subjects and banal materials monumental and thoroughly contemporary.

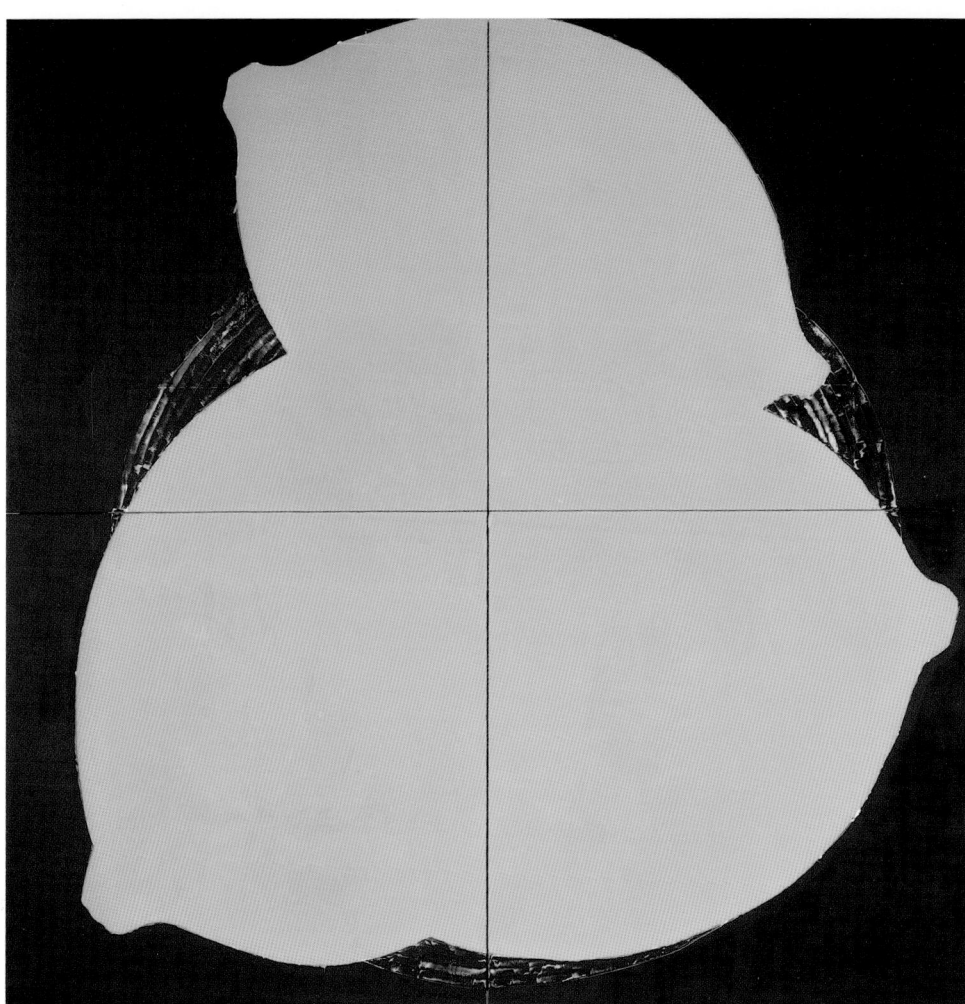

Later, one discovers that reality cannot be captured, that the things we make always represent just them-selves. — Gerhard Richter

Gerhard Richter ｜ German, born 1932 ｜ **Abstract Painting (594-1)** ｜ 1986 ｜ Oil on canvas ｜ 88 ⅝ x 78 ¾ inches
Gift of The Fabergé Society in honor of Sydney and Frances Lewis and Museum Purchase, The Arthur and Margaret Glasgow Fund, 97.129

Most of Richter's works have been abstractions, but during his remarkably varied career, he has moved freely between abstraction and realistic landscapes, portraits, and still lifes. He has used a wide array of styles and subjects to suggest the infinitely varied ways we perceive the world and to underscore reality's elusiveness and resistance to representation. To create the brilliant colors and sweeping strokes in *Abstract Painting (594-1),* Richter used large squeegees as well as brushes.

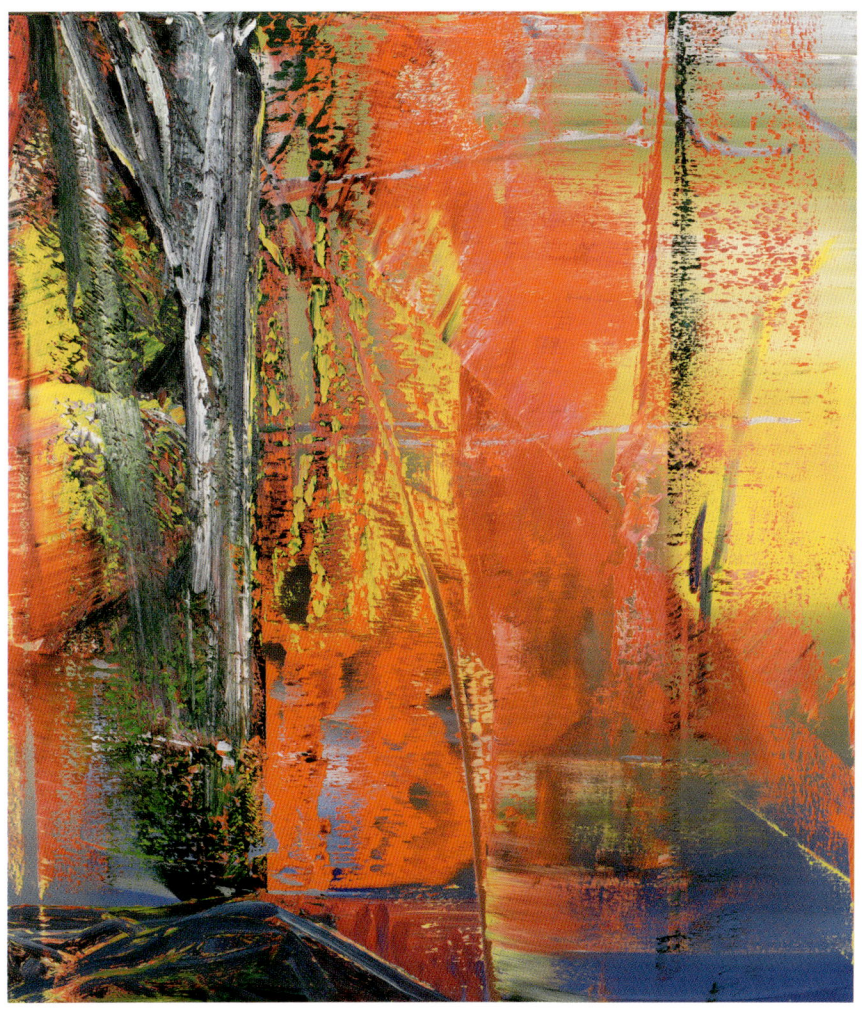

When an artist uses a conceptual form of art, it means that all of the planning and decisions are made beforehand and the execution is a perfunctory affair. The idea becomes a machine that makes the art.

— Sol LeWitt

Sol LeWitt | American, born 1928 | Detail of **Wall Drawing #541** | 1987 | Ink wash on wall | Dimensions vary with each installation | Museum Purchase, The Sydney and Frances Lewis Endowment Fund, 99.34

In the mid-1960s, LeWitt was a founder of Conceptual Art, an international movement that stressed an artwork's idea above its physical form. LeWitt himself installed his early wall drawings, but trained assistants now execute his plans—an approach that underscores his longstanding emphasis on the idea rather than the process or the object. LeWitt has compared himself to a composer who writes the score but doesn't necessarily perform the music.

LeWitt made his first wall drawings in 1968, using hard lead pencils directly on the wall. In the early 1980s, he began using soft cloths to apply ink washes, achieving the fresco-like effects seen in this work. The colors come from layering transparent washes of red, yellow, blue, and gray directly on the wall rather than mixing them beforehand. The cubes here are isometric drawings that represent three-dimensional forms on two-dimensional surfaces. LeWitt tilts and crops the forms to create the illusion that the images continue past the plane of the wall.

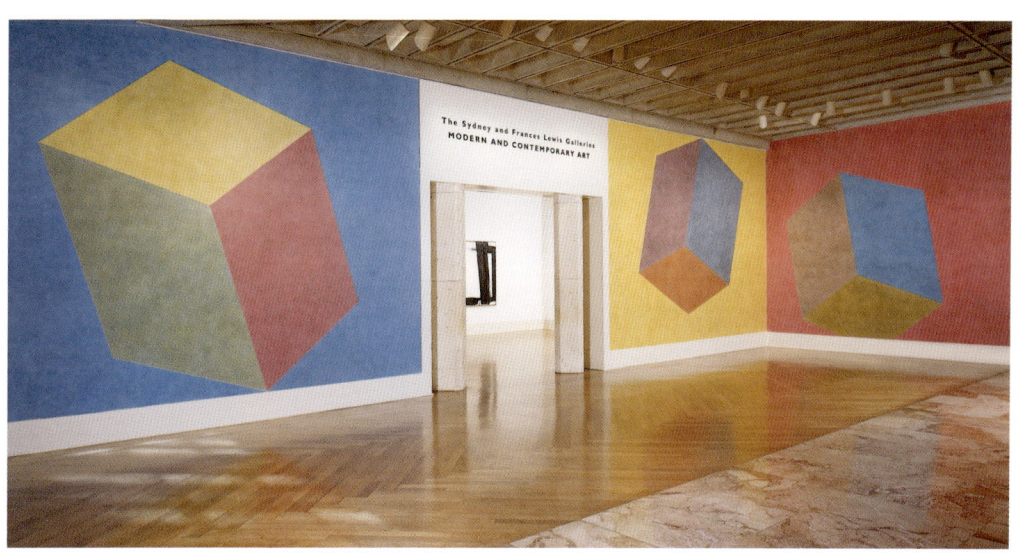

> In the end there is not so much to talk about but something to experience with the eye. Painting is very specific, but is not specific to things you can say.
>
> — Vija Celmins

Vija Celmins | American, born in Latvia, 1938 | **Untitled (Galaxy)** | 1988–92 | Oil on canvas mounted on wood panel | 16 ¼ x 18 ⅜ inches | Museum Purchase, The Adolph D. and Wilkins C. Williams Fund, 93.8

Since the early 1960s, Celmins has focused on a narrow range of subjects, repeated in drawing, painting, and occasional sculptures. Her works are usually small-scale, devoid of expressive gesture, bright color, and obvious composition. Within their closely defined limits, however, Celmins's images of deserts, oceans, and night skies reward viewers with glimpses of infinity.

Celmins, though, resists symbolic interpretation. She emphasizes the physical presence of her images, rather than their emotional or metaphorical possibilities, and her process reflects this. For the galaxy paintings, Celmins used small souvenir photos of night skies, on which she traced a grid to help her render the image with greater accuracy. Found images help Celmins distance herself from her subjects, removing them from the realms of personal experience and memory. Her interest lies in the act of translating the photographic image onto paper or canvas. Intense scrutiny and close involvement with her materials are not only her means, but her subject.

I think my paintings are a kind of dream, and about dreaming. — Elizabeth Murray

Elizabeth Murray ┊ American, born 1940 ┊ **Summer Wind** ┊ 1997 ┊ Oil on canvas on wood ┊ 120 x 107 x 3½ inches ┊ Museum Purchase, The Sydney and Frances Lewis Endowment Fund, 99.35

Murray's lively painting style, poised on the line between figuration and abstraction, played an important part in reinvigorating painting in the late 1970s and 1980s. Her complex paintings—often multi-paneled and irregularly shaped—monumentalize domestic objects and incidents, from teacups and tables to crying babies and family chaos. The stretched and distorted figure in *Summer Wind* (the dark form at the bottom whose ribbon arms and akimbo legs spread across the image) reshapes our concept of space and perspective and evokes associations ranging from a reclining figure engaged in breezy summer dreams to classical images of fallen heroes, their heads lowered toward the ground.

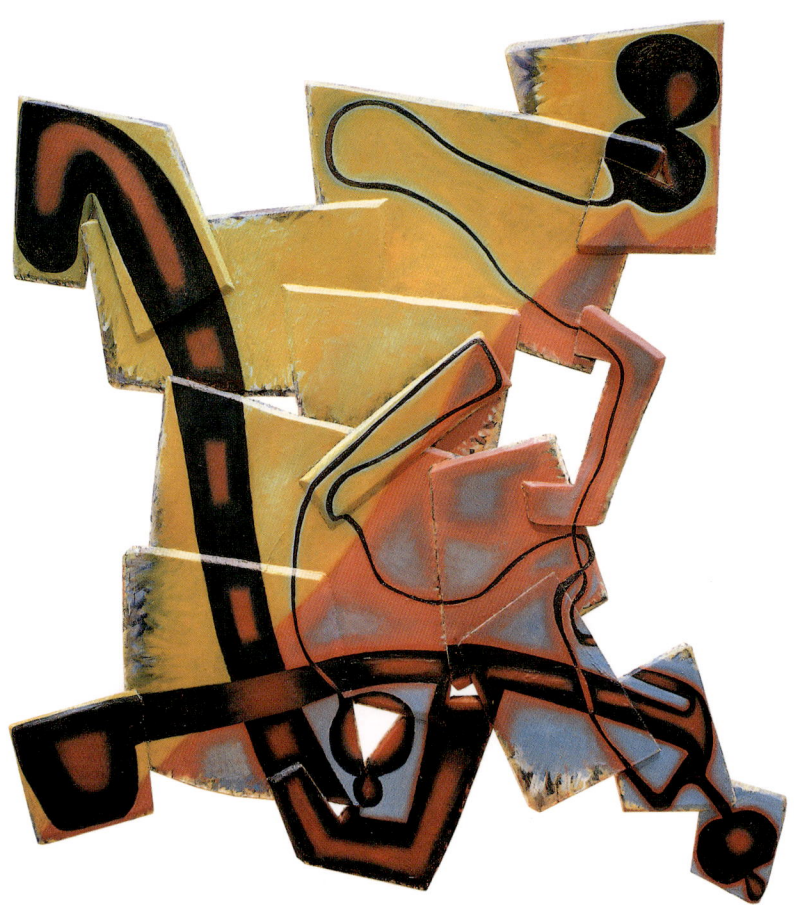

Painting can reflect our current environment. It has to be radically reinvented to be relevant to the present. I want my paintings not to be nostalgic or sentimental—that means they have to be about this moment.

— David Reed

David Reed | American, born 1946 | **#341** | 1993/1995/1999 | Oil and alkyd on linen | 36 x 144 inches | Museum Purchase, The National Endowment for the Arts Fund for American Art, 2000.10

Reed is fascinated with technology and media. The even lighting of *#341* suggests the glow of TV; its brighter colors have the intensity of Technicolor; and the extended horizontal format resembles CinemaScope. Reed also delights in the past. His signature ribbonlike forms recall the folds of garments in Renaissance and Baroque paintings. The luscious colors he uses also reflect his passion for those periods.

The abstract, gestural forms of Reed's paintings cause comparisons with Abstract Expressionism, in which the artist's brushstrokes record his creative impulse. Reed's looping gestures, however, are carefully crafted. He builds up layers of translucent glazes, opaque paint, and synthetic resins; masks off some areas and completely removes others; and sands and burnishes the surface. Reed worked on *#341* in three phases, completing it in 1999.

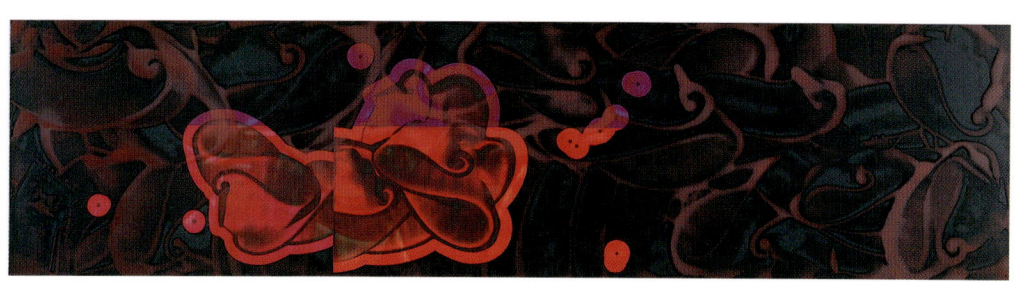

The iron and scorch pieces started . . . with my see-ing an iron on the street for many days and noticing it had a face on it that looked like a West African mask, a Dan. — Willie Cole

Willie Cole | American, born 1955 | **Fast Track Home** | 1999 | Scorched canvas | 72 ¼ x 73 ¼ inches | Museum Purchase, The National Endowment for the Arts Fund for American Art, 99.37

Drawing upon a rich tradition of artists who make art from everyday objects, Cole created *Fast Track Home* by pressing superheated electric irons onto canvas to make a complex pattern of light and dark scorch marks. Three generations of women in Cole's family were housekeepers; the use of irons refers to that history.

But the scorch marks' broader cultural references include scarification, African masks, crucifixes, and the gestural brushwork in Abstract Expressionist paintings. The white dashes along the marks' edges reminded the artist of highway lines receding into the distance and also of migrating geese flying in a vee formation, hence the title *Fast Track Home.*

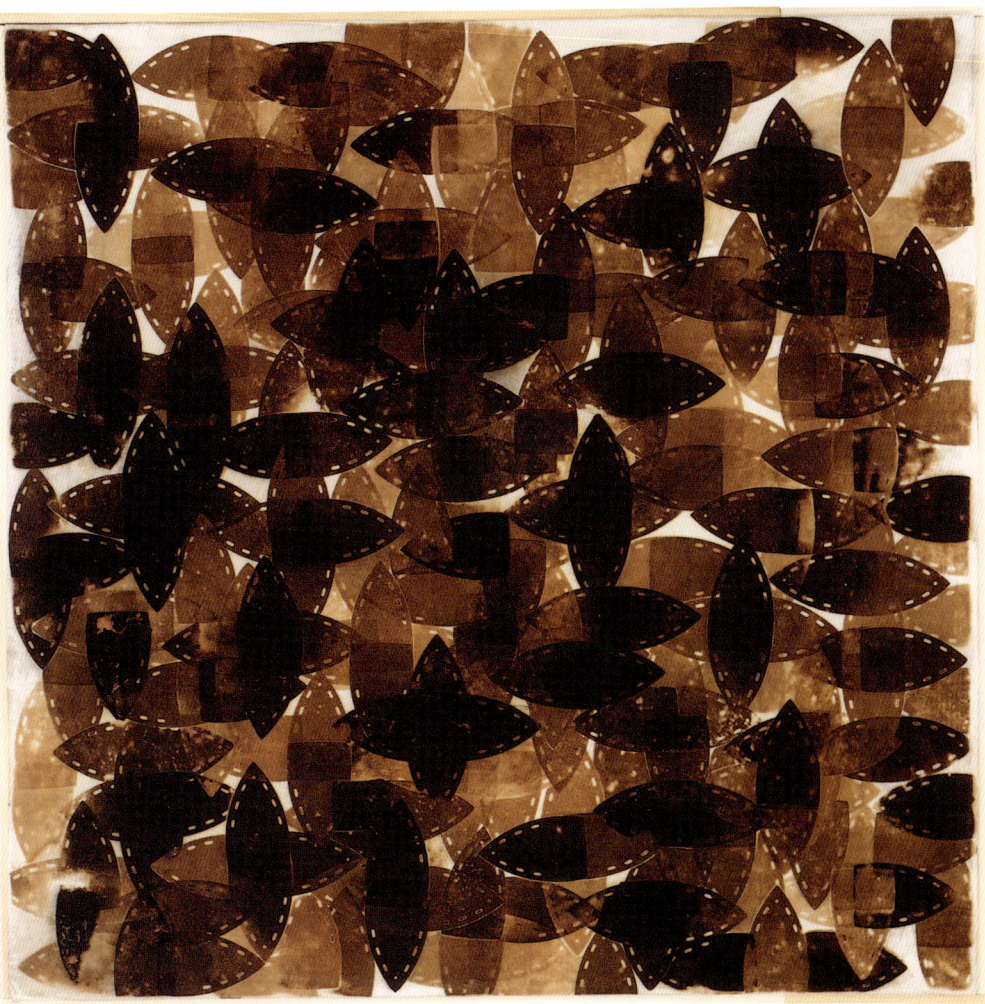

My challenge is how to develop something which is neither personal nor cultural, but somewhere in between. . . . People do not necessarily need to understand in-depth miniature painting to then understand what is happening in my work. — Shahzia Sikander

Shahzia Sikander | Pakistani, born 1969 | **Monsters Within** | 2001 | Watercolor, dry pigment, vegetable color, and tea on hand-prepared *wasli* paper | 15 x 11 9/16 inches | Museum Purchase, The Adolph D. and Wilkins C. Williams Fund, 2002.535

Sikander has adopted the formalized art of traditional Indian and Islamic miniature painting as the basis for personal expression. A Pakistani artist who makes her own brushes, paper, and paints, Sikander belongs to the first generation that has returned to the actual techniques of this traditional Eastern medium and has transformed it with methods and motifs from contemporary Western art.

This painting uses subtle layers of colors and combines realism, abstract pattern, and loose organic forms. A fully modeled self-portrait of the artist appears at the lower left, while a flatly rendered figure crouches to her right. Another abstracted crouching figure at the upper left merges human and bird forms. These disparate styles and hybrid forms signal Sikander's interest in bringing together diverse cultures and traditions in the space of a single image.

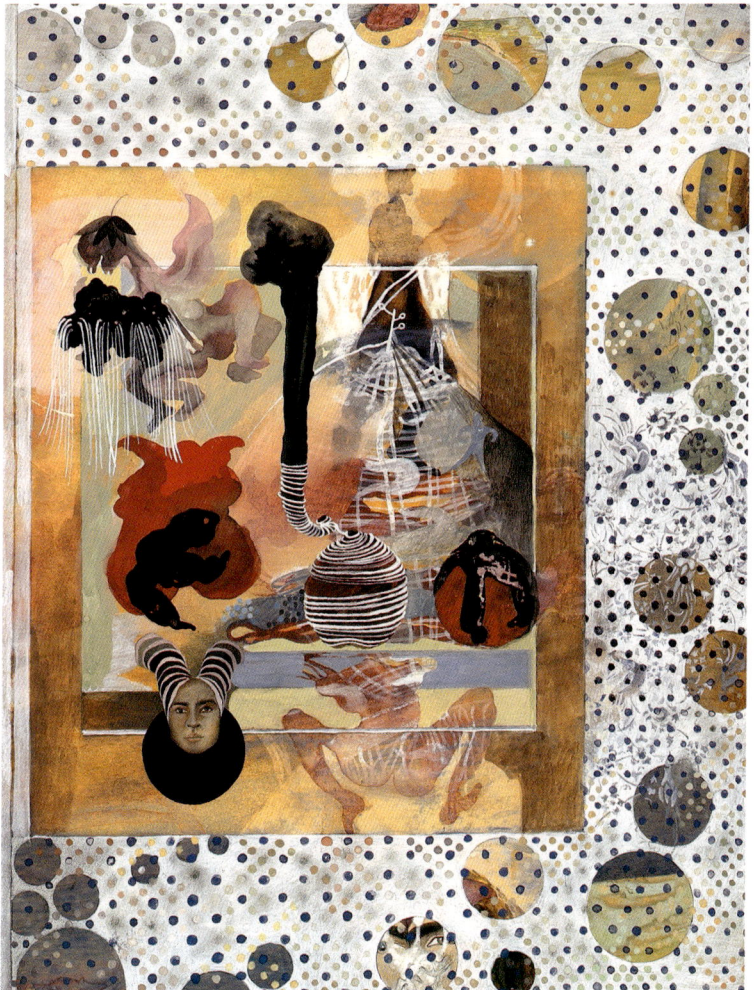

You have a choice: either you are going to make safe art or you are going to take chances. And I wanted to take chances. Here I've depicted a terror scene, which I have never actually experienced. . . . But still I am giving myself permission—through Surrealism in a way—by making the scene and in a way not meaning it, like it's a dream. —Inka Essenhigh

Inka Essenhigh | American, born 1969 | **Green Wave** | 2002 | Oil on panel | 60 x 72 inches | Museum Purchase, The Kathleen Boone Samuels Memorial Fund, 2003.4

Essenhigh is part of a rising generation that keeps painting fresh in an age of advanced technology and media saturation. In works such as *Green Wave,* she combines traditional picture-making with imagery inspired by virtual reality and cartoons.

Here, a tiny pink hand holds back a massive wave frozen in the moment before crashing. An eye glaring from the right adds both fury and lunacy. The curling crest that forms an upper lip meets a jawlike swell below to make a giant mouth poised to swallow the feminine creature at water's edge. She appears to be a hybrid of sea anemone and Kabuki heroine. Essenhigh suggests that this being, who even sports the remnants of an airplane lifejacket with ties and a whistle, is a survivor.

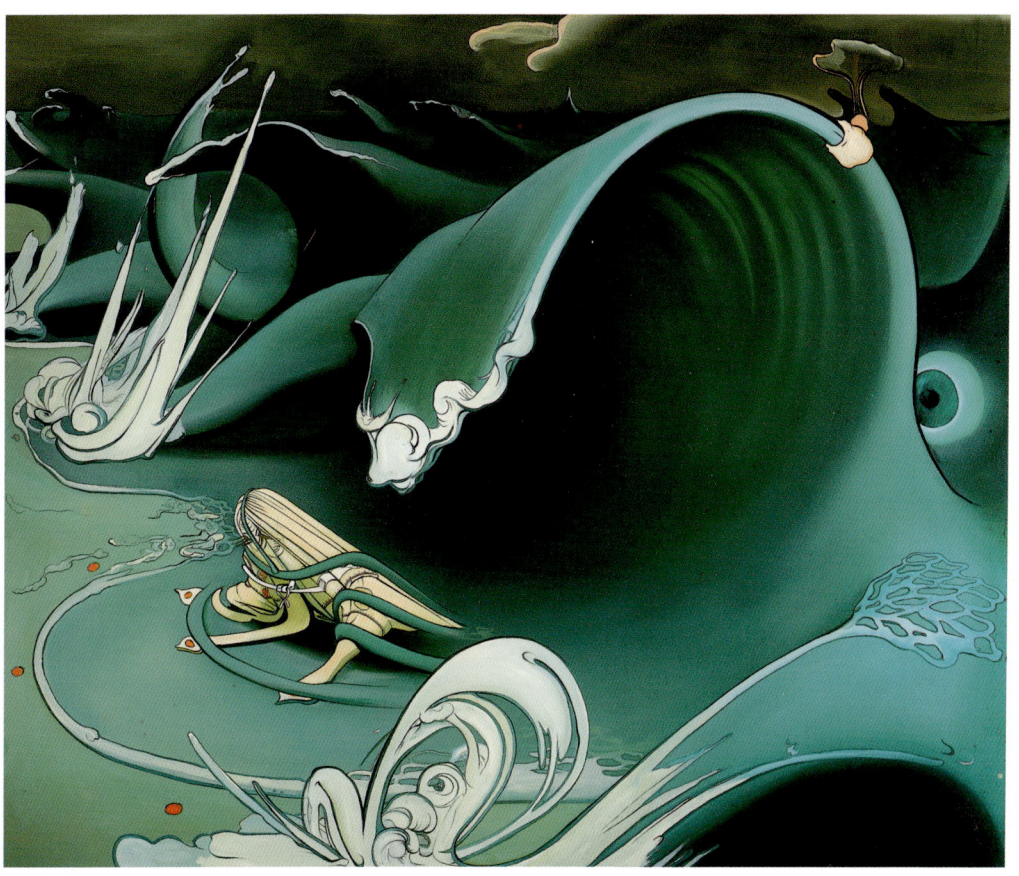

This translation or transmutation of hip-hop in Korea and Japan was a very strange awakening for me. There was a peculiar mix of performance or theater for some and a real way of life for others . . . the way it is at home. —iona rozeal brown

iona rozeal brown ¦ American, born 1966 ¦ **a3 blackface #59** ¦ 2003 ¦ Acrylic on paper ¦ 49 ¾ x 38 inches
Gift of Dr. and Mrs. Lindley T. Smith, 2004.67

These portraits by brown, who writes her name in the lower case, unite African-American and East Asian cultures. Her paintings resemble nineteenth-century Japanese ukiyo-e woodblock prints, but they present contemporary urban characters influenced by hip-hop. The artist found inspiration for these "Afro-Asiatic allegories" in Tokyo.

There she discovered *ganguro,* a fad among Japanese youths who imitate African Americans to the extent of artificially altering their appearance. In her work, brown adds a further twist to this cultural borrowing by appropriating samurai imagery and references to Japanese art history, theater, and fashion.

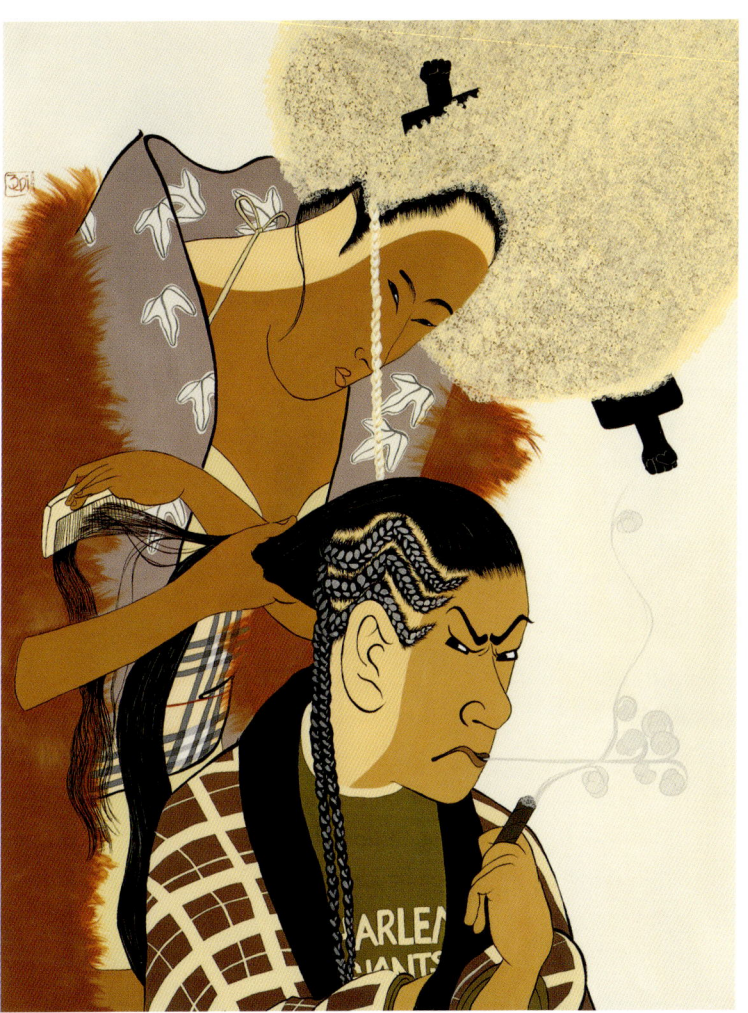

I want the kind of psychological space that feels seductive or Baroque in the sense of a space that you enter into. A slippery encompassing space, that's what I've been after. — Julie Heffernan

Julie Heffernan | American, born 1956 | **Self-Portrait in a Coral Bed** | 2003 | Oil on canvas | 80 x 45 ¼ inches
Museum Purchase, The Kathleen Boone Samuels Memorial Fund, 2003.9

In creating her allegorical self-portraits, Heffernan draws inspiration from dreams, observation, and historical styles, such as seventeenth-century Dutch and Spanish art. She has called all of her works self-portraits since the mid-1990s, although none of the figures particularly resembles her. Instead, they are psychological or metaphorical studies that arise from contemporary artists' renewed interest in narrative and allegory, and in expressing this interest through the human figure.

The girl seen here displays the opposing elements of fire and water like symbols of divinity or essential being. She stands waist-deep in a forest pool before lusciously painted coral, her head engulfed in flames. The small colorful globes falling from her hands also seem pregnant with meaning, recalling classical signs of fertility and abundance. The fire's suggestion of halo or crown underscores the girl's importance—though her specific identity remains deliberately vague, in keeping with contemporary approaches to allegory.

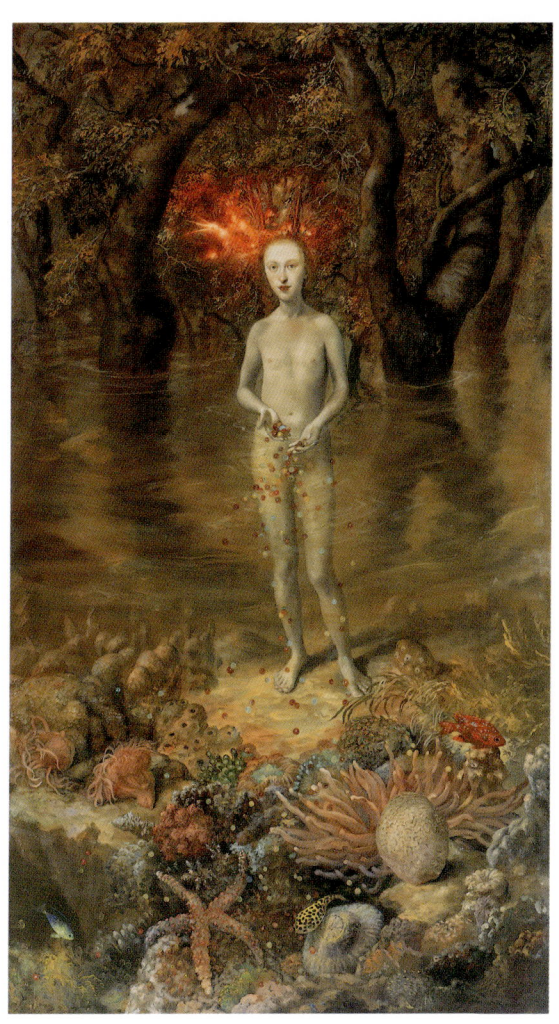

Ambiguity is the strongest weapon artists have at their disposal. You can play with the layers of interpretation and avoid getting into trouble. —Farhad Moshiri

Farhad Moshiri | Iranian, born 1963 | **S4M53** | 2004 | Oil on canvas | 71 $^7/_8$ x 92 $^1/_8$ inches | Museum Purchase, The Kathleen Boone Samuels Memorial Fund, with additional funds provided by Dr. and Mrs. G. Dastgir Qureshi and Mary and Donald Shockey, Jr., 2004.68

Moshiri returned to Tehran after studying at the California Institute of the Arts in the 1980s. Like many post-revolutionary Iranian artists, he makes works that address the interface between Islamic and non-Islamic cultures while refraining, for political reasons, from direct critique. *S4M53* derives its unusual title and subject from a coded numeric writing system used to transcribe and condense long Islamic religious texts.

Here, a sample of coded text is greatly enlarged and repeated in several directions to create a deliberate cultural hybrid: Eastern sacred script merged with Western abstraction. Moshiri built up the painting in layers of low-quality oil paint, which he prizes for its brittleness, and finished by folding and crushing the completed canvas. The fragile network of cracks conveys the sense of ancient material in the process of decay. Gridlike creases that resemble oversized tiles in a mosque strengthen this impression. Moshiri brings past and present together in uneasy union, commenting indirectly on the tensions in contemporary Iran between tradition and modernity.

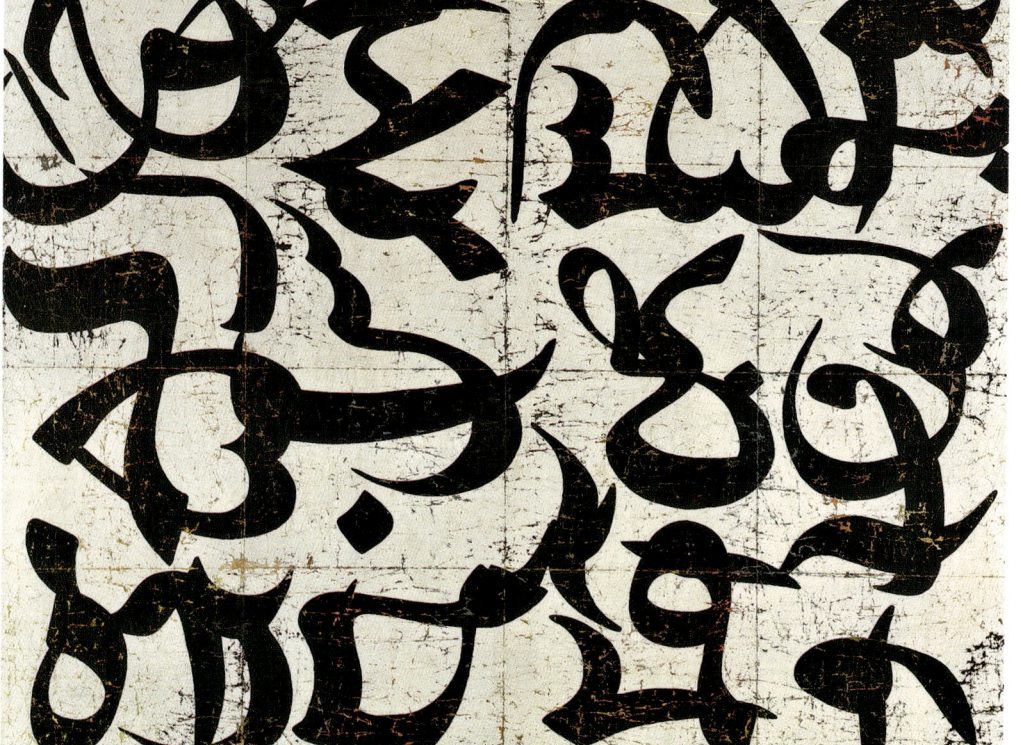

I'm interested in describing this as a system . . . a whole cosmos, and that is the overall painting, while the little minute detail marks act more like characters, individual stories. Each mark has agency in that sense—individual agency. —Julie Mehretu

Julie Mehretu | American, born Ethiopia, 1970 | **Stadia III** | 2004 | Ink and acrylic on canvas | 107 x 140 inches | Museum Purchase, The National Endowment for the Arts Fund for American Art, and partial gift of Jeanne Greenberg Rohatyn, 2006.1

Mehretu's monumental paintings address contemporary themes of power, colonialism, and globalism with dramatic flair. She adapts imagery from architecture, city planning, mapping, and the media. At the same time, her bold use of color, line, and gesture makes her works feel like personal expression.

Stadia III belongs to a series of three *Stadia* paintings dealing with the theme of mass spectacle. Conceived in the wake of the U.S.-led invasion of Iraq in 2003, the series reflects Mehretu's fascination with television coverage that transformed the war into a kind of video game—as many at the time commented—and in the spectrum of nationalistic responses that she witnessed during travels to Mexico, Australia, Turkey, and Germany. The series also reflects her interest in the international buildup to the 2004 Summer Olympics in Athens.

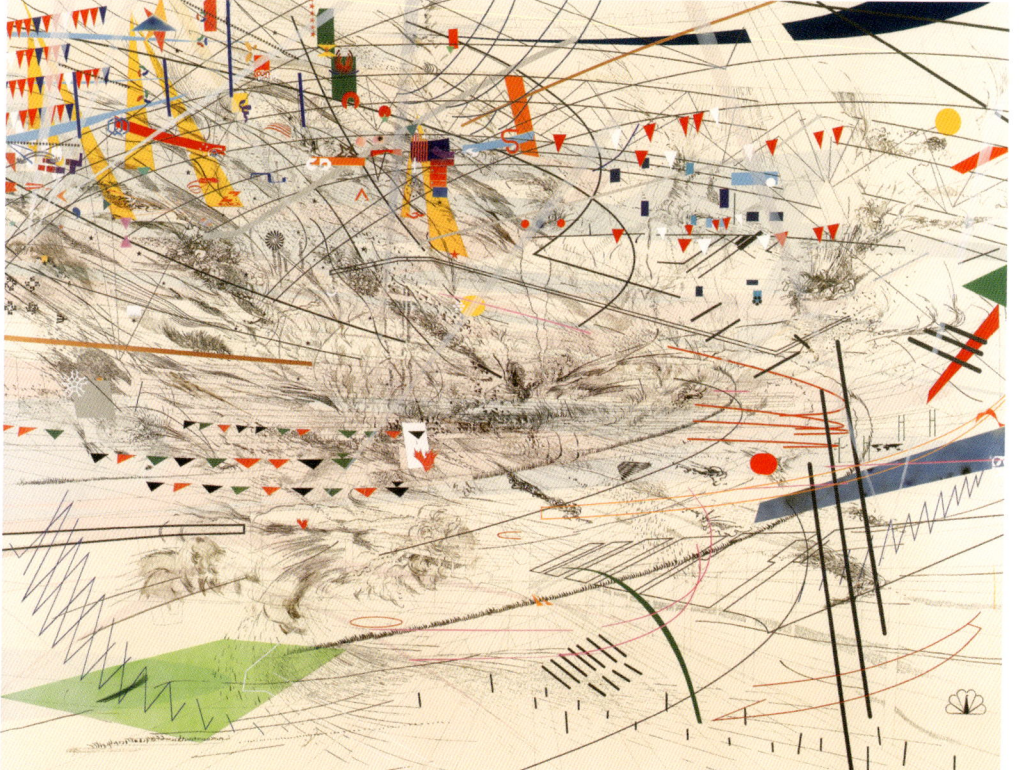

I'm trying to communicate complex and poetic concepts with a cold, graphic, and authoritative visual vocabulary. — Ryan McGinness

Ryan McGinness ¦ American, born 1972 ¦ **He Who Pays the Piper, Names the Tune** ¦ 2005 ¦ Car paint and acrylic silk-screened on board ¦ 96 x 60 inches ¦ Gift of the Fabergé Society of the Virginia Museum of Fine Arts, 2006.4

McGinness gained attention in 1999 with his book *flatnessisgod,* an outgrowth of his interest in design, illustration, and popular culture. He has since developed those interests further in painting and sculpture, creating a highly decorative, semi-abstract Pop Art based on anonymous universal design icons. McGinness transforms signs and symbols by drawing them in his notebooks and adjusting, revising, or reinventing them.

After refining them further on the computer, he silkscreens them onto brightly colored grounds. Like Andy Warhol, he uses this mechanical means of reproduction in a painterly way, welcoming smudges, blurs, and off-registration, while at the same time embracing the erasure of the artist's hand.

McGinness's flat, clean-edged style presents fantastic visions of outmoded pageantry and contemporary life, hiding recognizable emblems—stags, unicorns, griffins, aerosol cans, skateboarders, hand-grenades, candelabra, a courtly dancer, a guillotine—within a rococo confection of colorful swags and arabesques.

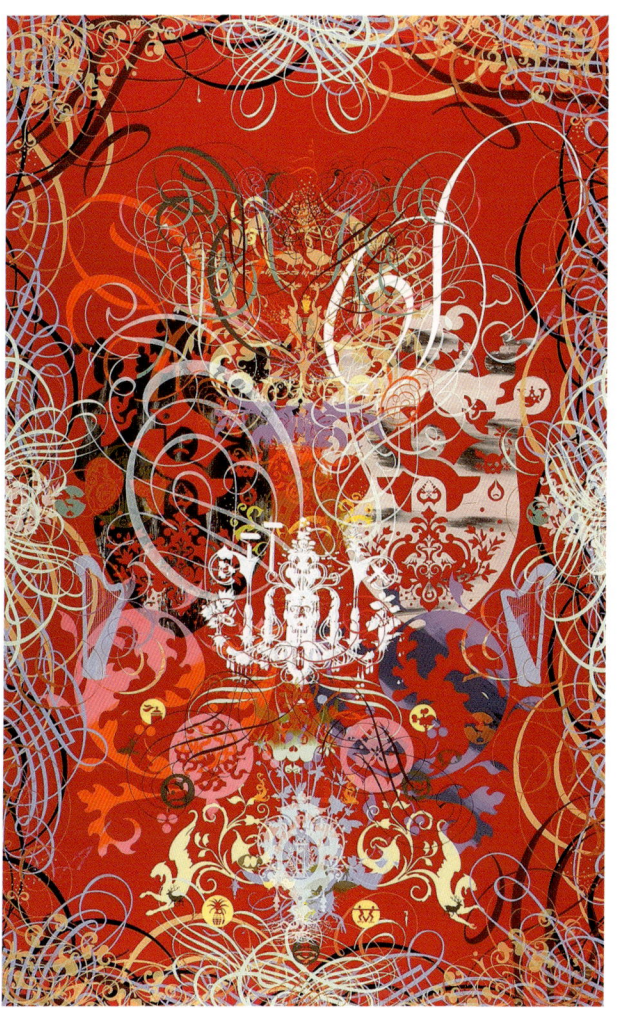

I want to aestheticize masculine beauty and to be complicit within that language of oppressive power while at once critiquing it. . . . I think it's always important not to shut the work down with any sense of high-art audience versus black-people-in-the-street audience. —Kehinde Wiley

Kehinde Wiley | American, born 1977 | **Willem van Heythuysen** | 2006 | Oil and enamel on canvas | Canvas size 96 x 72 inches | Museum Purchase, The Arthur and Margaret Glasgow Fund, 2006.14

Kehinde Wiley's lavish, larger-than-life images of African-American men play on Old Master paintings. His realistic portraits offer the spectacle and beauty of traditional European art while simultaneously critiquing the absence of people of color.

Wiley's *Willem van Heythuysen* references a 1625 painting of a Dutch merchant by Frans Hals, whose bravura portraits helped define Holland's Golden Age. Wiley's model, from Harlem, New York, here takes the name of the original sitter from Haarlem, the Netherlands, whose pose and attitude he mimics. Despite the wide gold frame and the vibrantly patterned background whose Indian-inspired tendrils encircle his legs, this subject's stylish Sean Jean street wear and Timberland boots keep him firmly in the present and in urban America.

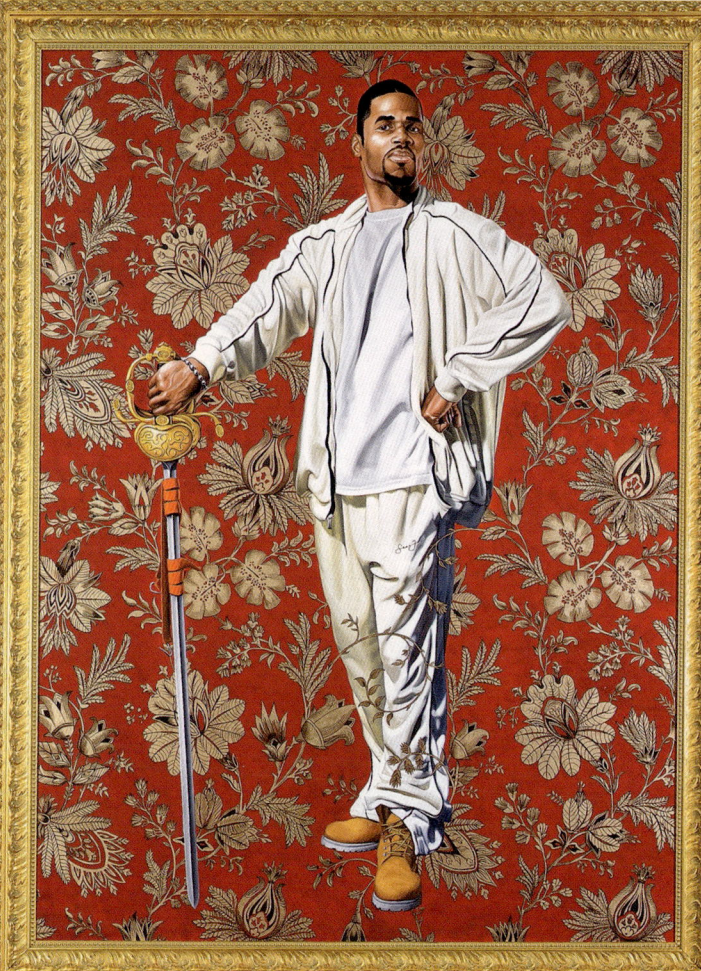

Sculpture | Video Art

To most people who look at a mobile, it's no more than a series of flat objects that move. To a few, though, it may be poetry. — Alexander Calder

Alexander Calder ⋮ American, 1898–1976 ⋮ **Hanging Mobile** ⋮ 1951 ⋮ Painted steel ⋮ 26 ½ x 66 inches radius
Gift of Philip L. Goodwin, 51.20

Calder's "mobiles," hanging or standing abstract sculptures whose parts move with air currents, are a notable innovation of twentieth-century art. Shortly after making his first mobile in 1931, Calder acknowledged that abstract paintings by Modernists Mondrian, Léger, and Miró had inspired his work. He wanted to see such colorful geometric and biomorphic shapes in motion.

Calder's early training as a mechanical engineer and his interest in astronomy also played a role. He described the new works in terms of such celestial phenomena as planets orbiting in a solar system.

Calder wrote the Virginia Museum of Fine Arts, which commissioned this mobile, to offer several color choices, adding, "If you would prefer it all black, I will make it that way. If such a mobile is all black or all one color it is much easier to see it as a complete unit. . . . I vary them, making some sombre, and others brilliant."

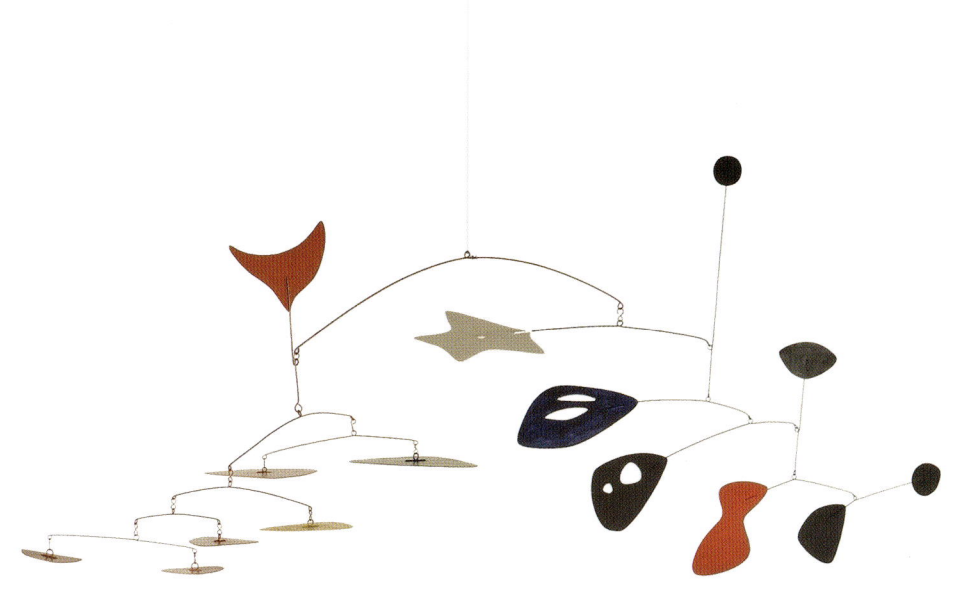

[T]he reclining figure gives the most freedom, compositionally and spatially. . . . It is free and stable at the same time. It fits in with my belief that sculpture should . . . last for eternity. —Henry Moore

Henry Moore ⫶ English, 1898–1986 ⫶ **Reclining Figure (Exterior Form)** ⫶ 1953–54 ⫶ Bronze ⫶ 45 x 87 x 32 inches
Museum Purchase, The Arthur and Margaret Glasgow Fund, 62.25

One of the most celebrated twentieth-century artists, Moore pioneered Modernism in Britain and spread its tenets internationally. Although he was known during the thirties and forties for his commitment to direct carving in wood and stone, after World War II Moore favored bronze casting, often for major government commissions. This official embrace led some to see his art as academic, forgetting that his early work received severe criticism for attacking the sanctity of the human form.

Moore's biomorphic abstraction reflects his interest in earlier Modernists—Arp, Brancusi, Miró, Picasso—and in non-Western and Archaic art. Organic forms such as bones, shells, and stones also inspired Moore's work, as did pastoral landscapes and the human figure. The reclining figure particularly occupied his attention, accounting for around a third of his works. In this example, large voids punctuate an abstracted body, creating strong tension between positive and negative forms. The smooth, curving contours invite the eye to glide along them, slipping in and out of what Moore called "pools of space."

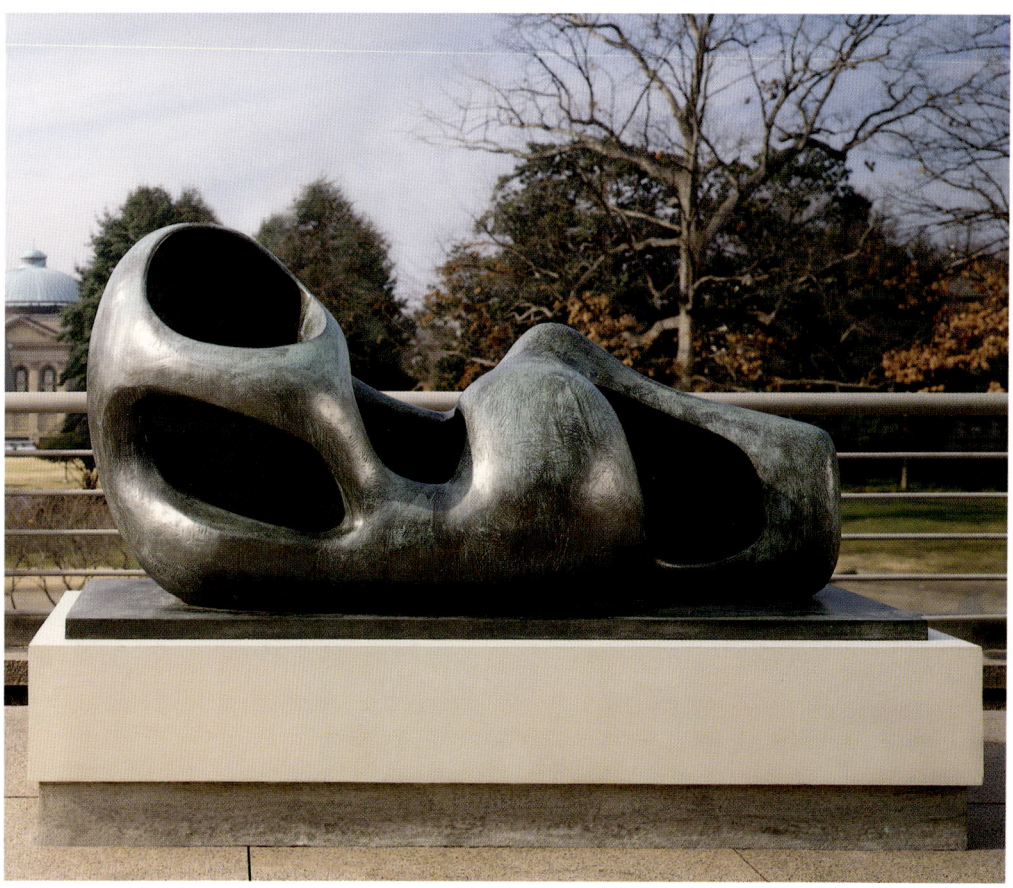

> The definition of sculpture for me is stance and attitude. All sculpture takes a stance. If it dances on one foot, or even if it dances while sitting down, it has a light-on-its-feet stance. — John Chamberlain

John Chamberlain | American, born 1927 | **Johnny Bird** | 1959 | Enameled steel | 59 x 53 x 45 ½ inches | Gift of Sydney and Frances Lewis, 85.370

Chamberlain's sculptures—salvaged automobile parts welded into complex masses—often transform his materials so completely that it is difficult to tell that they once were pieces of cars. *Johnny Bird* builds around a central axis and gains further interest from juxtapositions of color, texture, and irregular forms. Chamberlain's vigorous manipulation of these elements associates his work with Abstract Expressionism, although his use of found materials, and his willingness to embrace popular culture as represented by the car, links his work to the generation following, including Jasper Johns and Robert Rauschenberg.

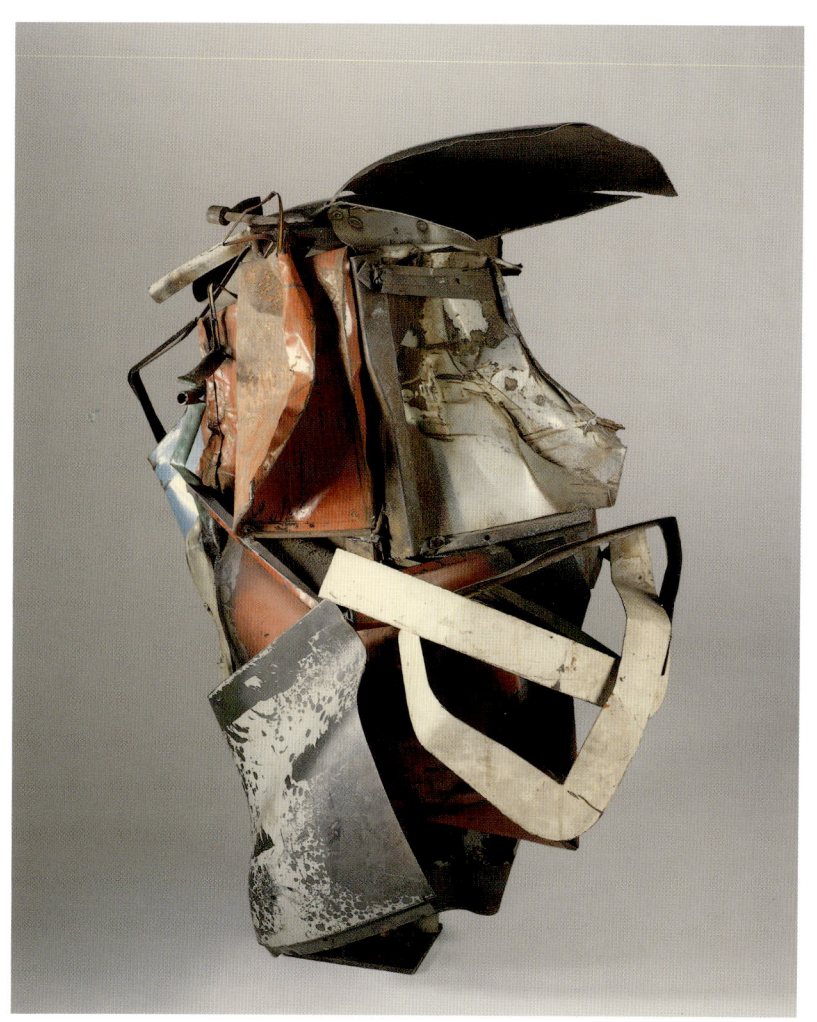

The Pop artists did images that anybody walking down Broadway could recognize in a split second—comics, picnic tables . . . refrigerators, Coke bottles—all the great modern things that the Abstract Expressionists tried so hard not to notice at all.

— Andy Warhol

Andy Warhol | American, 1928–1987 | **Brillo Soap Pads Box** | 1964 | Silkscreen ink and synthetic polymer house paint on wood | 17 x 17 x 14 inches | Gift of the Andy Warhol Foundation for the Visual Arts, Inc., and Museum Purchase, The Arthur and Margaret Glasgow Fund, 94.11

Warhol's reproductions of commercial packing boxes mimic banal everyday objects. These wooden boxes, hand-made to the exact dimensions of their cardboard prototypes, were painted light brown or bright white and silk-screened with appropriate logos. These sculptures are one example of the way Warhol eroded the boundary between commerce and fine art to make the two indistinguishable. Warhol's 1964 exhibition at the Stable Gallery in New York crammed hundreds of these boxes into the space, in effect transforming the gallery into a supermarket warehouse.

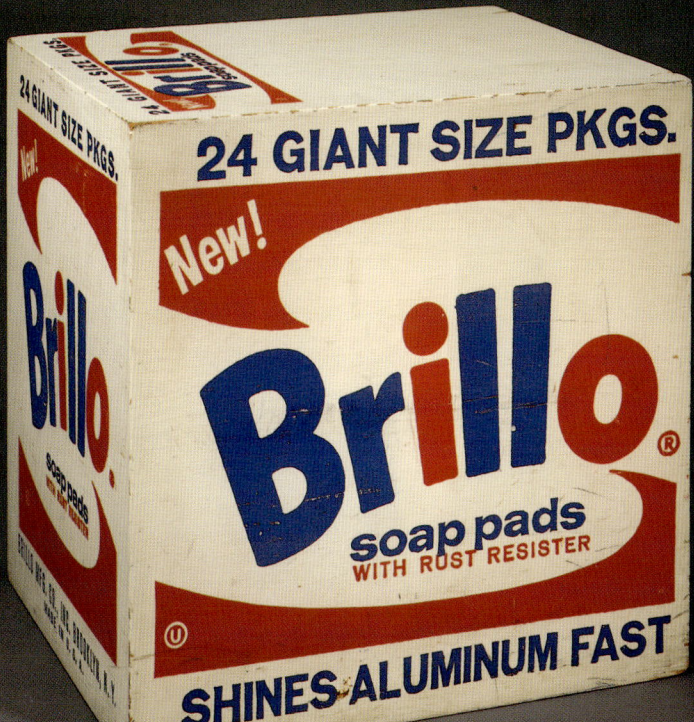

I suppose you can call me a Surrealist. But one should really say I am concerned with realism . . . [which] means the real with mystery. . . . I want to show reality in such a way that it evokes mystery.

— René Magritte

René Magritte | Belgian, 1898–1967 | **Madame Récamier** | 1967 | Bronze | ca. 67 1/4 x 90 x 40 inches, overall installation | Gift of Sydney and Frances Lewis, 91.484a–f

Shortly before his death, Magritte conceived the idea of making a series of sculptures derived from eight of his paintings. Like the canvas that preceded it, this sculpture is based on a celebrated portrait by French painter Jacques-Louis David (1748–1825). David's neoclassical painting depicts an aristocratic woman, Madame Récamier, reclining on a daybed.

While Magritte faithfully reproduced the bed, the footstool, the lamp, and the drapery that appear in the painting, he replaced the seated figure with an L-shaped coffin. His unexpected substitution transforms an image of elegant repose into a disquieting evocation of a more permanent rest.

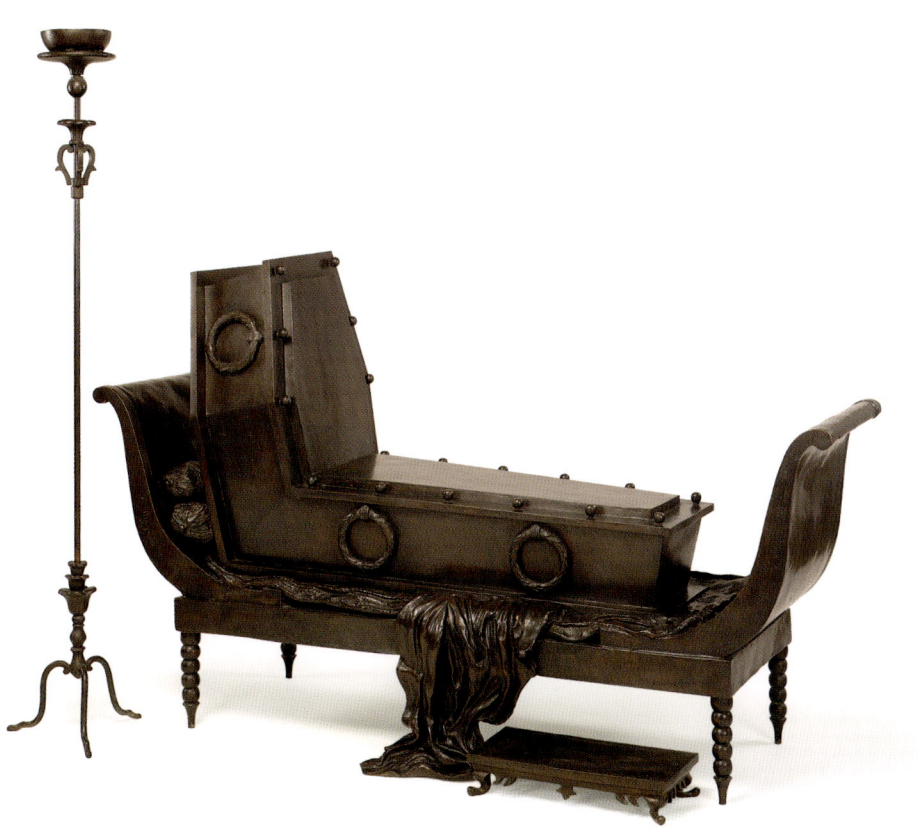

For me, the sphere is a perfect, almost magical form. Then you try to break the surface, go inside and give life to the form. — Arnaldo Pomodoro

Arnaldo Pomodoro | Italian, born 1926 | **Rotating Sphere** | 1968–69 | Bronze | 75 ¼ inches diameter | Gift of Mr. and Mrs. Lloyd U. Noland, Jr., 75.8

During the 1960s, Pomodoro's large-scale bronze sculptures became sought-after outdoor works for private and public collections. Pomodoro cites painting—especially the slashed canvases of fellow Italian Luciano Fontana and the dynamic energy of Jackson Pollock's painted surfaces—as a major influence on his three-dimensional pieces. Early-twentieth-century sculptor Constantin Brancusi's polished geometric forms also inspired Pomodoro's work, but he combined Brancusi's perfection with deliberate imperfections and rough surfaces that suggest the passage of time. Pomodoro's spherical works date from the early 1960s; in 1967 a massive sphere became one of the signature works of the Montreal Expo.

In *Rotating Sphere,* dark voids gouged into the highly polished form address relationships between past and present, nature and technology. The reflective surface distorts its surroundings, changing continually with light and movement. Violent ruptures of the perfect surface introduce tensions that Pomodoro likens to the anxieties of contemporary life but that also suggest futuristic landscapes.

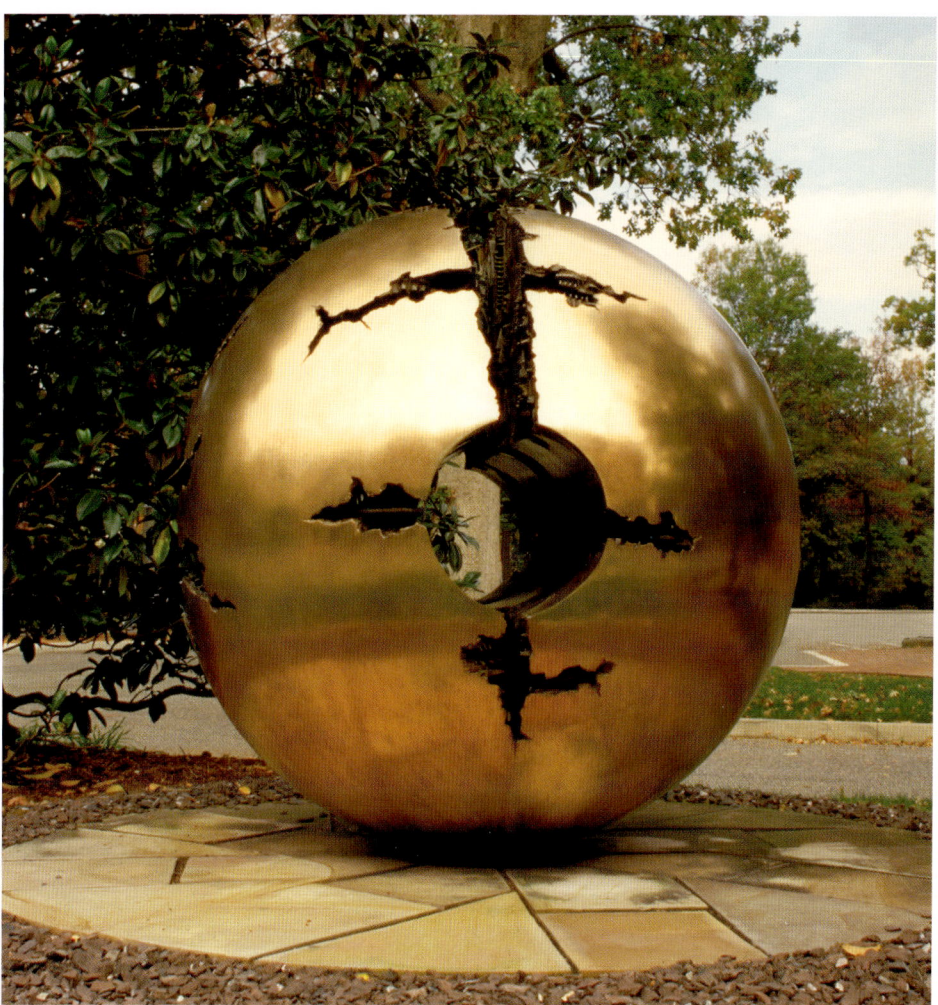

A direct investigation of the properties of these materials is in progress. . . . Considerations of gravity become as important as those of space. The focus on matter and gravity as means results in forms which were not projected in advance. . . . Random piling, loose stacking, hanging, give passing form to the material. —Robert Morris

Robert Morris ⏐ American, born 1931 ⏐ **Untitled** ⏐ 1970 ⏐ Industrial felt ⏐ 72 x 144 x 18 inches (varies) ⏐ Gift of The Sydney and Frances Lewis Foundation, 72.47

Morris began his series of felt works in 1967, shortly after becoming known for simple, rigid, boxlike sculptures that helped define Minimalism. His soft, flexible sculptures signaled a new emphasis on process rather than object—a shift many of his peers also made, called Anti-Form.

Morris made this visually complex work simply by cutting nine slits in a thick rectangular sheet of industrial felt, then hanging it on the wall at eye level. Gravity determines the final composition, which changes somewhat whenever the work is re-installed. Partly hanging and partly resting, it bridges wall and floor, the realms of painting and sculpture. Its pliable material, slits, and bulges suggest the body.

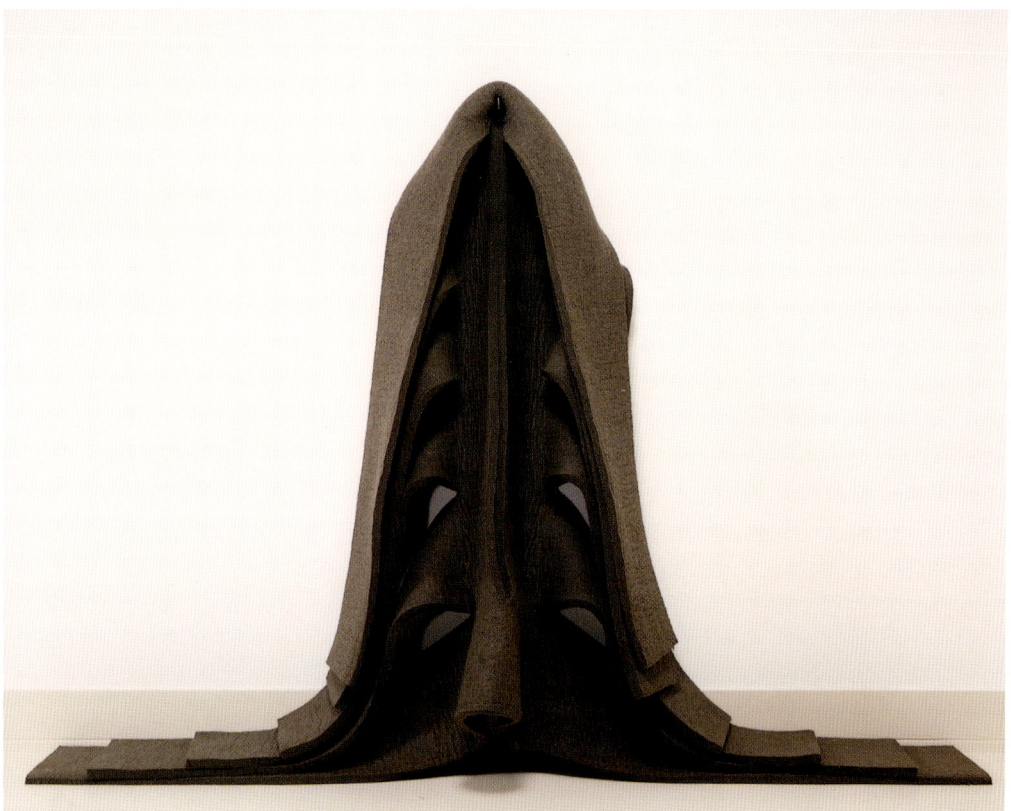

I'm interested in everyday types of things that people do—the common denominator, those things that are down-to-earth, non-elitist. —Duane Hanson

Duane Hanson ǀ American, 1925–1996 ǀ **Hard Hat Construction Worker** ǀ 1970 ǀ Painted polyester resin, clothes, wood, metal, plastic, found objects ǀ 47 ½ x 35 x 42 inches ǀ Gift of Sydney and Frances Lewis, 85.401 ǀ © Estate of Duane Hanson/Licensed by VAGA, New York, NY

Hanson began making his ultrarealistic sculptures around the same time that such artists as Chuck Close, Richard Estes, and Robert Cottingham began their precise illusionistic paintings using photography. Hanson, however, worked directly from life, making casts of parts of his models' bodies, filling the molds with liquid polyester resin, and reinforcing the resin with fiberglass. Then he painted, posed, and dressed the assembled parts.

Although based on individuals, each of Hanson's works is a type, an unremarkable Everyman or Everywoman. *Hard Hat Construction Worker* is a contemplative piece that recalls earlier sculptures, particularly Rodin's well-known *Thinker*.

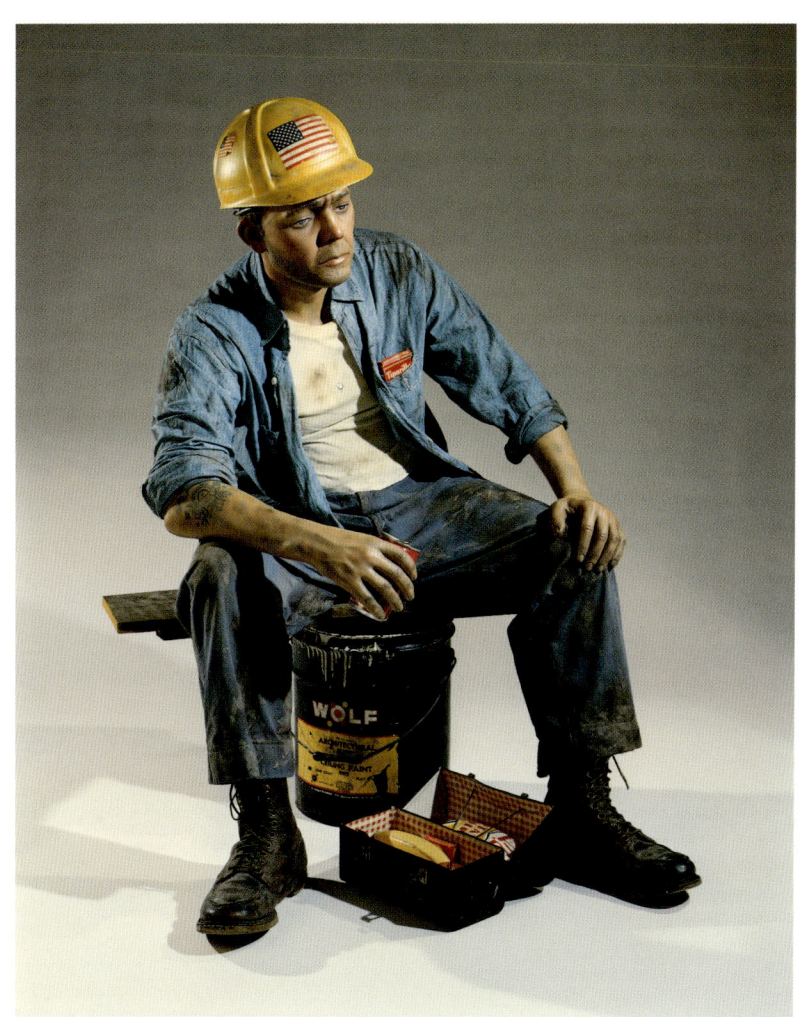

I am for an art that takes its forms from the lines of life itself, that twists and extends and accumulates and spits and drips, and is heavy and coarse and blunt and sweet and stupid as life itself. —Claes Oldenburg

Claes Oldenburg ¦ American, born in Sweden, 1929 ¦ **Clothespin Ten Foot** ¦ 1974 ¦ Cor-Ten steel, stainless steel ¦ 120 x 24 x 44 inches ¦ Gift of Sydney and Frances Lewis, 85.510

One of the original Pop artists of the early 1960s, Oldenburg made such common commercial items as food, clothes, and household appliances seem strange and extraordinary by enlarging them, changing their materials, and simplifying their forms.

On an airplane in 1967, Oldenburg held a clothespin up to the window and conceived a truly colossal urban sculpture. In 1976, he installed his first large-scale permanent public sculpture, a forty-five-foot-tall steel clothespin, in downtown Philadelphia. The ten-foot-tall version seen here suggests architectural scale but also suggests the body, or perhaps two tall bodies embracing.

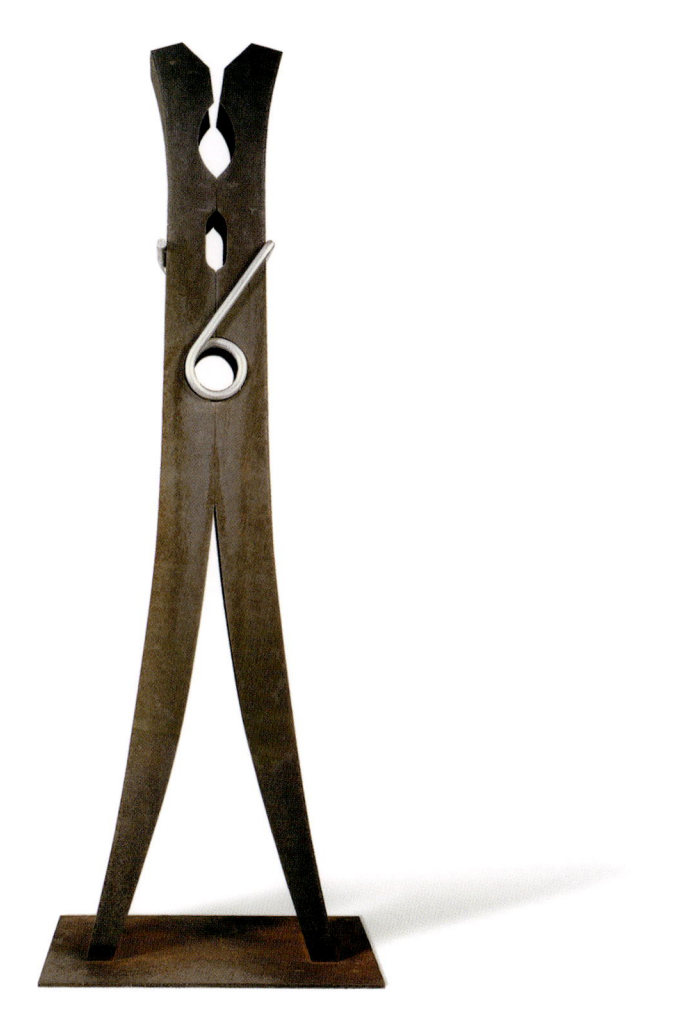

It has become increasingly clear to me that the core of my work resides in an area of my mind which can very well be approached geographically.

— Rafael Ferrer

Rafael Ferrer ⋮ American, born Puerto Rico, 1933 ⋮ **Map for the Poets** ⋮ 1974 ⋮ Wood, lead, copper ⋮ 49 x 46 inches ⋮ Gift of Ivan Karp, 74.30.5

Ferrer's art addresses his own Puerto Rican heritage as well as each individual's search for identity and personal meaning. In the 1970s, Ferrer developed images and artifacts for an imaginary primitive culture. *Map for the Poets* charts its unknown terrain and also suggests the human form.

This simple wall-mounted construction crosses the usual boundary between painting and sculpture. By incorporating natural materials and figurative references, it also updates and enriches the abstract reductivist vocabulary of Minimalism and Conceptual Art out of which Ferrer's work developed.

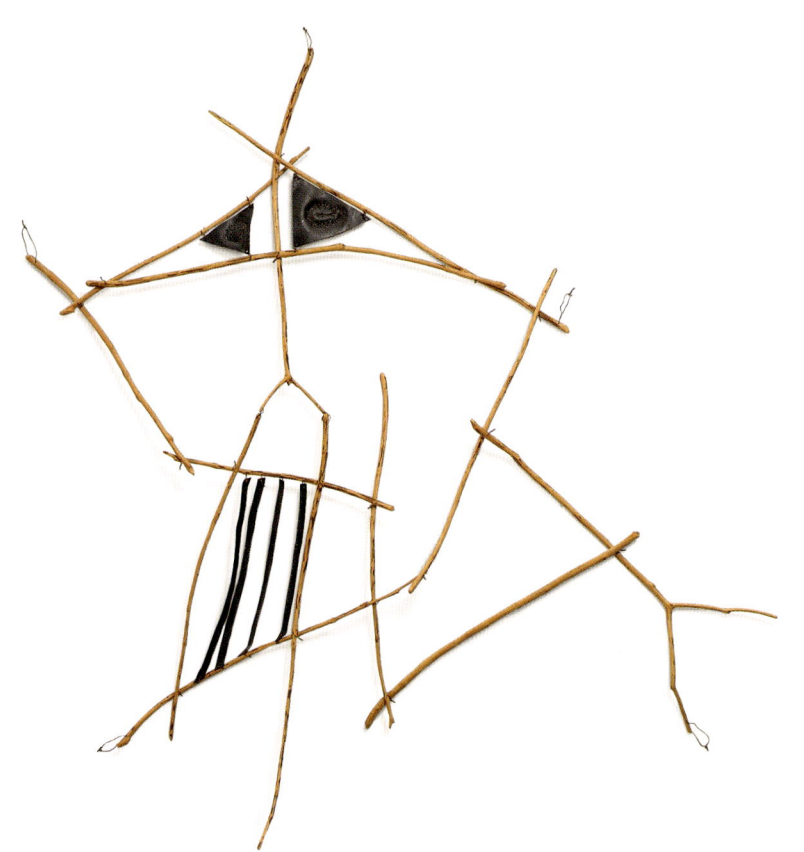

Instead of going to an art store, we'd go to the hardware stores, or to the five-and-dime. . . . I took some pins and glue and saw immediately that it made fantastic textural sculpture. . . . It connected with my past too—that silver tradition and Byzantine gold. —Lucas Samaras

Lucas Samaras | American, born in Greece, 1936 | **Box #89** | 1974 | Mixed media | 8 x 13 x 10 inches | Gift of Sydney and Frances Lewis, 85.441

Working in a range of media, Samaras has followed his own path, alternately joining and veering from the mainstream. Unconventional materials, craft techniques, and obsessive modes of composing characterize his work. One of Samaras's signature forms is the elaborately decorated box; he made a numbered series of 135 between 1962 and 1989. Samaras's boxes beckon and threaten in equal measure, and have been likened to reliquaries and fetish objects.

Box #89 bristles with densely packed stainless-steel straight pins. When opened, it reveals an odd assortment of keepsakes surrounding Samaras's image beneath a glass pyramid and chicken wire. These objects suggest autobiography, and a small silver-lidded container holding cut-up black-and-white photographs of a male nude seems to promise further revelation. Ultimately, however, *Box #89* offers enigma, allusion, and provocation—hallmarks of Samaras's self-referential art.

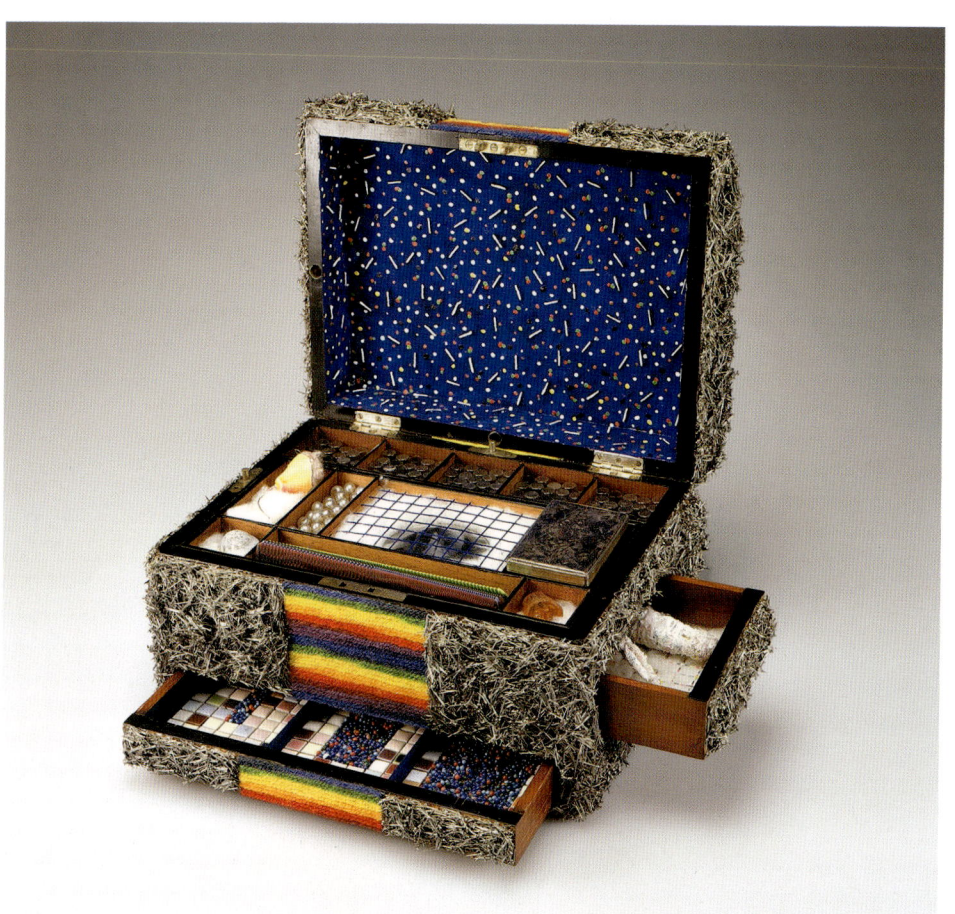

She was restless, twitchy, something seemed to be bothering her and he was in an oblivious state. I thought it was important to catch this quality, and their moods, so separate from each other's.

— George Segal

George Segal ¦ American, 1924–2000 ¦ **Blue Girl on Black Bed** ¦ 1976 ¦ Painted plaster, wood ¦ 44 x 82 x 60 inches ¦ Gift of Sydney and Frances Lewis, 85.444.1–2 ¦ © The George and Helen Segal Foundation/Licensed by VAGA, New York, NY

The models for these figures were two of Segal's friends, a photographer and his wife, whom the artist recalls above. From his first life cast in 1961, Segal's art has been a unique amalgam of Abstract Expressionist surfaces, Pop Art subjects, and the artist's own inquiry into contemporary life.

Segal wrapped his models in fast-drying, plaster-soaked bandages that he removed and reassembled for the final cast. The resulting sculptures probe the shifting moods of everyday situations. Rather than leaving these two plaster figures unpainted, as he usually did, Segal used flat, unrealistic colors to deepen the piece's emotional impact.

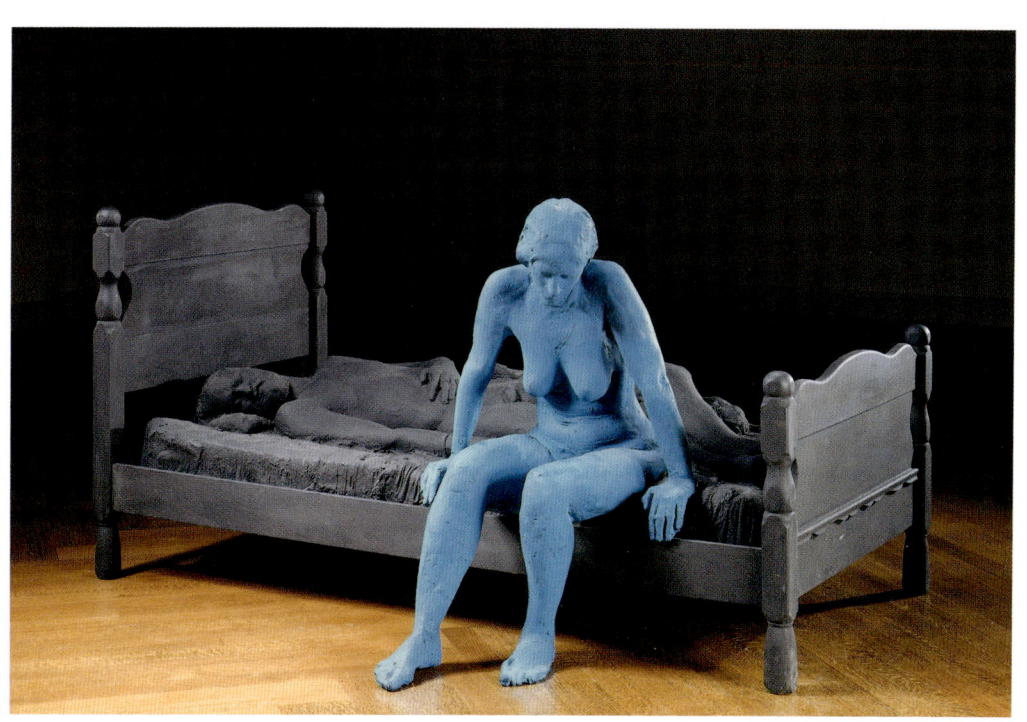

I think painting and sculpture proceed from the same vision. . . . In drawing some simple still lifes I thought, "just cut the drawing out and then you have a sculpture." I elaborated on that quite a bit. —Roy Lichtenstein

Roy Lichtenstein ⋮ American, 1923–1997 ⋮ **Lamp II** ⋮ 1977 ⋮ Painted bronze ⋮ 84 ¼ x 27 ⅝ x 17 ⅝ inches Gift of Sydney and Frances Lewis, 85.511

Although known primarily as a painter, Lichtenstein made sculptures throughout his career. These mostly grew from his paintings, but they grappled with such sculptural relationships as solid/void and image/volume. Like his paintings, Lichtenstein's sculpture shows his interest in images that read as both abstract and representational, and his ability to present familiar things with great economy.

Lamp II belongs to a group of painted bronzes depicting common household items. Here, shafts of light become solid forms that support a hanging fixture. Some beams reach the ground, forming a pool of yellow light. Short diagonal lines suggest shading. Using a limited palette of yellow, green, and white with thick black lines, Lichtenstein captures weightlessness in solid form—as he had done with reflections, smoke, and steam. His playful inversion of the tangible and intangible extends to the idea of making a nearly flat, see-through sculpture: the work reads first as a painted image, then as a solid, larger-than-life object in real space.

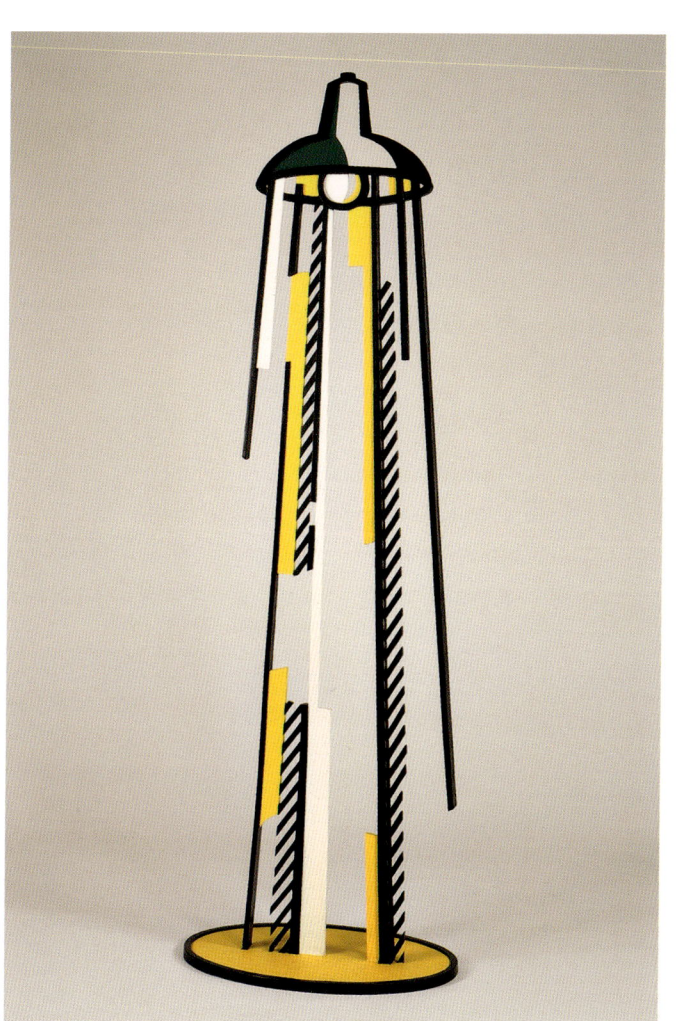

When an artist uses a multiple modular method, he usually chooses a simple and readily available form. The form itself is of very limited importance; it becomes the grammar for the total work. — Sol LeWitt

Sol LeWitt ⁞ American, born 1928 ⁞ **1 2 3 4 5 6** ⁞ 1978 ⁞ Painted wood ⁞ 99 ¼ x 29 x 29 inches ⁞ Gift of The Sydney and Frances Lewis Foundation, 85.555

LeWitt, a founder of Conceptual Art, rejected Abstract Expressionism's glorification of the artist's own thoughts and emotions and emphasized instead a rational, objective approach to form. The meaning of LeWitt's work—in sculpture, works on paper, and wall drawings like that on page 87—lies in its concepts and planning; its physical form is merely a way to communicate these concepts in visual terms.

This sculpture continues a series of open modular cubic structures LeWitt began in the mid-1960s. This imposing tower comes from a simple routine for multiplication—1x1, 2x2, 3x3, etc.—that results in adding one more row to each descending level of stacked cubes. The top cube is a single module, while the bottom cube is 6 x 6 x 6 units. This basic formula yields surprisingly complex visual results as the viewer peers into the work from various angles.

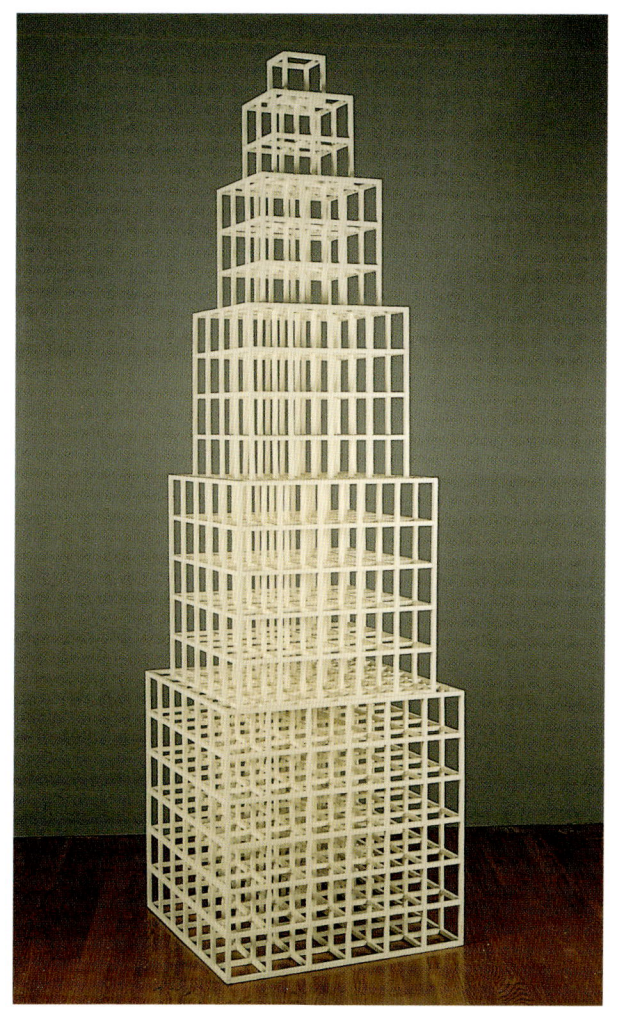

> For me, they mimicked the giant clots of mud and sticks left over in riverbeds after a flood/thaw—a direct relation to my own thoughts taking form and direction after a "flood" of emotion. —Deborah Butterfield

Deborah Butterfield | American, born 1949 | **Large Horse** | 1978 | Steel armature, chicken wire, mud, sticks, paper pulp, dextrine, plaster, and fiberglass shreds | 54 x 100 x 53 inches | Gift of Sydney and Frances Lewis, 85.367

Butterfield's *Large Horse* counters the tradition of equestrian sculptures—warhorse stallions with great men astride them. This horse might appear to be resting, but splintered branches pierce its body. Butterfield conceives of these horses—her exclusive subject over a thirty-year career—as metaphorical substitutes for herself; they grow out of a lifelong interest in riding and schooling them. Her alter ego here resembles an equine Saint Sebastian, raising pithy notions of artistic suffering.

Butterfield, who matured as an artist during the 1970s, shares with other Post-Minimalist sculptors, including Martin Puryear (page 164) and Ursula von Rydingsvard (page 162), an interest in unorthodox materials and processes, intense physicality of the object, and openness to allusion. Butterfield's work is more tied to recognizable form than many of her peers, but her mud-and-stick pieces signaled a decisive break with her earlier naturalism and marked a turn toward greater expressiveness.

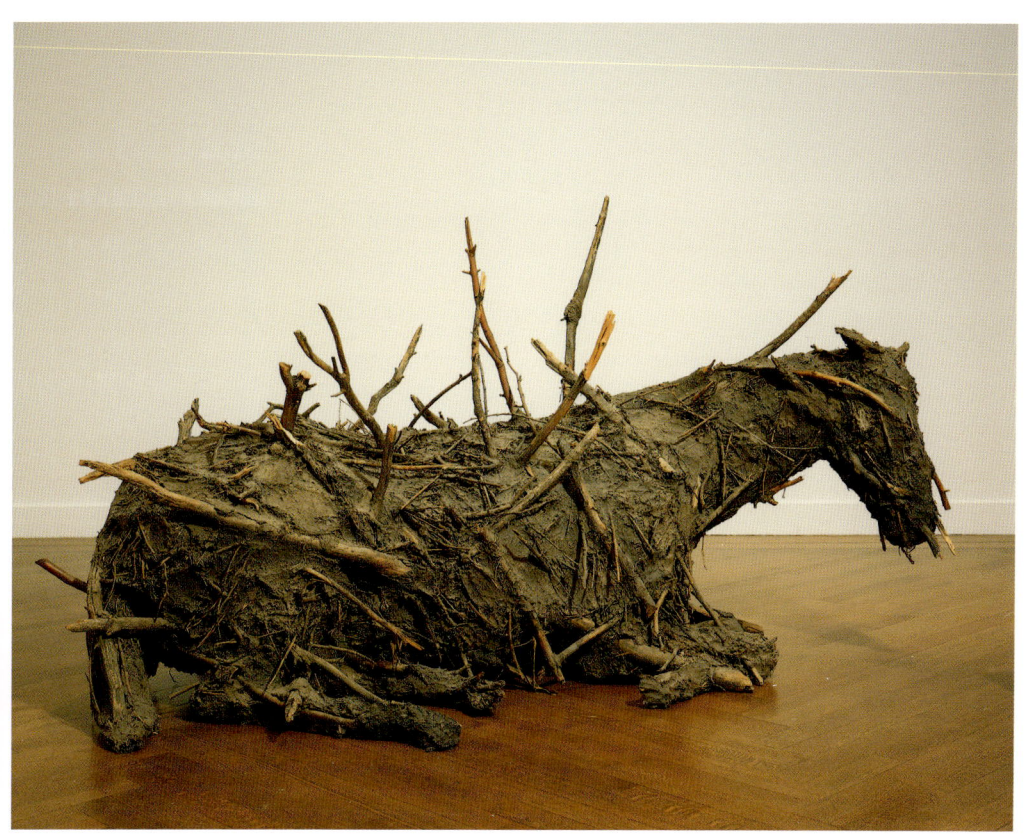

After twenty-five years, I see that all of the head sculptures are self-portraits that refer to the bondage of my childhood. —Nancy Grossman

Nancy Grossman ⁞ American, born 1940 ⁞ **House** ⁞ 1969–70 ⁞ Leather, wood, lacquer ⁞ 16 ¼ x 6 ¾ x 8 inches
Gift of Sydney and Frances Lewis, 85.399a–b

Originally a painter and draftsman, Grossman began making sculpture in the mid-1960s, inspired in part by her friendship with sculptor David Smith. The series of forty-three heads, begun in 1968 and completed by 1972, grew out of drawings whose feeling of restrained motion and emotion Grossman wanted to make more palpable. The intricate wooden heads she carved remain unseen beneath the dark leather.

Grossman meant the heads to evoke the clenched fist of the black-power salute and the beauty of black. She also connects them to literary and artistic "outsiders"—monsters and other sub- and superhuman beings, including Prometheus and the protagonist of Mary Shelley's *Frankenstein.*

Grossman traces their origins to an equestrian girlhood and to the tack—bridles, halter, lip straps, and martingales—that she used. These bound heads, both menacing and pathetic, relate to issues of oppression that she felt keenly as a woman artist during the years of Vietnam, Black Power, and the assassinations of Martin Luther King, Jr., and Robert F. Kennedy.

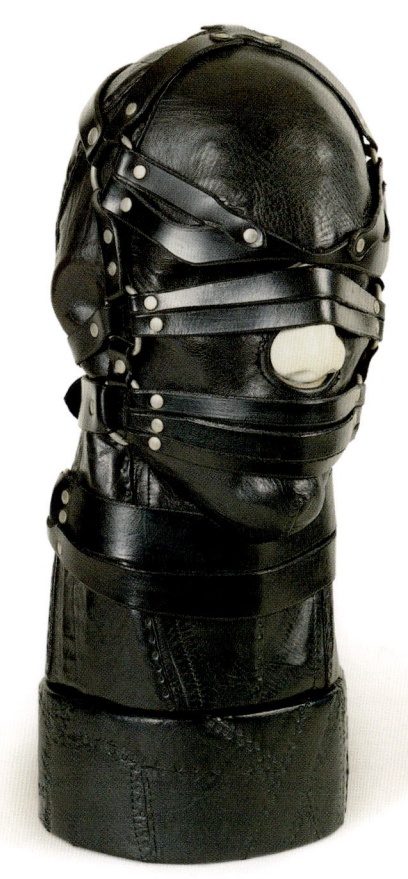

Between myself and the material with which I create, no tool intervenes. I select it with my hands. I shape it with my hands. My hands transmit my energy to it. . . . They reveal the unconscious. —Magdalena Abakanowicz

Magdalena Abakanowicz | Polish, born 1930 | Detail of **Seated Figures** | 1974–79 | Burlap and glue, steel stands
Eighteen figures, each 41 x 20 x 26 inches | Gift of The Sydney and Frances Lewis Foundation, 98.2.1a/b–18a/b

Abakanowicz is one of several European artists who focused their art on social concerns and nontraditional materials in the mid-1970s. *Seated Figures* is the first of many such sculptural groups Abakanowicz made. These glue-stiffened burlap figures seem identical, but closer inspection reveals subtle differences.

Abakanowicz's chilling representations of the human form reflect the domination of her native Poland by successive totalitarian regimes, but they also speak to such universal concerns as the tension between group and individual identity. In addition, their fragmentary forms allude to the missing heads and limbs of ancient statuary.

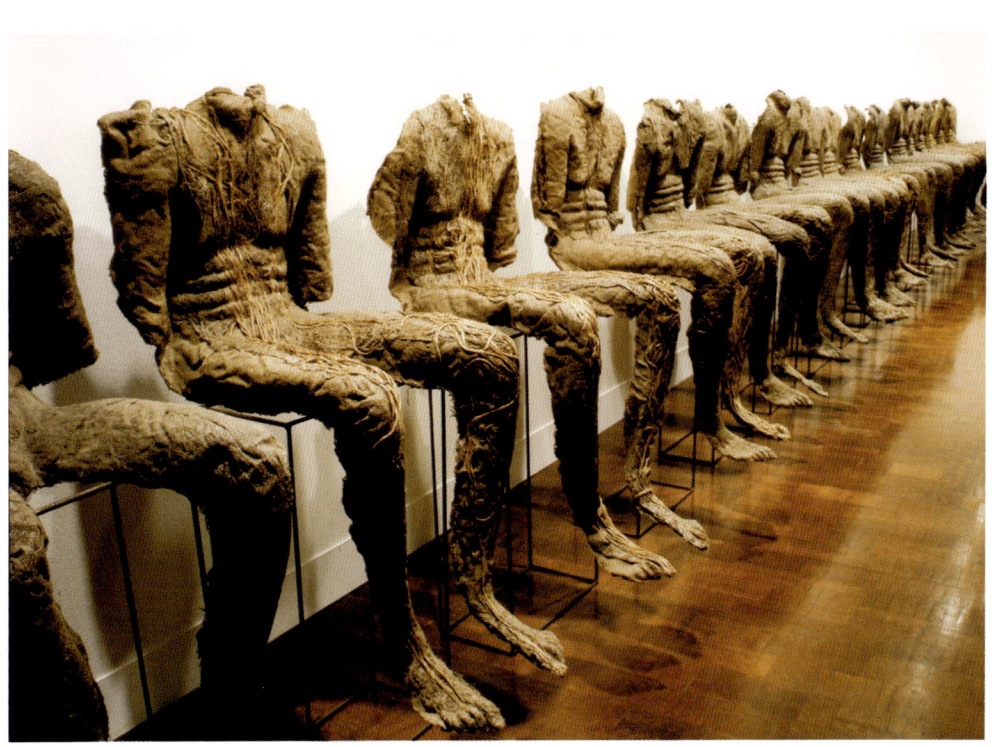

My work is not about sculpture in the traditional sense, volumes, and planes. . . . I am making drawings and paintings in space. — Robert Arneson

Robert Arneson | American, 1930–1992 | **A Likeness of Francis B.** | 1981 | Glazed ceramic | 75 x 26 x 19 ½ inches | Gift of Sydney and Frances Lewis, 85.357a–b | © Estate of Robert Arneson/Licensed by VAGA, New York, NY

Arneson, a San Francisco–area sculptor, is best known for ribald ceramic self-portraits from the early 1970s and hard-hitting antinuclear works from the 1980s. Arneson used white earthenware clay and brilliant low-fire glazes for these sculptures, which he considered paintings in three dimensions. He also produced sculptural portraits of important twentieth-century artists, including Picasso, Pollock, and Duchamp, paeans to modernist heroes done with Arneson's characteristic blend of humor, irreverence, and the grotesque. Each also reflects its subject's artistic style.

For *A Likeness of Francis B.,* Arneson used the strong oranges and blues Bacon favored and combined three aspects: frontal likeness; shadowy profile; and, on the back, grimacing caricature. The use of serial views, particularly a triptych of faces, also reflects Bacon's method, as does the macabre distortion of human anatomy, which captures something, too, of Arneson's own angst and turbulence in the early 1980s.

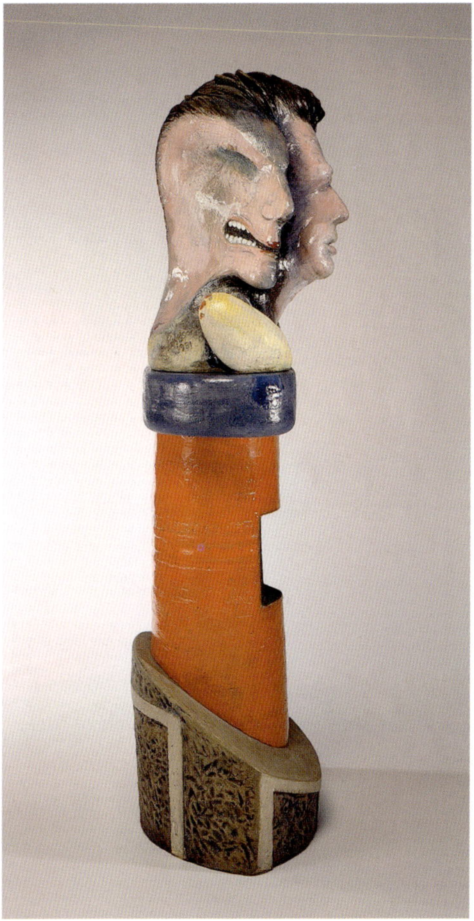

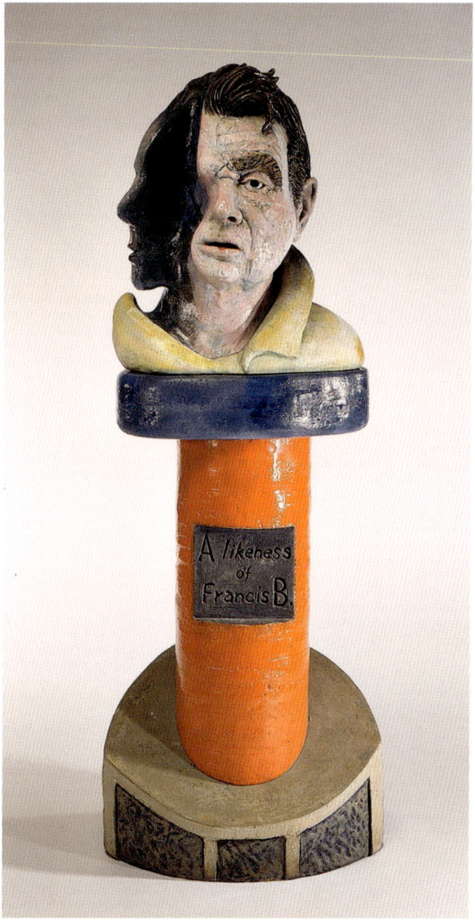

A likeness
of
Francis B.

If you consider what conveys situation and meaning and feeling in a human figure, the range of expression is in fact far more limited than the device of investing an animal—a hare especially—with the expressive attributes of a human being. — Barry Flanagan

Barry Flanagan ⋮ Welsh, born 1941 ⋮ **Large Leaping Hare** ⋮ 1982 ⋮ Gilded bronze and steel ⋮ 96 x 108 x 78 ¾ inches ⋮ Gift of Sydney and Frances Lewis, 85.385a–b

Flanagan's cavorting hare, a continuing subject he began making in the early 1980s, combines humor and sophistication with a poke in the ribs. Flanagan started his career in the 1960s by rejecting prevailing formalist tastes for welded-steel sculpture. He experimented instead with limp lengths of rope, unfinished wooden poles, and soft cloth forms filled with sand or plaster—informal, impermanent, organic anti-objects that tested the limits of sculpture.

Flanagan returned to traditional sculptural materials—stone in the 1970s and bronze in the early 1980s—but not to traditional practices. The hare was one of the first figures Flanagan made when he began casting in bronze. Flanagan's hare, a witty and iconoclastic effort to deflate avant-garde orthodoxy and academicism, looks like a hare rather than an abstraction. Gilding ennobles the slender leaping creature, as does his perch atop a Minimalist pyramid of crossed steel battens.

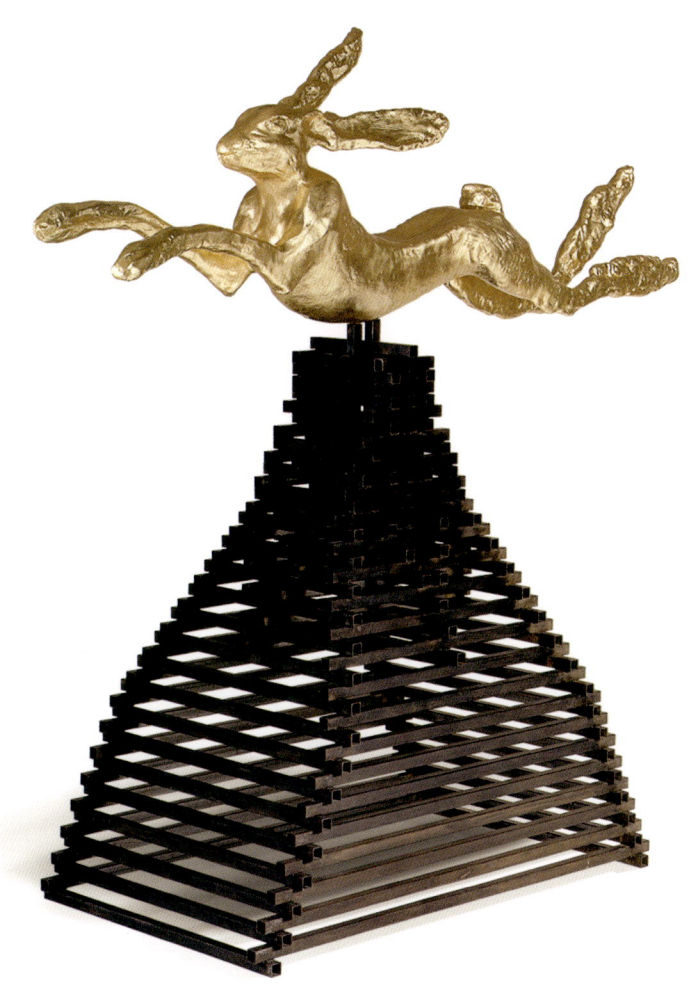

Nature in landscape *becomes* the figure. — Bryan Hunt

Bryan Hunt | American, born 1947 | **Conductor** | 1982 | Bronze | 146 x 54 x 31 inches | Gift of The Sydney and Frances Lewis Foundation, 85.407

Hunt came to New York in the early 1970s during the heyday of Minimalism. He sought to reconcile that movement's abstract and severely reduced geometric forms with his interest in expressive gesture and recognizable imagery. In 1977, Hunt began his best-known body of work, a series of cast-bronze waterfalls. The gouges, scrapes, and ripples marking these elongated and austere forms preserve the artist's touch.

At over twelve feet tall, *Conductor* reflects Hunt's interest in monumental sculpture, for which bronze has long been a medium. By presenting an isolated fragment of nature, *Conductor* lends the cascade a dreamlike quality. Because the work seems supported by arms and legs, it also suggests the human body. Hunt brings a sense of draftsmanship to *Conductor,* creating interplay between its solid form and its linearity and between the figure's integrity and the fluidity of water.

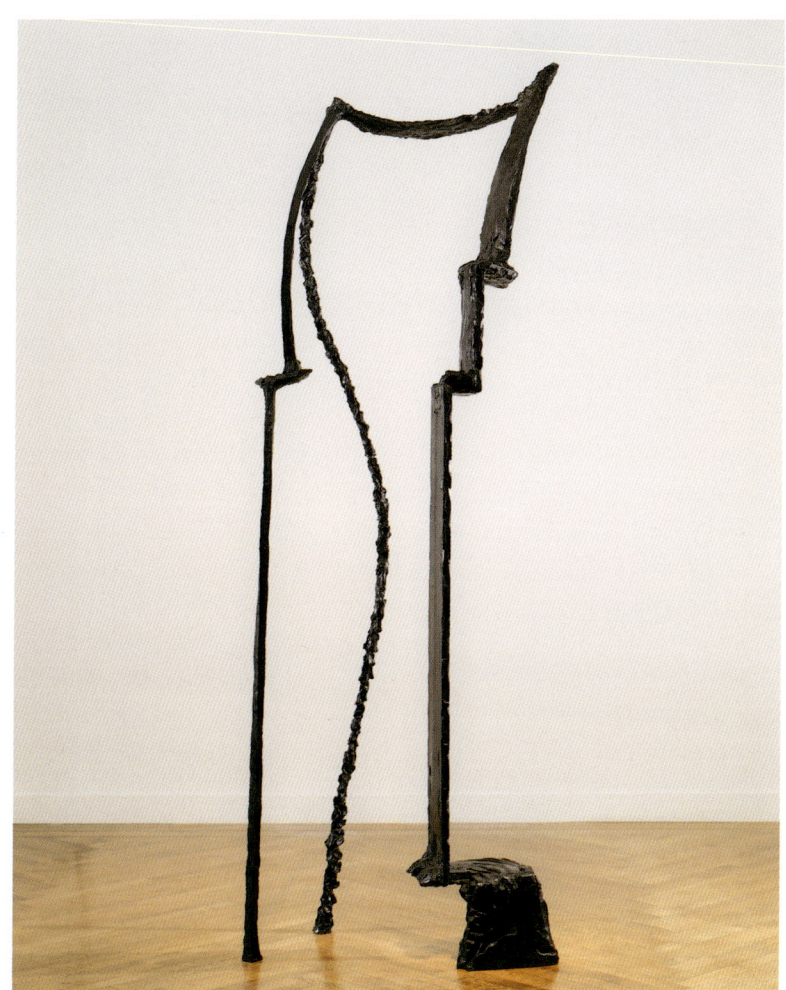

It isn't necessary for a work to have a lot of things to look at, to compare, to analyze one by one, to contemplate. The thing as a whole, its qualities as a whole, is what is interesting. —Donald Judd

Like Pop Art, Minimalism rejected the dynamic brushstrokes and emotional content of Abstract Expressionism. No evidence of the artist's hand appears in Judd's elegantly proportioned metal boxes. Austere and intellectually challenging, Minimalist sculpture and painting emphasized clearly defined geometric forms and pristine, unembellished surfaces.

These boxes were commercially manufactured to Judd's precise specifications; each is one meter high and one meter wide. Judd also specified the hanging height and interval between the paired boxes. This piece focuses on color, depth, interval, edge, sheen, light and shadow; the boxes look to no world beyond their own.

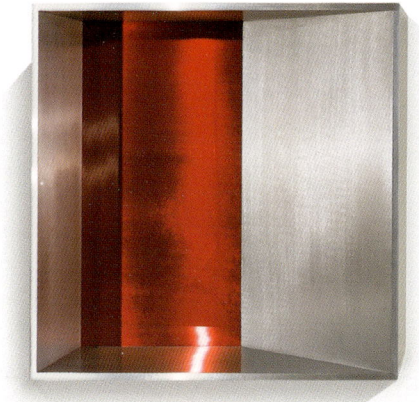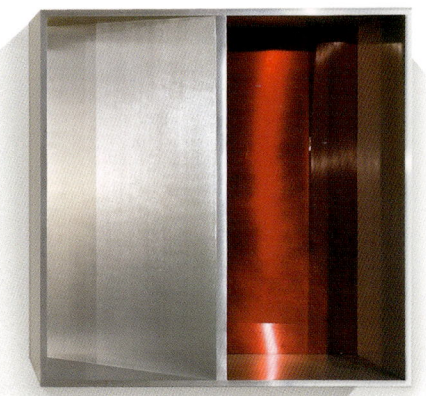

What I'm trying to put into my work is what I am, culturally, anthropologically. . . . This tradition is something I ate with my food as a child, because I was born in a certain place. — Sandro Chia

Sandro Chia | Italian, born 1946 | **Man and Vegetation** | 1983 | Bronze | 99 x 70 x 67 inches | Gift of The Sydney and Frances Lewis Foundation, 85.371 | © Sandro Chia/Licensed by VAGA, New York, NY

Born and raised in Florence, Chia was surrounded by Renaissance art from childhood. During the 1980s, he played a central role in Neo-Expressionism, a movement centered in Germany, Italy, and the United States whose revival of large-scale, aggressively gestural figurative painting often drew inspiration from past art.

Man and Vegetation shows a giant bronze figure claimed by vines and bricks. The figure's swollen and distorted form and active surface reflect Chia's painting style, giving the figure the presence in real space that Chia's two-dimensional figures have on their imaginary stages. This image of metamorphosis recalls classical myths, but here no specific narrative exists. Figures in transition recur throughout Chia's work as open-ended allegories: civilization and nature continue an endless cycle of decay and rebirth.

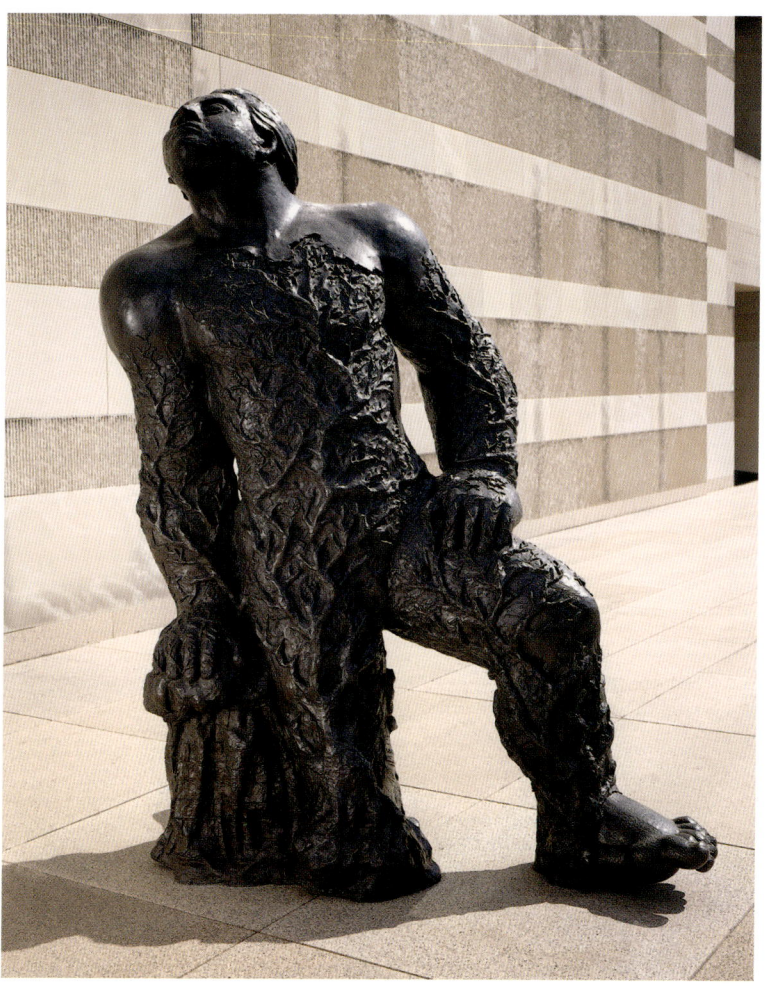

The mind constructs things on its own scale. And our ancient habit is still to conceive our head as our private chamber, a room we furnish and whose occupant is us. — Elizabeth King

Elizabeth King | American, born 1950 | **Portrait of M.** | 1983 | Porcelain, glass | 5 x 5 x 4 inches | Museum Purchase, The John Barton Payne Fund, 86.204

King's sculptures merge realistic portraiture with the uncanny. King bases them on direct observation, but she has also studied articulated mannequins, eighteenth-century automata, and Japanese Bunraku puppets. Her small figures have a surprising capacity to suggest thought and emotion.

King's precisely detailed *Portrait of M.* reflects her mastery of various crafts—she blew the glass eyes and cast the head in porcelain herself, carving its features further after removing it from the mold. Hyper-real, yet less than half the size of an actual head, this work examines the human form in an intimate and unsettling way.

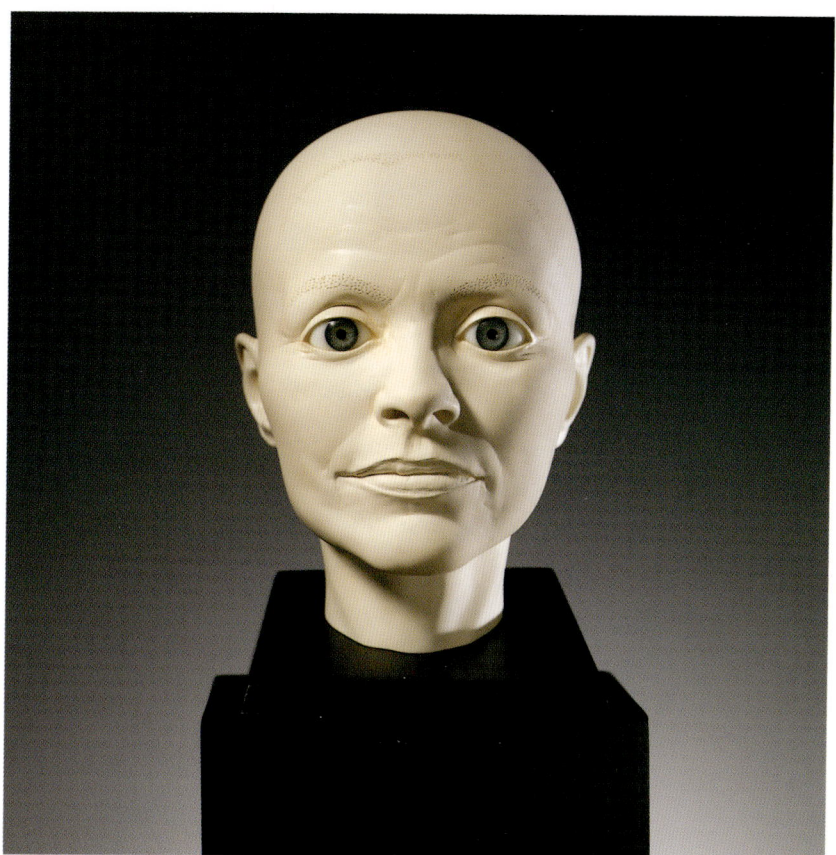

I'm interested in incorporating very ancient religions into contemporary imagery and ideas, keeping the ancient ideas alive so that they can serve a very useful purpose in everyday life. —Alison Saar

Alison Saar | American, born 1956 | **Untitled** from the installation **Crossroads** | 1989 | Wood and found metal objects | 72 inches high, width and depth vary | Museum Purchase, The Sydney and Frances Lewis Endowment Fund, 92.233a–qqq

Saar works in a wide range of media, including sculpture, drawing, printmaking, and installations. Traditions influencing her work include African art and American folk art. In this piece, paint, ceiling tin, nails, and other cast-off industrial objects transform a carved wooden figure into a totem that speaks of human suffering and perseverance.

Although Saar's intent is not primarily religious, this sculpture resembles the smaller *nkisi* figures from Congo in Central Africa. Nails driven into these power figures activate spiritual pacts between priests and supplicants that allow petitioners' requests to be heard by the deities and ancestors.

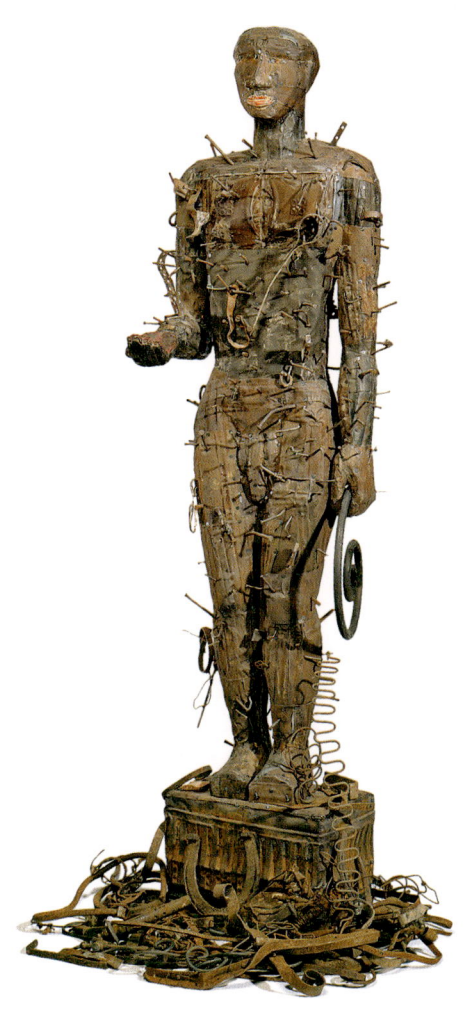

I flirt between . . . what's considered a landscape and . . . what would be considered farming implements, and then put in things that have to do with body parts, like a knee, or a leg or an arm, and negotiate some place between all of those. —Ursula von Rydingsvard

Ursula von Rydingsvard | American, born Germany, 1942 | **Girlie Girl** | 1991 | Cedar, graphite, with steel, mahogany, and felt | 116 x 116 x 44 inches | Gift of the Fabergé Society of the Virginia Museum of Fine Arts, 93.1

Von Rydingsvard was born to a Polish family who moved through various refugee camps before emigrating to the United States. Her early life gives insight into her ritualistic Old-World forms and their anxious surfaces, but her entry into the New York art world in the early 1970s also helps explain her work. Part of a generation who expanded the forms and practices of Minimalism, von Rydingsvard built her stacked pieces with multiple units of four-by-four-inch milled cedar beams. Improvisational saw-cuts made surfaces active, bringing spontaneity and emotional intensity to her industrial materials.

Here, graphite rubbed onto the irregularly angled cuts creates a craggy, weathered surface that evokes geological formations. At the same time, the dense row of towering forms suggests human figures—ancient totems or chorus girls with hands on hips and arms akimbo—at once dominating and vulnerable, serious and funny.

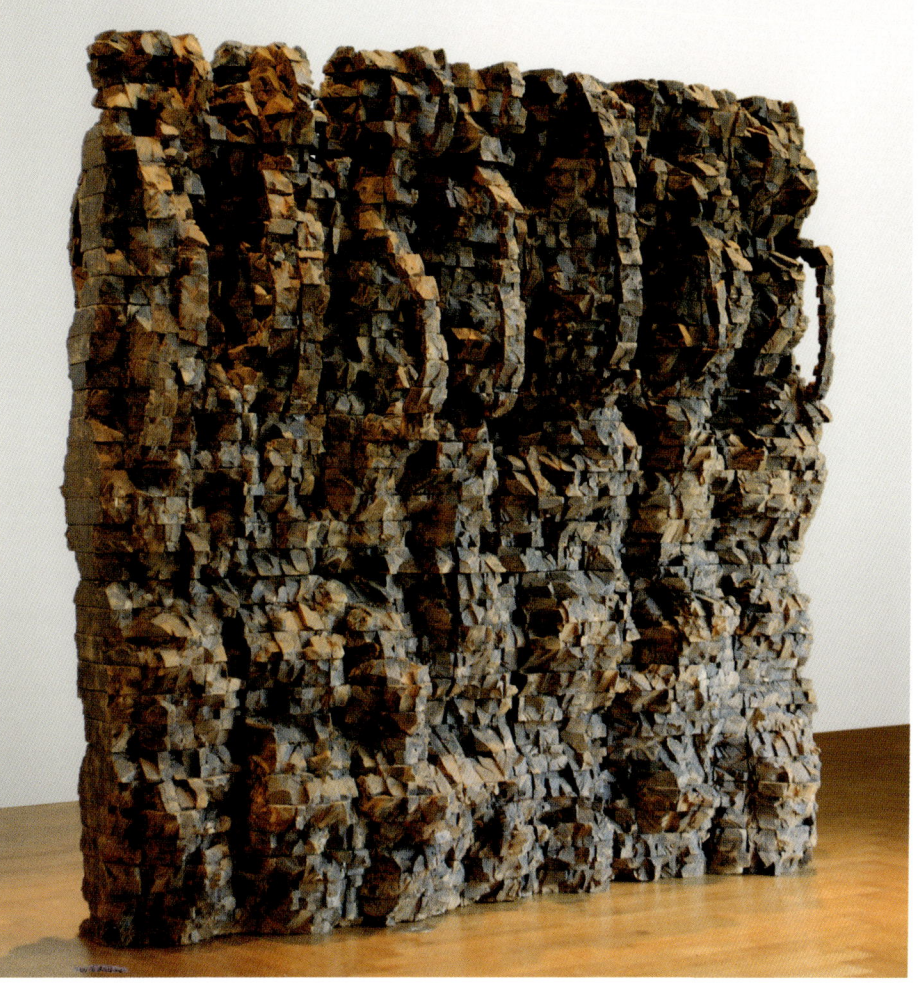

What I'm interested in is work that has a myriad
of associations but is also extremely pared down.

— Martin Puryear

Martin Puryear ⋮ American, born 1941 ⋮ **Untitled** ⋮ 1995 ⋮ Wire mesh, steel, tar, cedar, particleboard ⋮ Museum
Purchase, The Sydney and Frances Lewis Endowment Fund, 95.82

Puryear's abstract sculptures, while often simple in shape and materials, are richly
allusive. This combination of qualities links him to a group of artists loosely called
Post-Minimalists. The dark, monolithic form of this piece suggests a colossal head
or a primitive totem, although its asymmetry and its vessel-like quality recall organic
forms like seedpods or gourds. Puryear finished the piece—a metal grid overlaid
with squares of wire mesh—with a coating of tar. The coating defines the sculpture's massive form, but viewers can peer into the piece and out the other side.

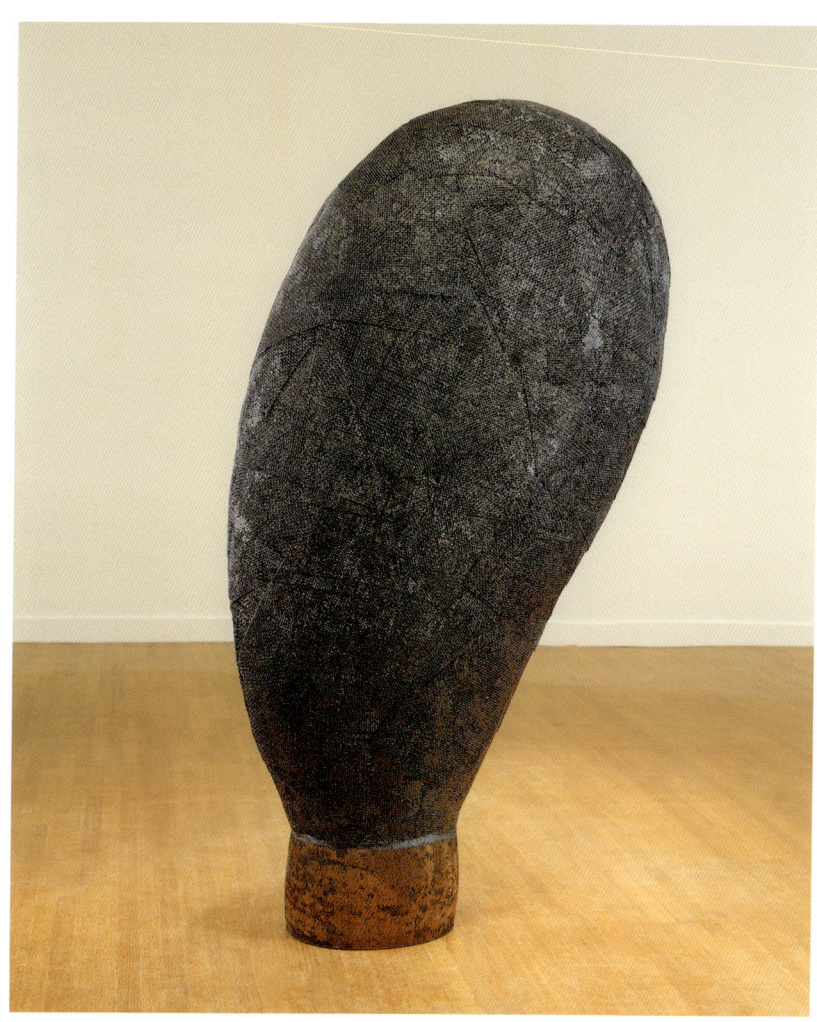

In making work that's about the body, I'm playing with the indestructibility of life, where life is this ferocious force that keeps propelling us. At the same time, . . . you can just pierce it and it dies. I'm always playing between these two extremes. —Kiki Smith

Kiki Smith | American, born 1954 | **Ice Man** | 1995–96 | Bronze | 79 1/4 x 29 1/8 x 11 1/2 inches | Museum Purchase, The Sydney and Frances Lewis Endowment Fund, 2004.1

During the 1980s, Smith's clay, paper, glass, and plaster representations of physical fragments and hidden organs addressed the degradation and disintegration of the human body—poignant responses to the AIDS crisis. In the early 1990s, around the time she focused on whole human figures, Smith began working in bronze. These developments were part of Smith's conscious effort to invest the European tradition of religious figurative art with fresh meaning.

Ice Man marks the culmination of this transition in Smith's work. Her inspiration for the piece came from the 1991 discovery of a 5300-year-old Stone Age man frozen in an Alpine glacier. The figure's isolated, atrophied form is perhaps an unlikely messenger of hope. But the work's mood of introspection and embrace of fragility suggest the preciousness of life, a life to which the figure appears to cling.

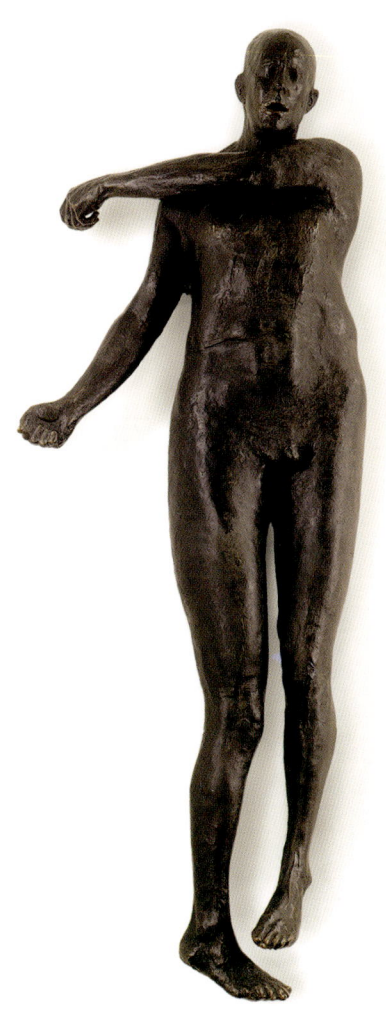

The real issue implied in "Art and Technology" is not to make another scientific toy, but how to humanize the technology and the electronic medium, which is progressing rapidly—too rapidly. —Nam June Paik

Nam June Paik ⏐ American, born Korea, 1932–2006 ⏐ **Buddha Watching TV** ⏐ 1974/1997 ⏐ Stone sculpture, soil, television, video camera, and wood base ⏐ 69 x 104 x 41 inches (varies) ⏐ Gift of Friends of Frances and Sydney Lewis, in memory of Sydney Lewis and to commemorate the Grand Reopening of the Lewis Galleries in 2000, 2000.96a–g

Paik, undoubtedly the single most important figure in the history of video art, established the medium in the early 1960s. *Buddha Watching TV* comes from one of his most celebrated video sculpture series. Paik created the original concept in 1974 and made this example in 1997.

Here, a stone Buddha head from Indonesia, partially embedded in dirt and signed dramatically across the back by Paik in Korean and English, appears to observe itself on television. A live image of the unchanging head is continually relayed to the monitor by the closed-circuit camera on the tripod. The Buddha thus generates and receives its own image in an infinite temporal loop, updating the act of contemplation for the age of technology.

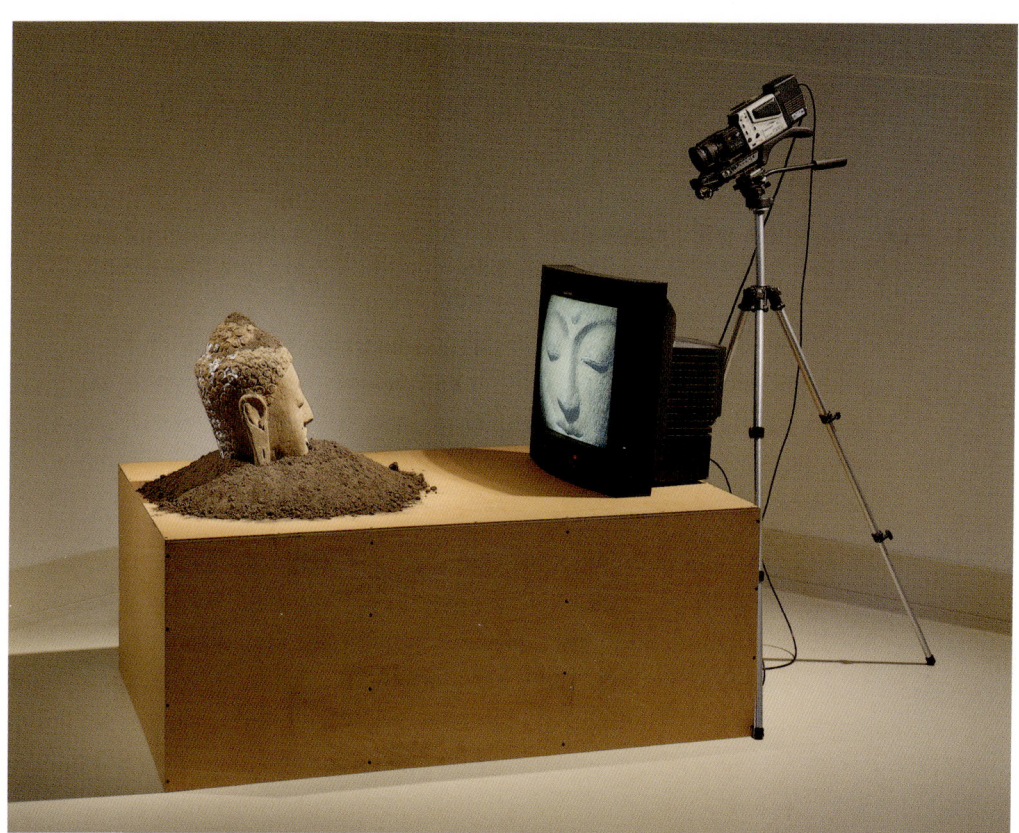

I draw inspiration from my surroundings. My life force is women—they are the source of growth and life.

— Ravinder Reddy

Ravinder Reddy | Indian, born 1956 | **Krishnaveni I** | 1997 | Painted and gilded polyester-resin fiberglass | ca. 75 x 72 x 73 inches | Museum Purchase, The Kathleen Boone Samuels Memorial Fund, 2001.230a–b

Reddy's work exemplifies a lively tendency among contemporary South Asian artists to combine indigenous traditions and an international perspective. Reddy's figures seem updated gods and goddesses drawn from Indian temple sculptures and religious mythology. Everyday Indian culture, however, including fashion, popular films, and the bazaar, is equally inspirational.

Postgraduate work at English art schools exposed Reddy to westernized abstract sculpture, including Cubism and Henry Moore's organic forms. American Pop Art, by Tom Wesselmann and Claes Oldenburg in particular, helped Reddy find the form and scale for his lively and sensual females. The figure's colossal size, stylized features, and gilded surface make her seem otherworldly. Her boldly painted lips and brows and the flowers in her hair, however, reflect common Indian fashion and its sources in Hollywood and Bollywood films. Krishnaveni, a popular female name in Reddy's home state of Andhra Pradesh, also refers to Radha, legendary consort of the god Krishna, who weaves colorful flowers into her *veni* (long braid) to seduce her lover.

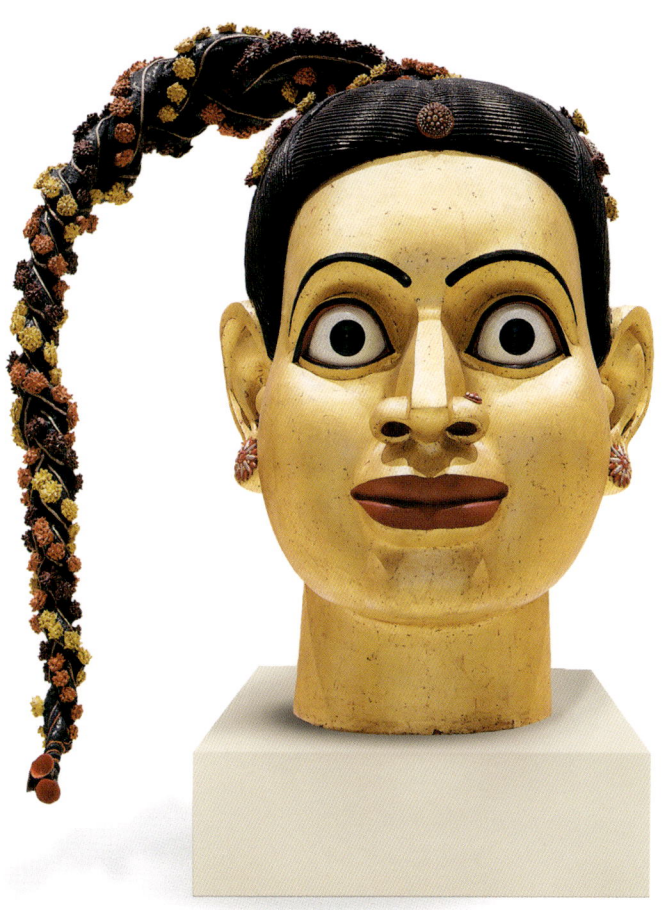

The performers hover at the threshold of stillness and immobility . . . maintaining a subtle connection to death and the inner emotional life that the traditional themes of the Deposition and Lamentation express. This is the unseen dimension referred to in the title.

— Bill Viola

Bill Viola | American, born 1951 | **The Quintet of the Unseen** | 2000 | Video installation (color video rear-screen projection) | Running time: 15 minutes, 19 seconds (continuous play) | Museum Purchase, The Sydney and Frances Lewis Endowment Fund, 2001.222

The Quintet of the Unseen pushes video art toward painting. It shows five people up close and in extreme slow motion as they exhibit intense feelings of anger, sorrow, rapture, fear, and grief. Their emotions build to an unbearable level, then crest, leaving the players drained and transformed. Although inspired in part by Viola's study of late Medieval and Renaissance painting, *The Quintet* contains no specific religious or mythological subject matter: allusions occur solely in each viewer's mind.

Viola recorded *The Quintet* on high-speed 35mm film as a single silent one-minute take. In transferring to video, he stretched the original action to more than fifteen minutes, accentuating each emotional nuance. By using a rear-projection installation, Viola underscores his reference to paintings: the translucent Plexiglas screen, resembles a painted surface on which the artist presents a timeless event.

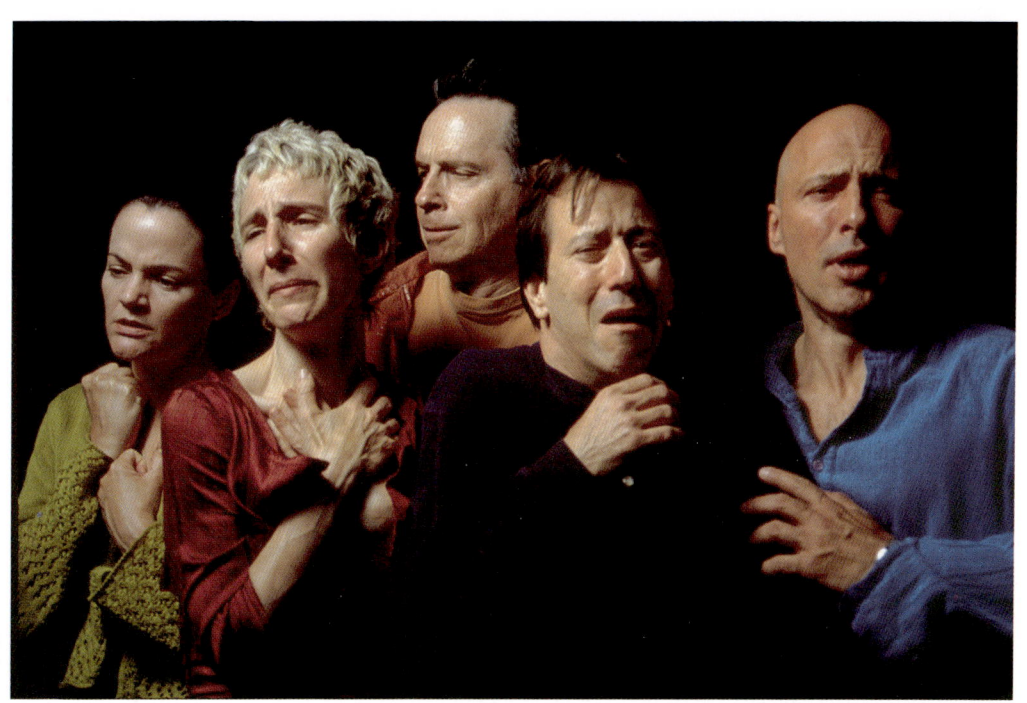

I'm always trying to give people, first, fun. If [people] look at my works, maybe people feel like . . . laughing or surprise. Then, next . . . [they] think something. —Yukinori Yanagi

Yukinori Yanagi | Japanese, born 1959 | **Dollar Pyramid** | 2000 | Colored sand, ants, plastic boxes, plastic tubes, plastic pipes | Fifteen boxes, each 17 x 25 inches; 100 x 149 inches overall | Museum Purchase, The Adolph D. and Wilkins C. Williams Fund, 2000.81.1–15

Dollar Pyramid uses colored sand in shallow plastic boxes to replicate a fragmented and enlarged dollar bill. After completing these meticulous sand paintings, Yanagi released thousands of live ants into the boxes. The ants tunneled through the boxes for weeks, eroding the overall image. Before it was completely destroyed, Yanagi removed the ants and fixed the sand permanently.

Yanagi first used ants as an unpredictable disruption in his art in the mid-1980s to explore his interest in social and political boundaries. Given the dollar's status as a worldwide symbol of capitalism, the ants' labor in *Dollar Pyramid* also has rich metaphorical possibilities. These industrious, anonymous workers paradoxically destroy the system in which they toil, an ironic twist on the dollar's usual associations with power and stability.

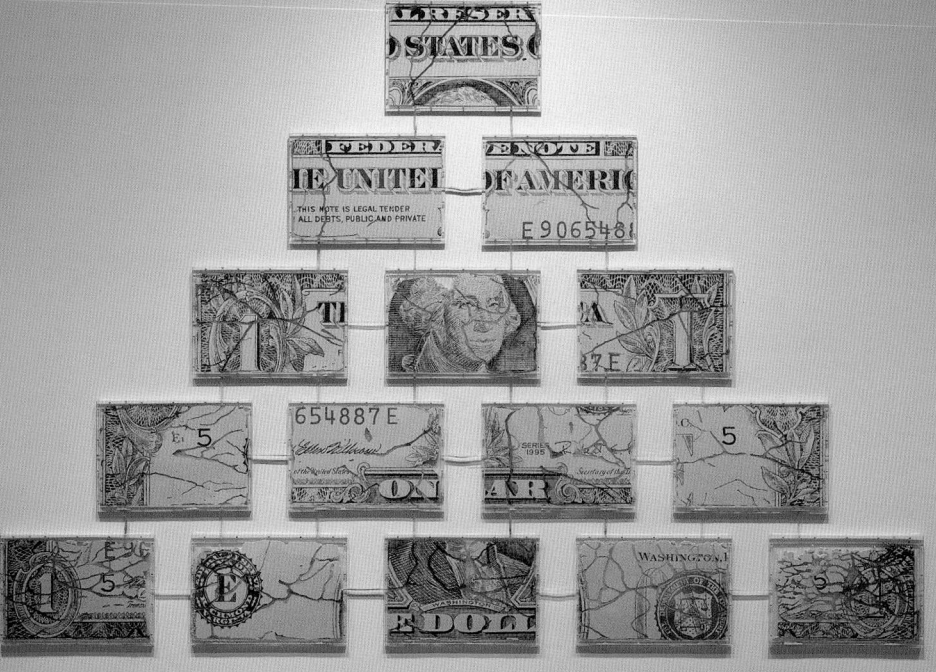

I see all media as being involved with a willing suspension of disbelief on the part of the viewer that does not end with the formation of the image—it continues into endless levels of interpretation.

— Tony Oursler

Tony Oursler | American, born 1957 | **Blue Husk** | 2001 | Digital video projection, hand-blown glass, fiberglass | Glass, 15 ¼ x 34 ½ x 12 inches; fiberglass, 15 x 17 x 9 ½ inches | Museum Purchase, The National Endowment for the Arts Fund for American Art, 2001.223

Oursler is best known for his video sculptures that redefine video art as a physical entity existing in the world of the viewer.

Blue Husk combines Oursler's interest in extreme psychological states with his other primary concern—the omnipresence of mass media. Oursler projects the face of actress Tracy Leopold (the persona for many Oursler works) onto a fiberglass form within a hand-blown glass "pod." Leopold's apparently stream-of-consciousness ruminations are actually a script. Oursler based his text on extensive research into the history of radio and television and on the phenomenon of psychics who claim to contact the dead using technology.

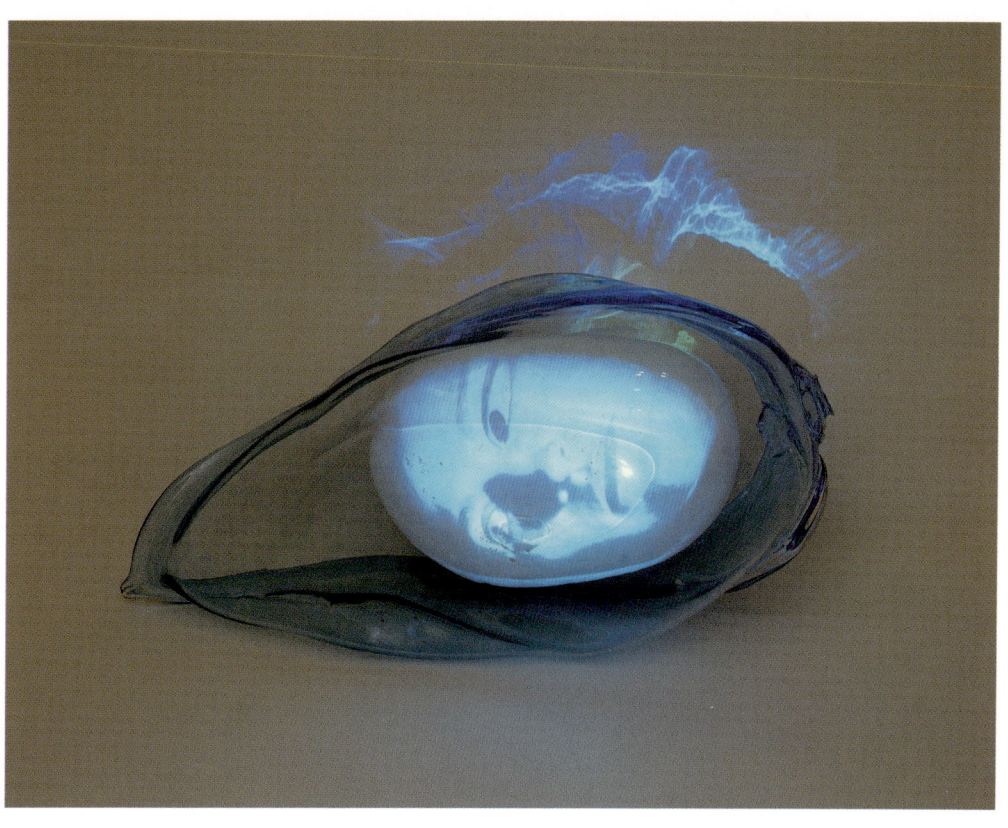

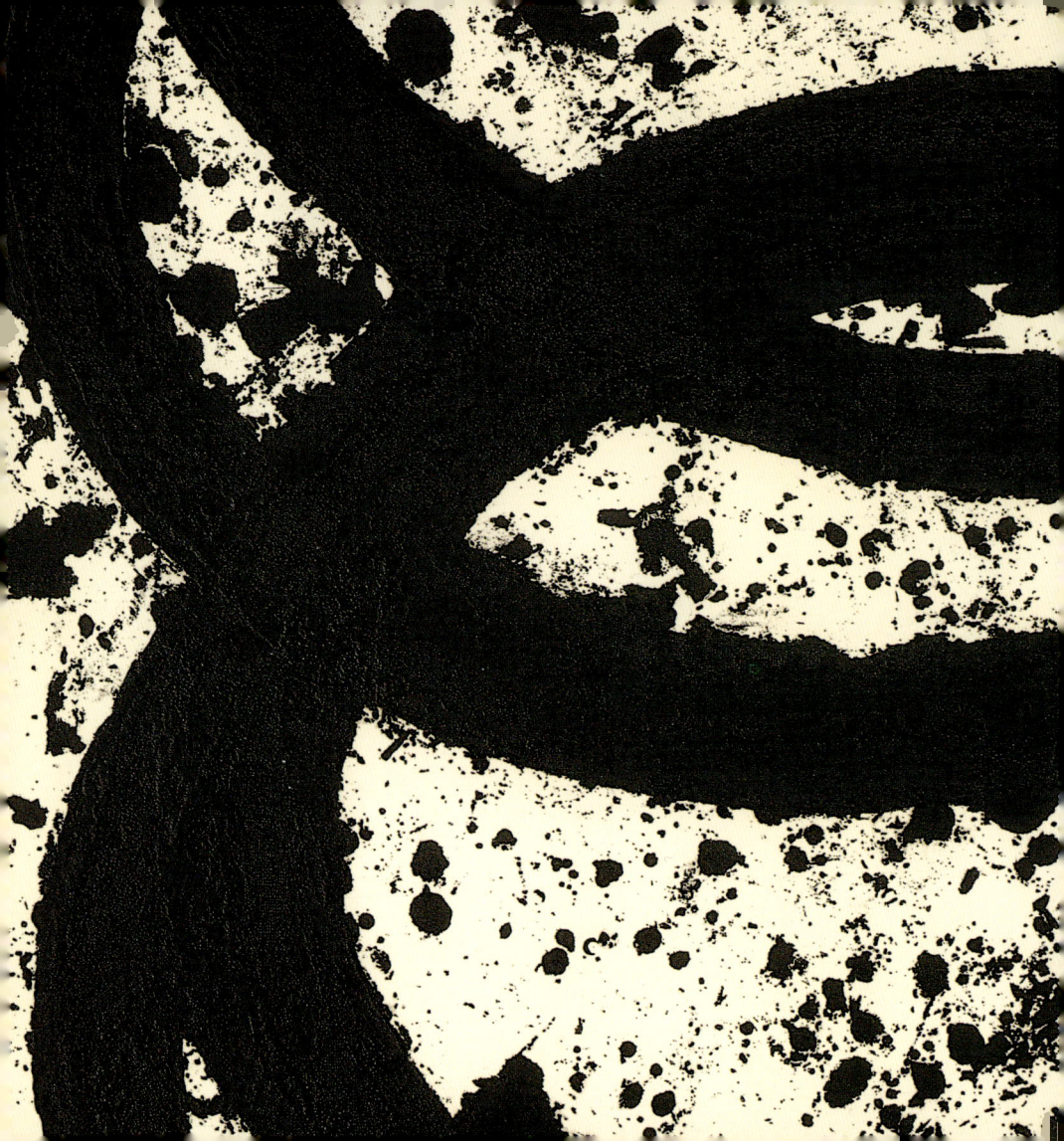

Painting is a feeling thinking, a material awareness of spirit, a sense of direct experience which transcends any intellectual method. — Richard Pousette-Dart

Richard Pousette-Dart ¦ American, 1916–1992 ¦ **Collage #1** ¦ 1950 ¦ Gouache, gilt, tape, scrap metal, canvas, printed advertising and packaging, and other materials ¦ 29 ½ x 21 ½ inches ¦ Museum Purchase, The John Barton Payne Fund, 54.12.4

Pousette-Dart, the youngest member of the original Abstract Expressionists, shared their concern with spirituality and the unconscious, which artists, writers, and thinkers of the time viewed as antidotes to the emptiness of modern life. Forging a style he called transcendental abstraction, Pousette-Dart sought a new symbolic language steeped in myth, metaphysics, and deep feeling. Like his peers, he drew inspiration from Native American, African, and Oceanic art, as well as from European and American modernism and the writings of Freud and Jung.

Collage #1 reflects Pousette-Dart's interest in dense surfaces and radiant light— mutually exclusive elements that, in his work, enhance each other to suggest the "material awareness of spirit." A thick black line, like church window leading, characterized his style throughout the 1940s. That line organizes the composition into an irregular grid, while geometric forms and webs of tracery fill the compartments. Shards of bright color lend the luminosity of stained glass, and over-painted materials—such as an exhibition announcement for Pousette-Dart at the Betty Parsons Gallery—create a tactile surface that includes autobiographical hints.

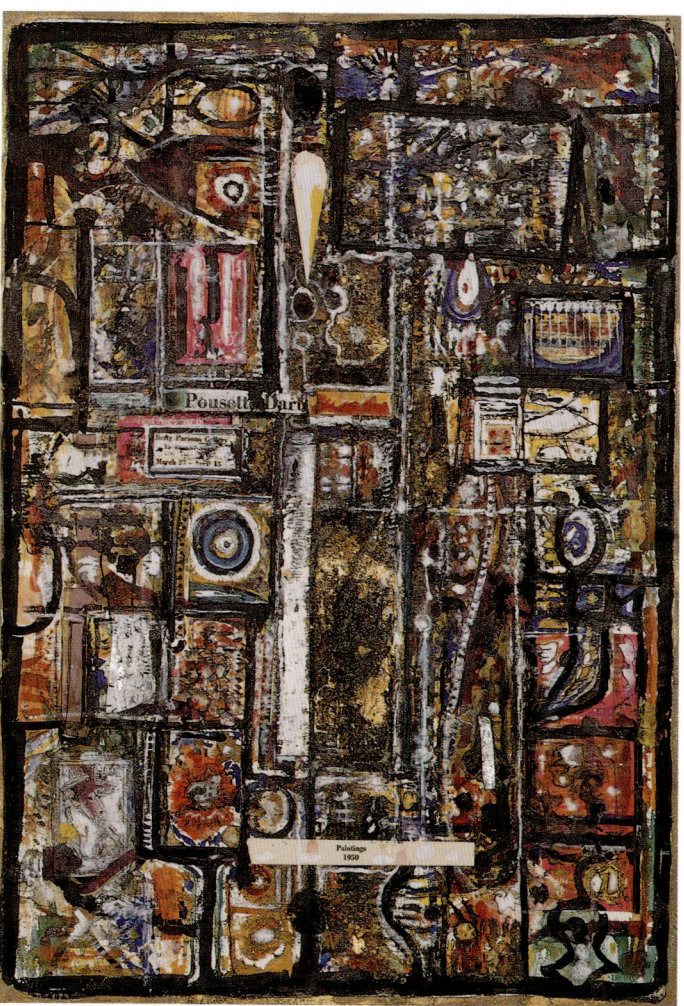

My mysticism is not only religious, but also nuclear
and hallucinogenic. —Salvador Dalí

Salvador Dalí ┊ Spanish, 1904–1989 ┊ **Trois Anges** (Three Angels) ┊ 1950 ┊ Watercolor and ink on paper ┊
11 x 14 ½ inches ┊ Gift of Mrs. Arthur Kelly Evans, 51.3

In the late 1920s, Dalí began the precise version of Surrealism that enabled him to make images he likened to "hand-painted dream photographs." By presenting the disturbing visions of his unconscious in brilliant detail, he hoped to lend credibility to the irrational realm of fears and fantasies. During the 1940s, however, Dalí rejected personal obsessions in favor of universal ones. Themes drawn from Catholicism, Renaissance art, and the explosion of the atom bomb, in particular, characterize his "classic" period.

Dalí's new nuclear mysticism included a special role for angels. His efforts to render the intangible idea of God using a visible symbol recalled his earlier drive to capture the workings of the unconscious. In addition, he believed angels were metaphysical phenomena like protons and neutrons: continually shifting elements that proved the spirituality of substance. Dalí's admiration for artists like Raphael and Leonardo also spurred his interest in angels. Though rendered with Dalí's Surrealist flair, the elegant, triumphant figures seen here have hallmarks of the High Renaissance.

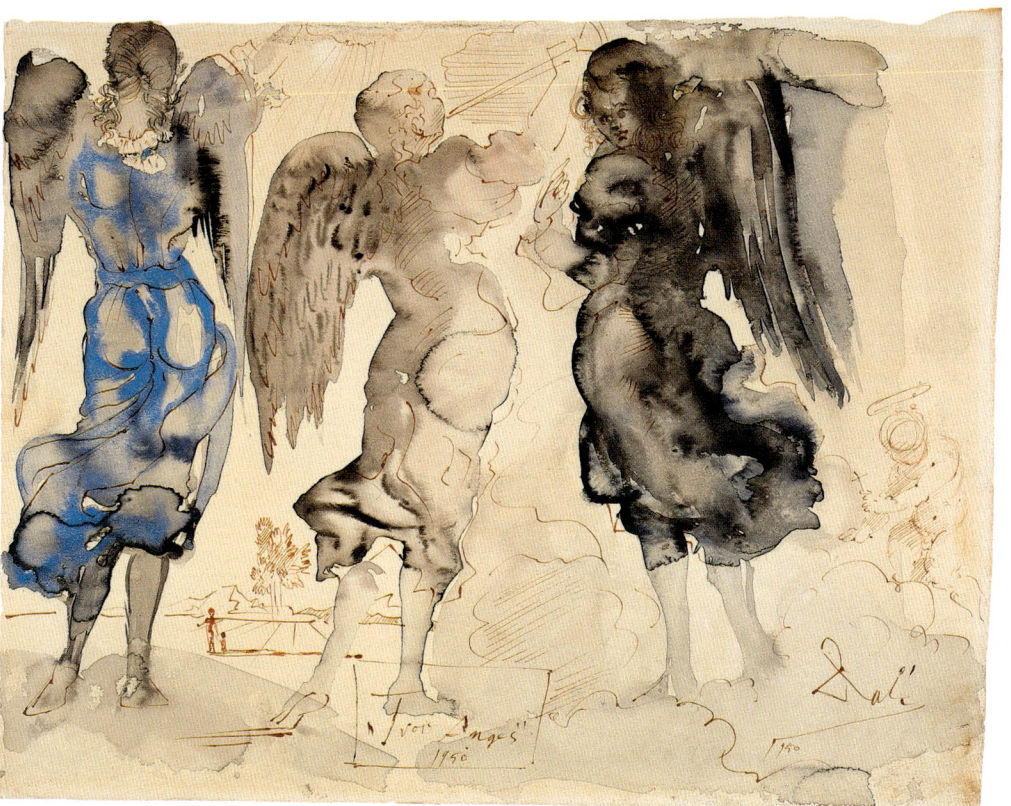

I know I shall be castigated by a large group of people today, but I was trained to assume that art related to the elusive quality of beauty and that the purpose of art was concerned with the elevation of the spirit (horrible Victorian notion!!). —Ansel Adams

Ansel Adams ┆ American, 1902–1984 ┆ **Bridalveil Fall** ┆ ca. 1952 ┆ Gelatin silver print ┆ 11 1/8 x 7 3/4 inches
Gift of Dr. and Mrs. Bernard J. Sabaroff, 86.206.2/4

During his sixty-year career, Adams's most constant muse was the mountains, forests, and rivers of California's Yosemite Valley and High Sierra. Adams made thousands of negatives and printed hundreds of images of this varied landscape.

Adams considered Bridalveil Fall "the most beautiful of all the Yosemite waterfalls." Its sunstruck water and shadowy cliffs offered the effects of light that interested Adams, as well as the monumentality he sought.

The museum's print appeared in Adams's *Portfolio III,* one of seven that featured what Adams considered his best images. These portfolios helped reestablish interest in the original photographic print as fine art, furthering one of Adams's lifelong missions.

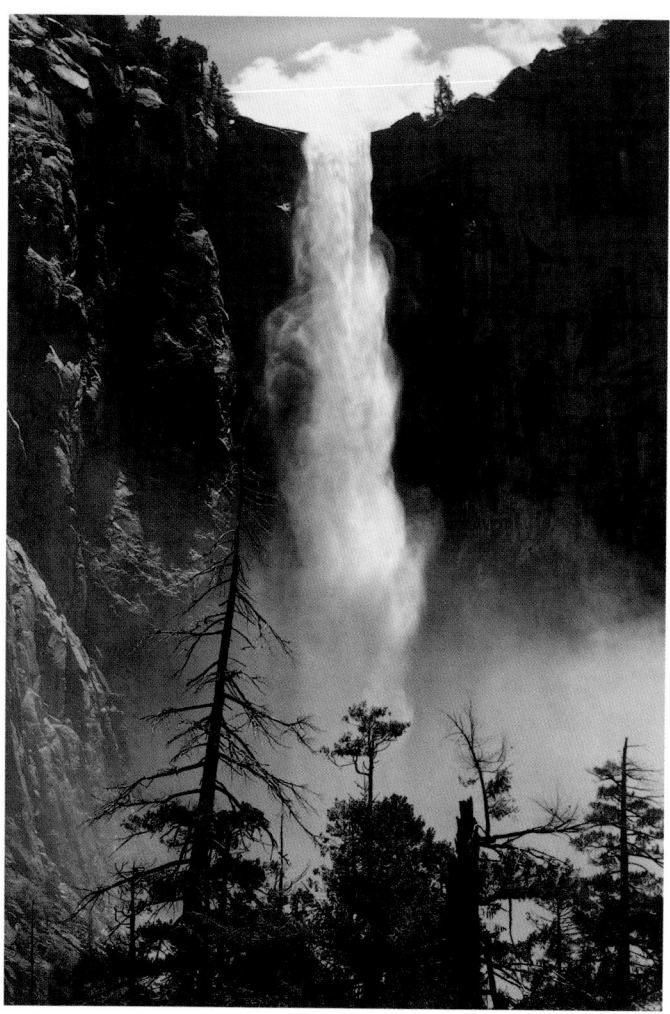

I walk around and put things in different positions
to break up the deadness of their eternal death.
I like to see dust move and crawl over an object like
a film. I like to see the objects scream and work
against their positions, against their size.   —Ivan Albright

Ivan Albright ¦ American, 1897–1983 ¦ **The Dead Doll** ¦ 1954 ¦ Lithograph ¦ 20 x 27 ⅞ inches ¦ Gift of Mr.
Gabe Wharton Burton in honor of Dorothy Haas Rautbord and in memory of Ryerson Williams Potter, 99.59

Once seen as an anomaly who clung to figurative realism against the advent
of Modernism, Albright now appears more clearly in relation to the work of
twentieth-century European and American realists, including Otto Dix, Lucian
Freud, Andrew Wyeth, and Grant Wood. Albright's early experiences as an army
medical artist set the course for such future themes as the contrast between life
and death and youth and age. (In 1943, MGM Studios commissioned Albright to
paint the famous version of the aged Dorian Gray seen in the 1945 movie.)

Albright considered *The Dead Doll* one of his most important images, and he made
several variations. Displaying his usual elaborate, nearly hallucinatory, articulation
of pattern and texture, this version presents the little figure in funereal splendor.
Although she is merely a doll, Albright's treatment of her here makes her seem a
dead and beloved person.

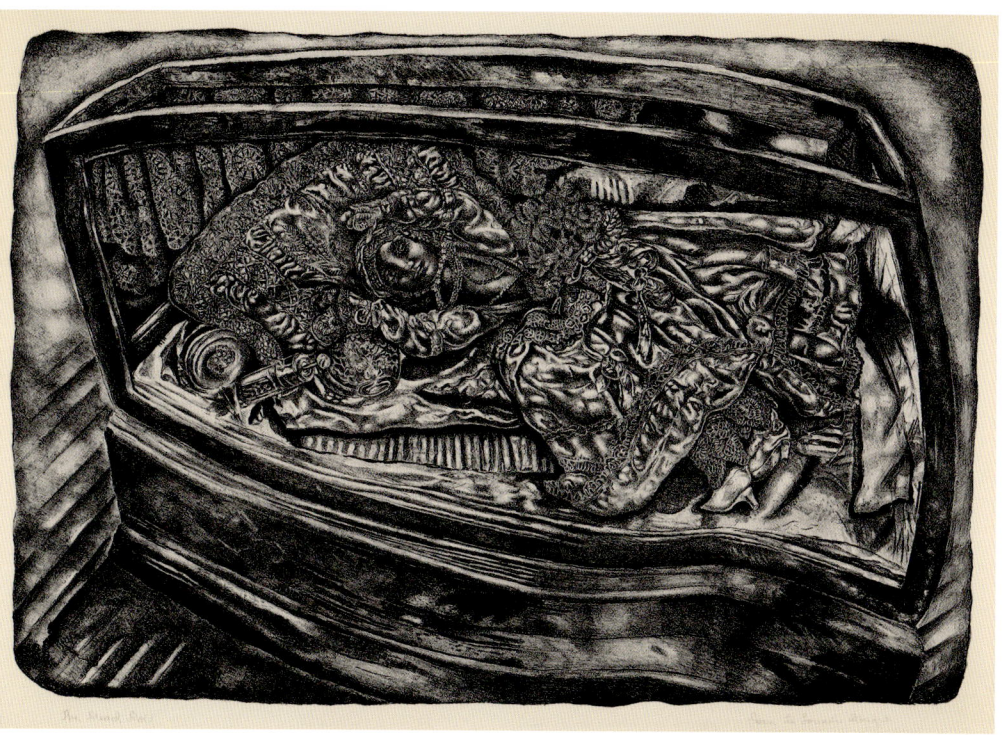

The Dream (?)

When you're a child, you see something that just excites you. And if it's a train, well, you're out of luck. Because you never lose it. — O. Winston Link

O. Winston Link | American, 1911–2001 | **The Birmingham Special Gets the Highball at Rural Retreat (NW 1634)** 1957 | Gelatin silver print | 16 1/8 x 19 5/16 inches | Museum Purchase, The A. Paul Funkhouser Endowment Fund, 2000.102

In the mid-1950s, Link, a successful commercial photographer, offered to document the Norfolk and Western Railway's steam-powered trains at his own expense. During the next five years, Link took seventeen trips to Virginia and West Virginia and shot over 2400 negatives, recording the vanishing era of the steam locomotive.

Making stop-action shots of speeding trains meant composing each scene before the train arrived. To capture the drama of night trains—his preferred subject—Link designed elaborate synchronized flash systems, sometimes firing up to sixty bulbs simultaneously. (In this image, for example, Link also included a single flash for the trainman's lantern.) Link's images of trains and railroading, among the most memorable ever produced, capture an important part of American history.

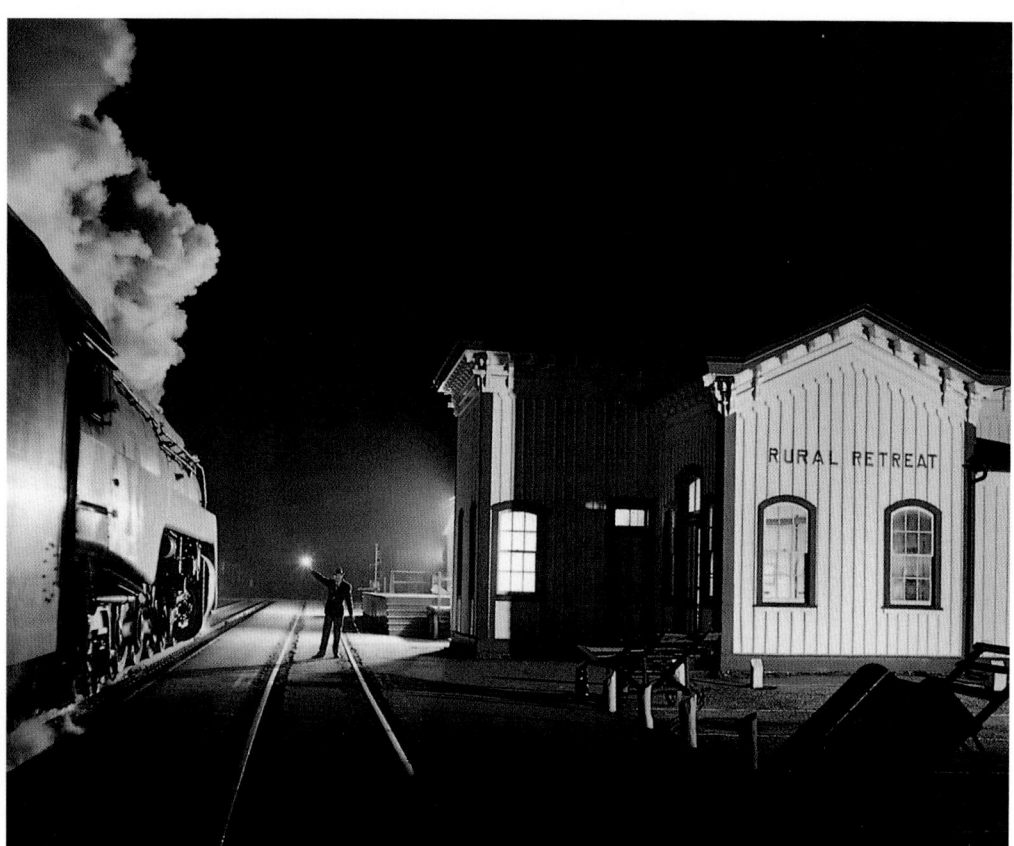

The collages are a kind of private diary . . . one that functions in an associative way for me. [They] offer a way of incorporating bits of the everyday world into pictures. —Robert Motherwell

Robert Motherwell ¦ American, 1915–1991 ¦ **Marine Collage** ¦ 1958 ¦ Oil and paper on board ¦ 18 x 15 inches ¦ Gift of the Dedalus Foundation, Inc., and Museum Purchase, The John Barton Payne Fund, 94.14 ¦ © Dedalus Foundation, Inc./Licensed by VAGA, New York, NY

Motherwell remains one of the best-known Abstract Expressionists, partly because of the scholarly writings in which he articulated the movement's aims. Graduate study at Harvard with philosopher Alfred North Whitehead led him to embrace abstraction as a way to discard nonessentials. Study at Columbia with art historian Meyer Schapiro convinced him to take up painting. He soon joined a group of artists—Jackson Pollock, Willem de Kooning, Mark Rothko, Franz Kline—who would define American art at midcentury.

Motherwell began making collages in 1943, exploring shapes, colors, and textures of painted and found elements, and combining gestural brushwork with paper fragments that carried personal meaning, as in this work, which includes part of a French journal (Motherwell worked in France for several months that year). The work's title probably refers to the artist's seaside studio in Provincetown, Massachusetts, where he spent summers after 1953; the image suggests a boat in rough water.

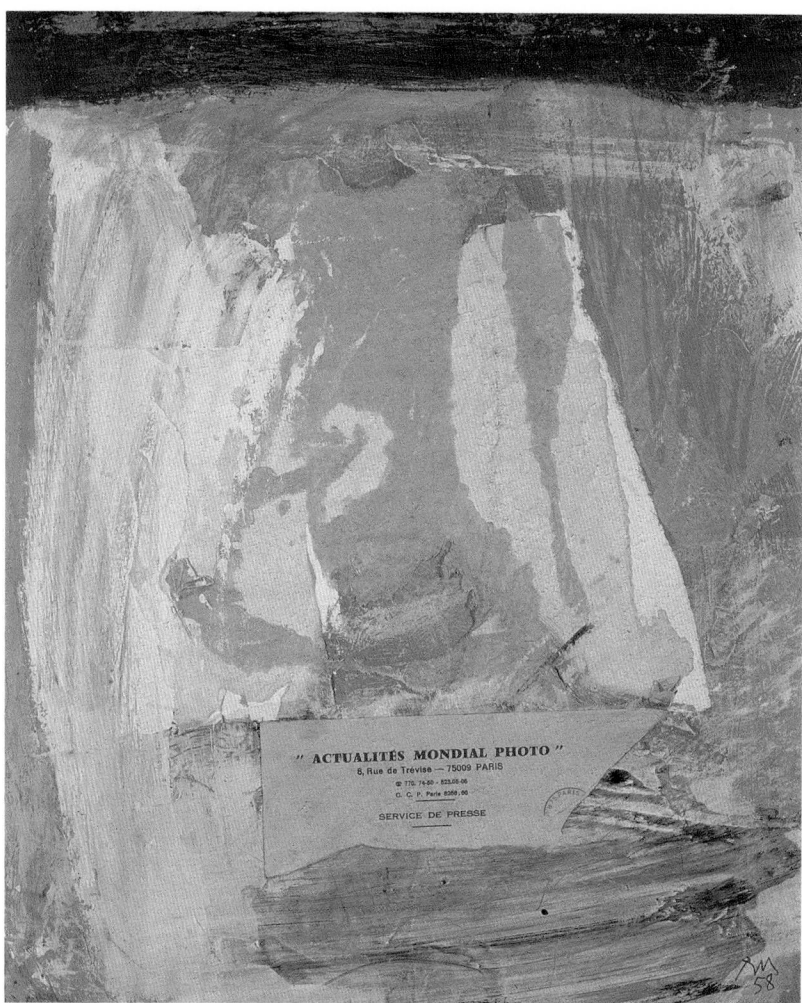

I use Negro subject matter because Negroes are closest to me. But I am trying to express a universal meaning for all men. . . . I've had my work in museums where I wasn't allowed to see it—but what I pour into my work is the challenge of how beautiful life can be. —Charles White

Charles White | American, 1918–1979 | **Guitarist** | ca. 1959 | Charcoal and gouache on illustration board | 44 x 38 inches | Gift of the Fabergé Society of the Virginia Museum of Fine Arts and Museum Purchase, The National Endowment for the Arts Fund for American Art, 2001.10

White is best known for his lifelong commitment to representing the human figure, especially in rich charcoal drawings. He emphasized African-American subjects, which he intended as symbols of the universal human conditions of suffering, joy, and dignity. In White's work, as in African-American culture, music is important; his friends included such prominent musicians as Paul Robeson and Harry Belafonte.

White's 1947 trip to Mexico with Elizabeth Catlett, then his wife, exposed him to the social realism of Mexican muralists Diego Rivera and David Siqueiros, and to the printmaking techniques of the Taller de Gráfica Popular (People's Graphic Workshop). This experience strengthened his commitment to a dramatic realist style and his choice of black-and-white drawing and printmaking over painting.

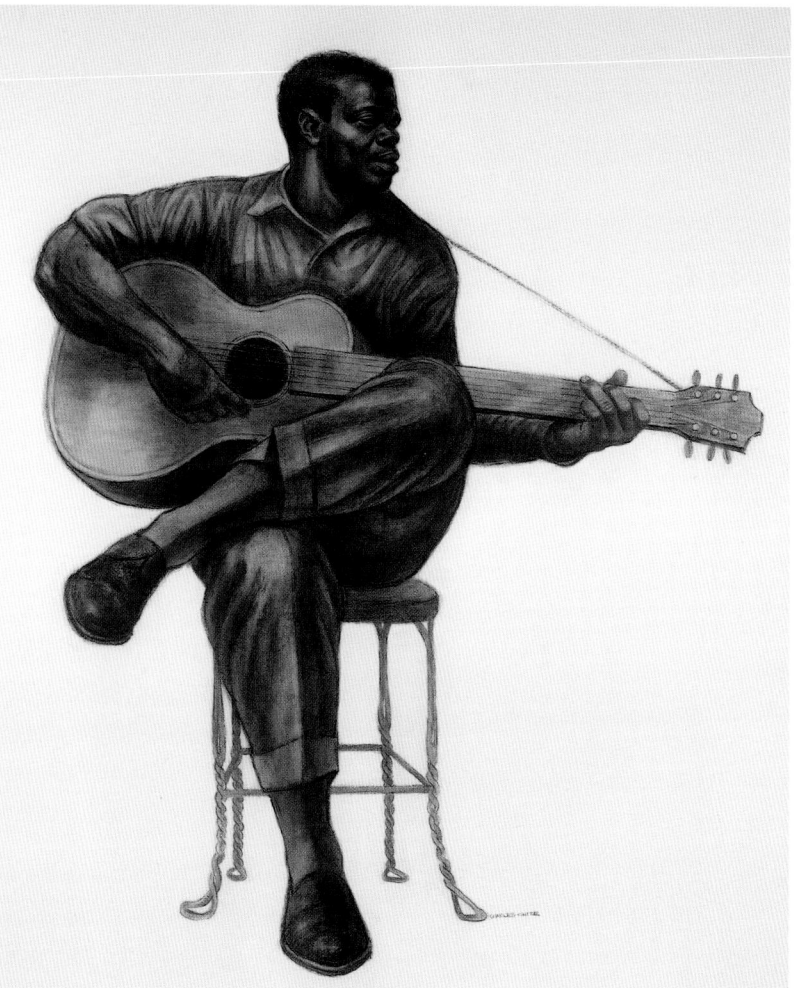

I've never been after an image of something or an illusion. I search for the realness, the real feeling of a subject, all the texture around it. . . . I want to come alive with the object. I want the primitive effect you get when you bring abstraction and the real together. —Andrew Wyeth

Andrew Wyeth | American, born 1917 | **Nick and Jamie** | 1963 | Dry brush watercolor on paper | 14 7/8 x 19 3/4 inches | Museum Purchase, the Mrs. Alfred I. du Pont Fund, 64.31

Nick and Jamie refers to Wyeth's sons, whose sacks of apples, the boys' stand-ins, wait in late-afternoon sun. One of America's most beloved painters, Wyeth's appeal lies in his realistic depictions of places untouched by encroaching technology and urbanism. Since the 1930s he has focused on the people, buildings, and landscape around Chadds Ford, Pennsylvania, where he grew up, and Cushing, Maine, where he has summered for decades. Wyeth came of age as an artist during the height of American Regionalist painting. His work's popularity surged in the 1950s and 1960s, when he defied Abstract Expressionism, Minimalism, and Pop Art.

Although Wyeth is considered a traditional realist, his work appears modernist in its abstraction of the visible world. Simplification, emptiness, odd angles, and ambiguous vistas create nostalgic or melancholy moods but also suggest contemporary alienation.

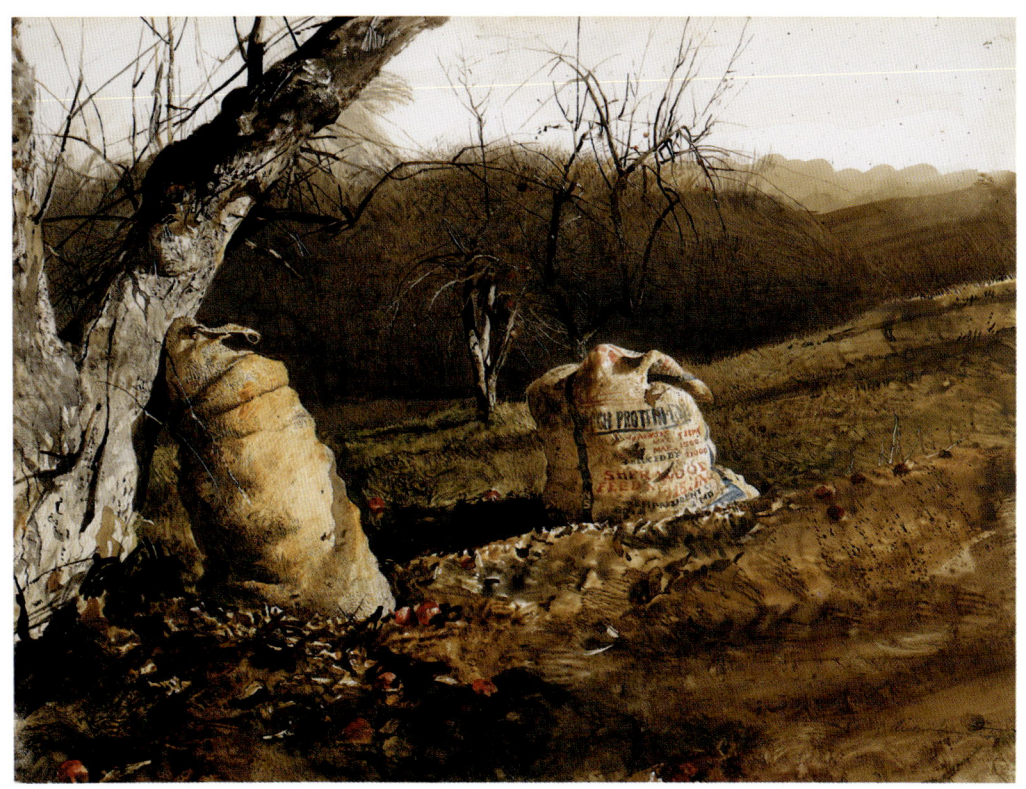

The mystery of a beautiful photograph really is revealed when nothing is obscured. We recognize that nothing has been withheld from us, so that we must complete its meaning. We are returned . . . to the sense and smell of its origin. —Emmet Gowin

Emmet Gowin | American, born 1941 | **Edith, Ruth, and Mae, Danville, Virginia** | 1967 | Gelatin silver print | 5 ½ x 7 inches | Museum Purchase with funds provided by the Museum Purchase Program of the National Endowment for the Arts and an anonymous donor, 91.22

Born and raised in Virginia, Gowin is closely identified with images of his family taken in and around Danville, where he was born and raised. Gowin left Virginia in 1965 to study photography at the Rhode Island School of Design with Harry Callahan, whose tender portrayals of his wife and daughter no doubt inspired Gowin's own interest in the intimacy and spirituality of the commonplace. Gowin returned to Danville for summers and holidays with his wife's extended family. His fascination with their lives made them his early subjects.

One of Gowin's best-known images, this work shows his wife, Edith, on the left, and her two sisters, Ruth and Mae, in the family backyard. Their physical closeness indicates a strong bond, underscored by their resemblance. Although this is an apparently candid glimpse of Gowin's family, the young women's graceful demeanor also suggests an allegorical dimension, perhaps the three Graces.

196

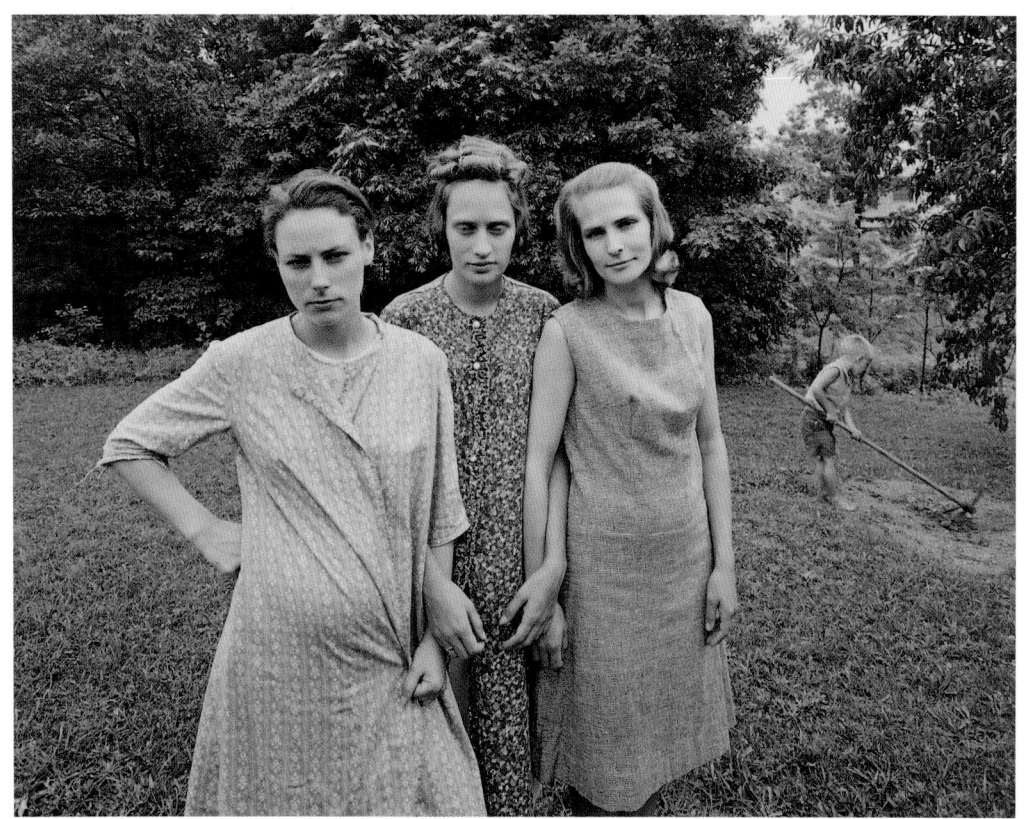

Most of the time when my photographs are interesting it's because the content is on the verge of overwhelming the form. — Garry Winogrand

Garry Winogrand ⏐ American, 1928–1984 ⏐ **New York City** ⏐ 1970 ⏐ Gelatin silver print ⏐ 9 x 13 ½ inches ⏐ Gift of an anonymous donor, 82.201.5/15

Inspired by Walker Evans's documentary photographs of vernacular American subjects during the thirties, Winogrand scoured the social landscape of the sixties for his subjects—people in the street, people at parties, people in airports, people at the zoo. But Winogrand embraced abundance, randomness, and tension, rather than seeking Evans's precision and balance, and he took a direct and candid approach to photography as personal expression over neutral documentation.

This image, sometimes called *Hard-Hat Rally, New York,* captures the turbulent political mood in America during the Vietnam War. Although usually dated 1969, the photograph documents a protest from May 1970, a month during which antiwar youth and pro-Nixon union workers clashed several times in New York. After beating students and bystanders at a Wall Street peace march on May 8, construction workers staged two rallies the next week. They carried signs denouncing Mayor John Lindsay, a Republican who opposed the war and the workers' attacks. The subject perfectly suits Winogrand's anarchic style; with his camera pushed up against the action, he captures a moment of true spectacle.

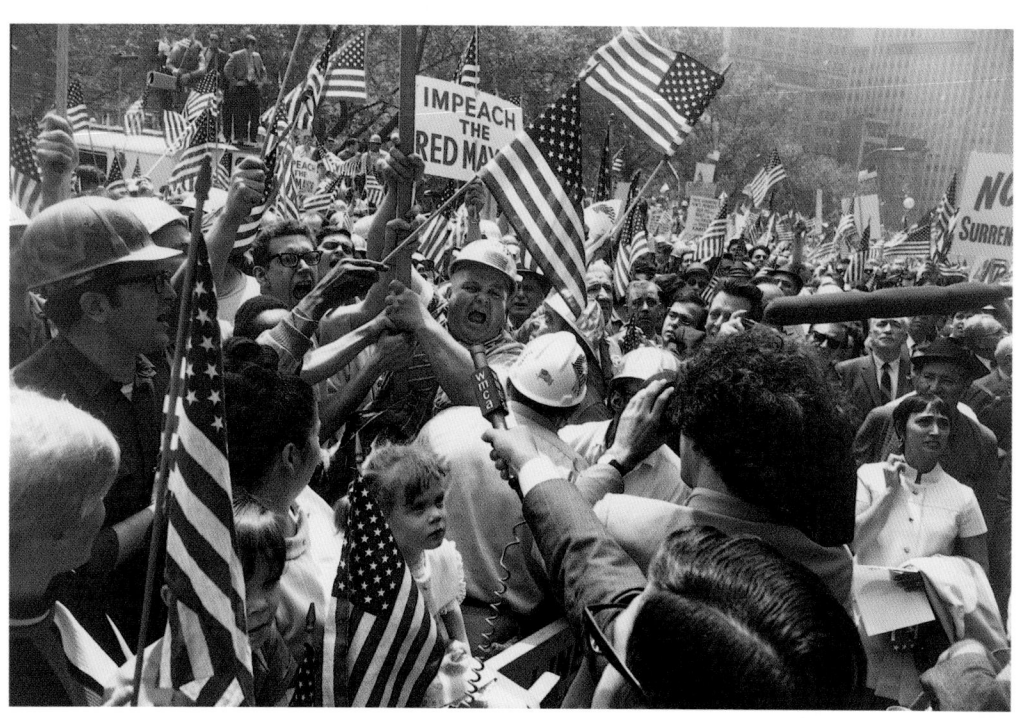

I had this notion of what I called a democratic way of looking around, that nothing was more or less important. — William Eggleston

William Eggleston | American, born 1939 | **Jackson, Mississippi** | 1972 | Dye transfer photograph | 19 x 25 ⅛ inches | Museum Purchase, The Museum Purchase Program of the National Endowment for the Arts, matching funds provided by the Volunteer Committees of Art Museums, 89.50

Eggleston gained notice in 1976 with a Museum of Modern Art exhibition and book of color photographs taken in and around Mississippi and his native city of Memphis, Tennessee. Critics struggled to reconcile Eggleston's saturated color, banal subjects, and snapshot aesthetic with high art photographic traditions. With a few exceptions, color work before Eggleston was associated with advertising, fashion, exotic images in *National Geographic,* and family snapshots and travel slides. Eggleston played on these vernacular associations in catapulting color photography to the medium's most advanced form. His subject, to an apparently perverse degree, was life's unremarkable moments.

Although Eggleston's work suggests the inherent value of such moments, he emphasizes the beauty of the dye-transfer color print at least as much. Here, color is the catalyst for a riot of competing patterns, in the midst of which Eggleston presents the frail female figure seen straight on and slightly above, as if he could hardly offer her the courtesy of composition. This vantage point compounds the idiosyncrasy and decay that some consider the Southernness of Eggleston's work.

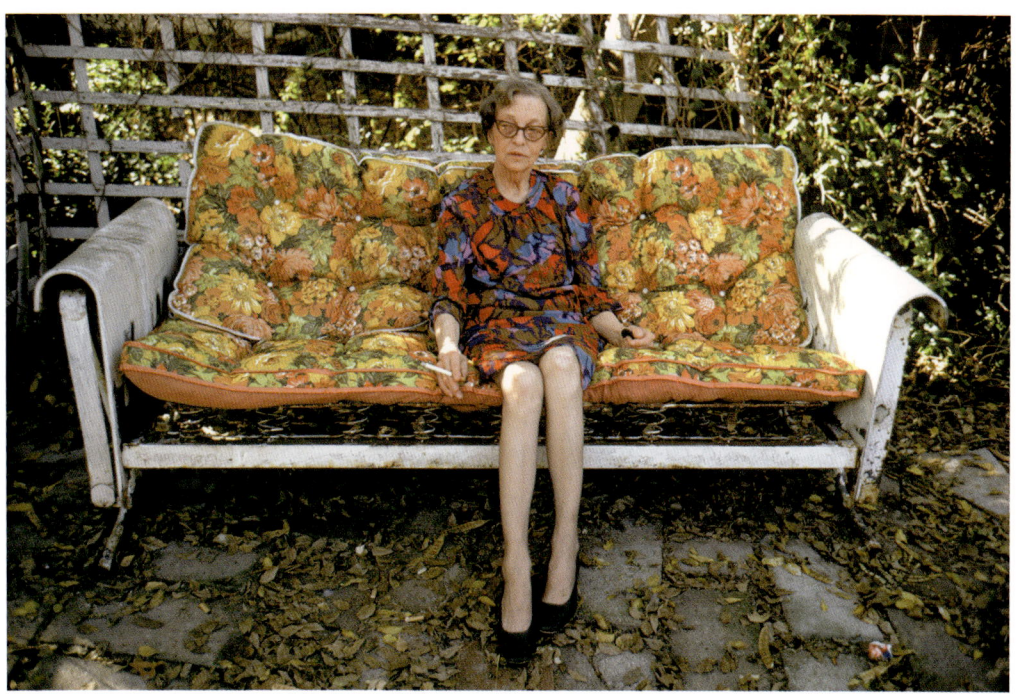

I am very close to the child's world in my creative process. I respond completely to all my instincts and channel them into the work. — Ray Johnson

Ray Johnson | American, 1927–1995 | **Marcel Duchamp's Mother's Potato-Masher** | 1973 | Graphite, ink, paint, and collage on paper and board | 19 ¾ x 14 ⅞ inches | Gift of Best Products, Inc., 90.12

Johnson is perhaps most closely identified with mail art, or, as he called it, the New York Correspondence School. For almost forty years he used the U.S. Postal Service to deliver informal drawn, printed, and collaged missives to friends, peers, and art-world professionals. Born of Johnson's resistance to the commercial gallery scene, his mail art was an alternative way to display his work and to connect broadly with an audience on his own terms. His work also shows Johnson's delight in playing the trickster—an insider and an outsider who knows everyone but is never fully known.

Mixed-media collage was Johnson's primary medium; its union of found and invented fragments perfectly suited his palimpsests of public and private meanings. This piece belongs to a group from the early 1970s featuring the potato-masher as a central motif. That group and other Johnson works share a fascination with celebrity. The title refers to Dadaist Marcel Duchamp, whose irreverent humor and use of found objects infuse Johnson's playful and mysterious homage.

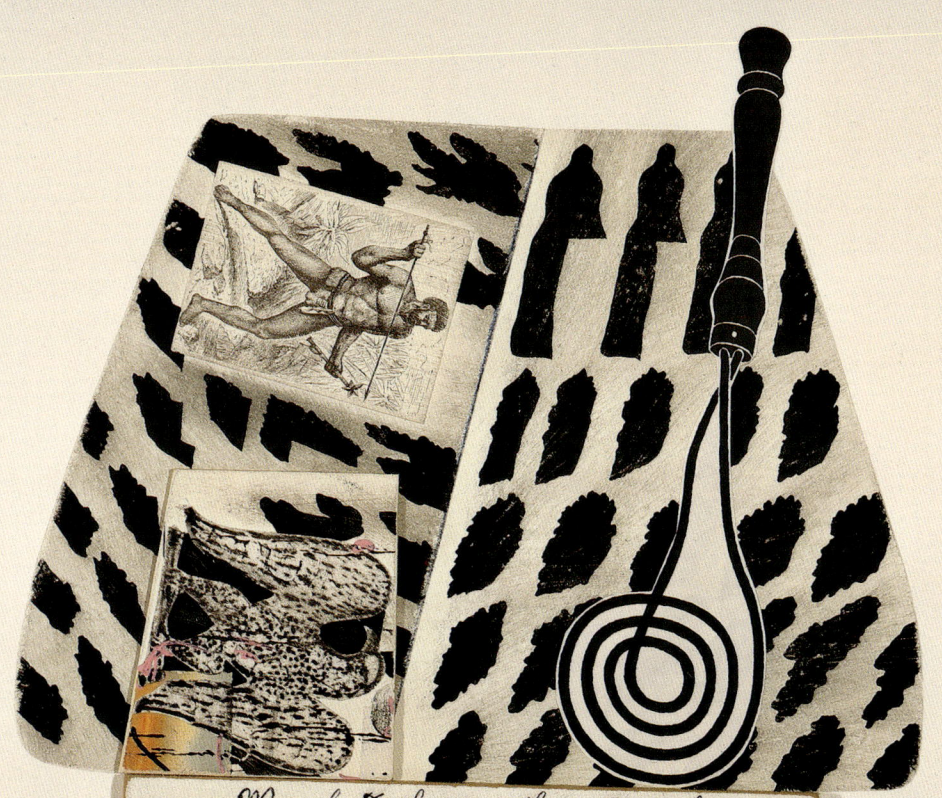

Marcel Duchamp's mother's potato-masher

MARCEL DUCHAMP 1887 - 1968

Ray Johnson 1973

I wanted a stupid, inarticulate, uninteresting mark that in and of itself could not be more interesting than the last mark or more beautiful than the next. . . . The imposition of rigorous, self-imposed limitations . . . seemed to open doors. —Chuck Close

Chuck Close ¦ American, born 1949 ¦ **Self-Portrait/Pastel** ¦ 1977 ¦ Pastel and ink wash on paper ¦ 30 ½ x 22 inches ¦ Gift of The Sydney and Frances Lewis Foundation, 85.531

For the past thirty-five years, Close has addressed a single subject—the human face. In a process Close likens to knitting, he takes, grids, and transfers photographs of his sitters to produce paintings, drawings, and prints. Originally considered a Photorealist, Close soon made clear his interest in the process and mechanics of representation, a focus that relates him to Minimalism and Conceptual Art.

As a young artist, Close needed an inexpensive and ever-ready model; since then, he has become his most frequent subject. This work, his only self-portrait in pastel, perfectly exemplifies Close's method of accumulating dispassionate and repetitive marks to create a remarkably accurate likeness. Rather than revealing the individual, however, Close uses the outward signs of his process—the grid and round marks formed by rotating the ends of pastel sticks—to emphasize the tension between his methods and structures and their capacity to create illusion.

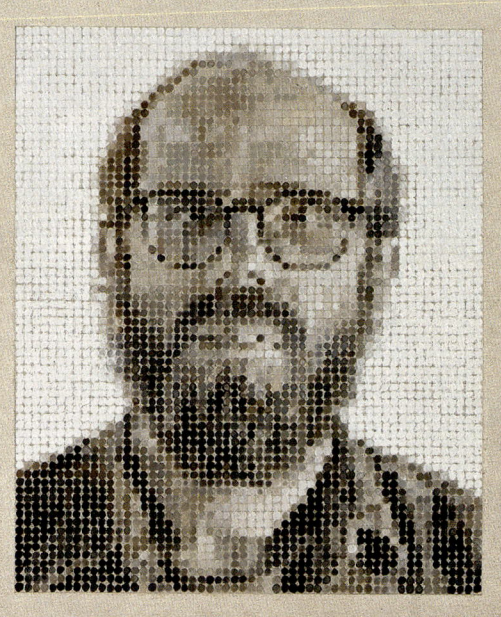

We are fascinated by the richness of the fabric of Our World and we honor the High-Mindedness of Man as the Ultimate Form and Meaning of Art. Beauty is Our Art. — Gilbert and George

Gilbert & George | Gilbert Proesch, English, born Italy, 1943; George Passmore, English, born 1942 | **The Tree** | 1978 | Sixteen gelatin silver prints | 23 ¾ x 19 ¾ inches each, 95 ¼ x 79 ⅜ inches overall | Gift of The Sydney and Frances Lewis Foundation, 85.390.1–16

Gilbert and George began collaborating in the late 1960s, first as live performance artists, and then, in the early 1970s, in making large, multi-paneled photographic works. *The Tree* is part of a 1978 series in which each piece focuses on an object from the everyday environment. In *The Tree,* a large, dark form rises out of a central void, framed by the artists' shadowy self-portraits. Each fractured and displaced element takes on new meaning in the company of the others: the self-portraits represent both specific individuals and mankind in general; likewise, the tree is a unique example photographed by artists and also a universal symbol for knowledge and growth.

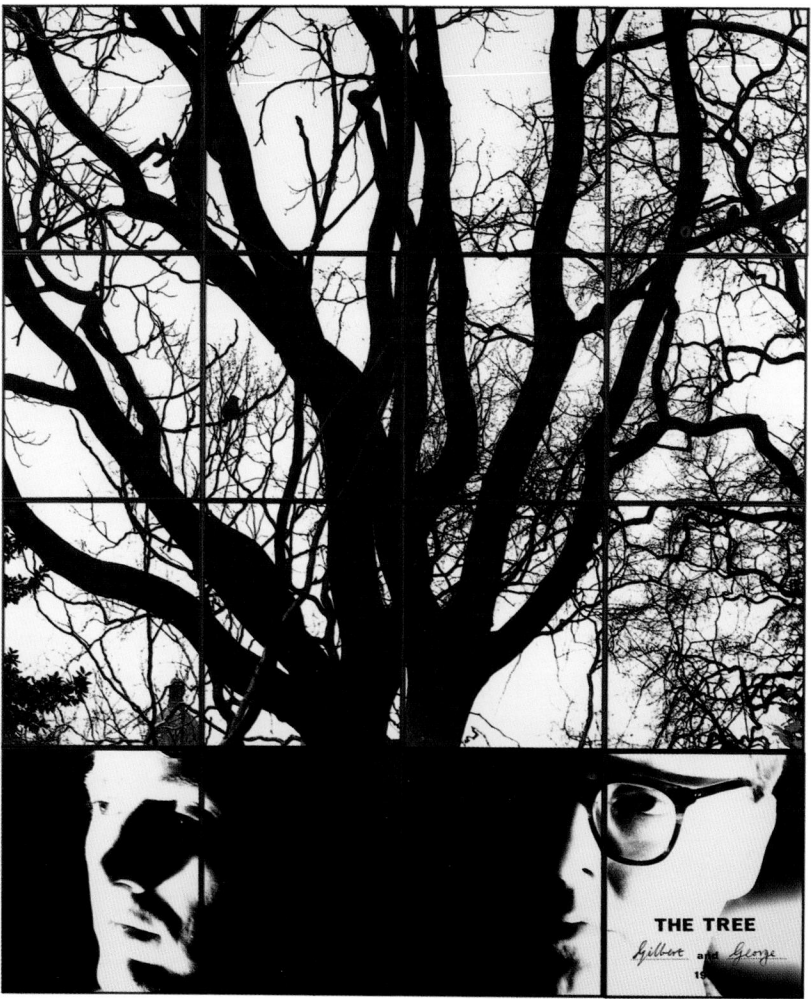

THE TREE
Gilbert and George
19

I was intrigued by a statement from Courbet, who, in reaction against the ecclesiastical work around him . . . said "Show me an angel and I'll paint it." I thought it would be marvelous to do an abstract angel: since there were no people with big wings sitting around posing, angels were probably the first non-geometric abstraction in painting. —Dorothea Rockburne

Dorothea Rockburne | Canadian, born 1932 | **White Angel #2** | 1981 | Folded paper | 70 x 46 inches | Gift of The Sydney and Frances Lewis Foundation, 85.570

Rockburne's concern with geometry and with rational, ordered thinking links her to Minimalism and Conceptual Art, out of which her work developed in the 1960s. After exploring mathematical permutations and ideal proportions like the Golden Mean, Rockburne sought inspiration in the compositional principles of earlier art.

The spare and elegant *White Angel #2* is deceptively simple. Paper folded in geometric patterns, it appears to focus solely on its own making. But it is actually part of a series based on the work of the early Renaissance painter Duccio. The title, as well as the work's folds and forms, refers to an angel guarding Christ's tomb in a painting in the Cathedral of Siena.

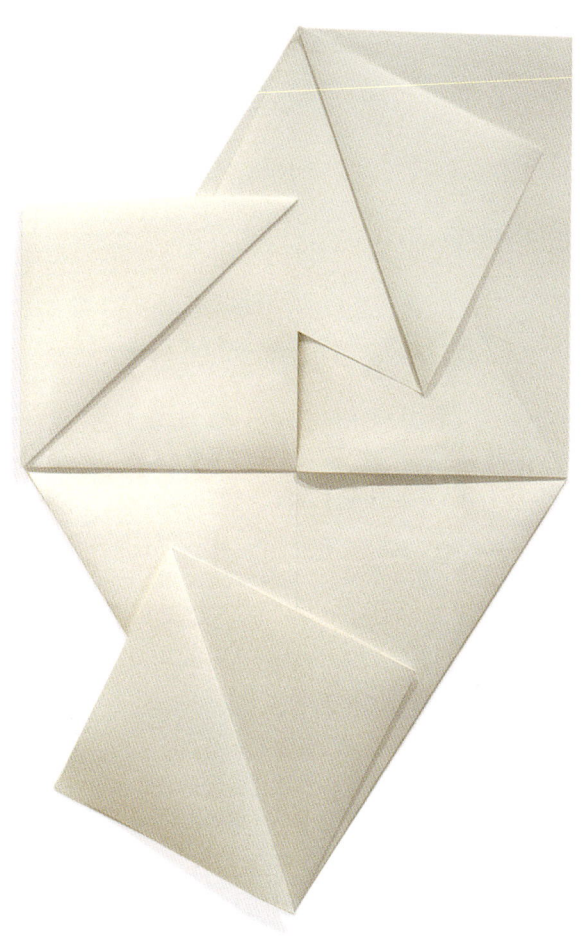

These are pictures of emotions personified, entirely of themselves, with their own presence. . . . I'm trying to make other people recognize something of themselves, rather than me. —Cindy Sherman

Cindy Sherman | American, born 1954 | **Untitled #119** | 1983 | Color photograph | 17 ½ x 36 inches | Museum Purchase, The National Endowment for the Arts Fund for American Art, 96.101

Sherman skillfully serves as actress, director, makeup artist, and costume and set designer in her striking photographs. Her images, in which she uses herself as the subject, adopt and manipulate familiar roles from drama, stereotypes, and fantasy. *Untitled #119*—in which Sherman poses as a colorful nightclub singer—was created as part of an advertising series commissioned for *Interview,* the magazine founded by Andy Warhol. The dramatic gesture, lighting, facial expression, and proximity to the camera make Sherman as much the focus of the photograph as the clothing that she is supposedly promoting.

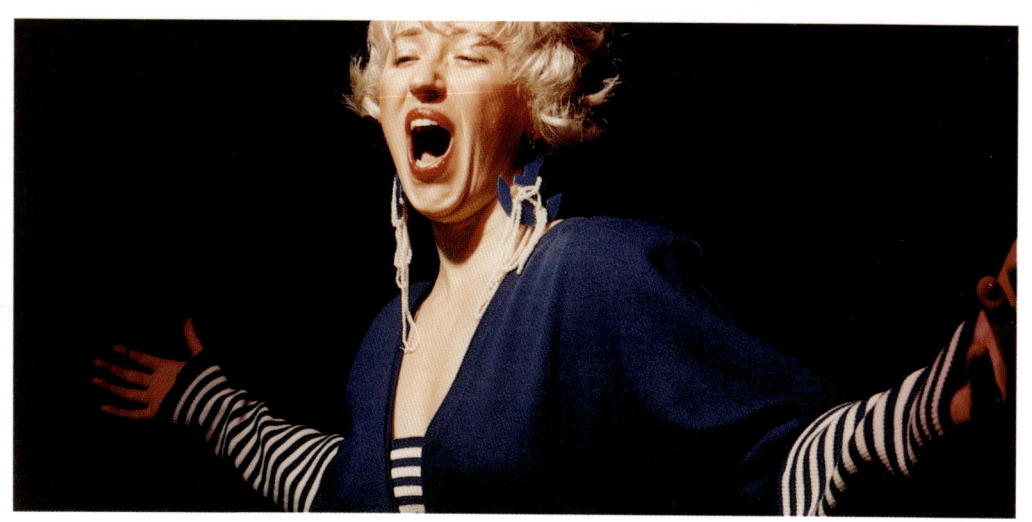

> Art's purpose is to sober and quiet the mind so that it is in accord with what happens. —John Cage

John Cage | American, 1912–1992 | **Series IV, #1** from **New River Watercolors** | 1988 | Watercolor on rag paper 26 ½ x 40 inches | Gift of Ray Kass and the Mountain Lake Art Workshop, and the Horton Fund of the Virginia Tech Foundation, 90.186

Known primarily as an experimental composer whose embrace of chance and silence revolutionized avant-garde music, Cage also devoted much of his later life to making visual art. Inspired in part by Zen Buddhism and the "readymades" of Marcel Duchamp, Cage's visual practice, like his music, also sought to downplay the individual ego and blur the distinction between art and everyday experience. Cage made drawings, watercolors, and prints, using the *I-Ching*—an ancient Chinese divination book—to make decisions without regard to individual taste and feelings.

Cage first experimented with watercolor during a 1983 visit to Virginia Tech in southwestern Virginia. He used the *I-Ching* to decide where to position smooth stones from the nearby New River on the paper before tracing their outlines in paint. As part of the Mountain Lake Workshop, Cage returned for longer sessions in 1988 and 1990. Using feathers as well brushes enabled Cage to incorporate the artist's gesture without reintroducing the subjective ego-driven expression Cage had so rigorously avoided throughout his career.

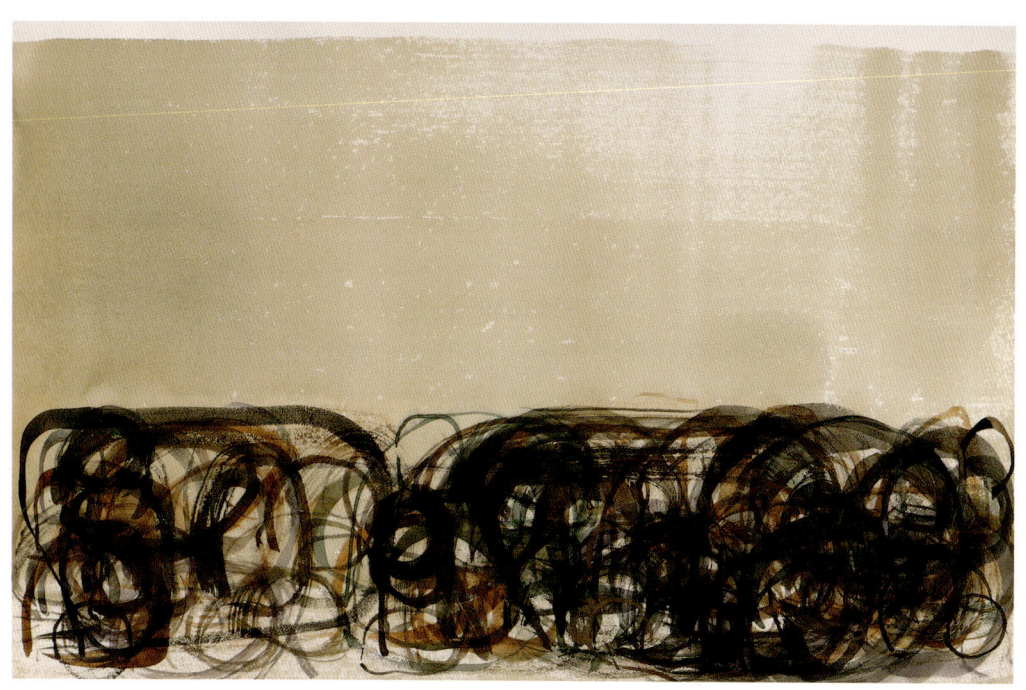

Talking about racism does not perpetuate it.

— Carrie Mae Weems

Carrie Mae Weems | American, born 1950 | **Blue Black Boy** | 1990 | Gelatin silver print toned blue; overmat, wood frame, Plexiglas with applied lettering | Three parts, each 16 7/8 x 16 7/8 inches | Museum purchase with funds provided by a grant from the Polaroid Foundation, 91.50.1–3

Weems makes social and psychological commentaries on race using the conventions of photographic documentation. By combining portraits and text that appear to reenact stereotypes, she addresses black experience.

The triptychs of the *Colored People* series draw upon Weems's interest in the range of African-American skin tones and refer to the skin-color caste system that exists in black communities. These tender portrayals of children are meant to affirm their identities as people of color.

Weems hand-tints each black-and-white picture with photographic dyes, then reinforces her message with titles such as *High Yella Girl, Red Bone Boy,* and *Magenta Colored Girl.* In *Blue Black Boy,* she has used a blue tint to enhance the young boy's rich, dark complexion.

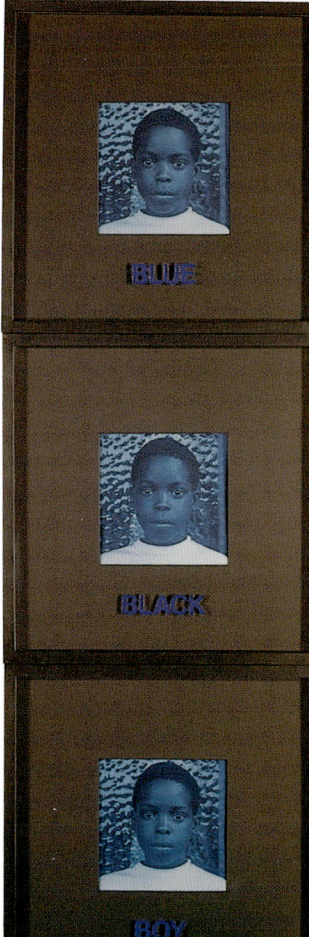

Feminist art is soft art, lightweight art, sewing art. This is the contribution that women have made that is uniquely theirs. . . . Women's art is less rigid, and it's open to all kinds of . . . innovations. —Faith Ringgold

Faith Ringgold ⎪ American, born 1930 ⎪ **Tar Beach II** ⎪ 1990 ⎪ Quilt (acid dyes screen-printed on bleached silk, and pieced commercially printed cotton) ⎪ 66 ¾ x 67 ½ inches ⎪ Gift of Marion Boulton Stroud, 2001.252

Ringgold has been an artist, social activist, art teacher, and community organizer since the early 1960s. In the 1980s, Ringgold began to make mixed-media "story quilts" that combined her interests in painting, quilting, and storytelling, as well as in arts from other cultures such as Tibetan *thankas* (religious paintings, often on fabric). Ringgold's quilts include texts that she wrote voicing the struggles and triumphs of fictitious women and children of color.

The narrator of *Tar Beach II* is eight-year-old Cassie Louise Lightfoot; the "tar beach" is the roof of her apartment building. Cassie imagines she can improve her family's station in life by flying over things and gathering them up. The George Washington Bridge, which looks to Cassie like a diamond necklace, is among these fantastic acquisitions. Ringgold made this work as part of an edition of twenty-four during a residency at Philadelphia's Fabric Workshop and Museum (her 1991 Caldecott Honor children's book, *Tar Beach,* was based on an earlier version).

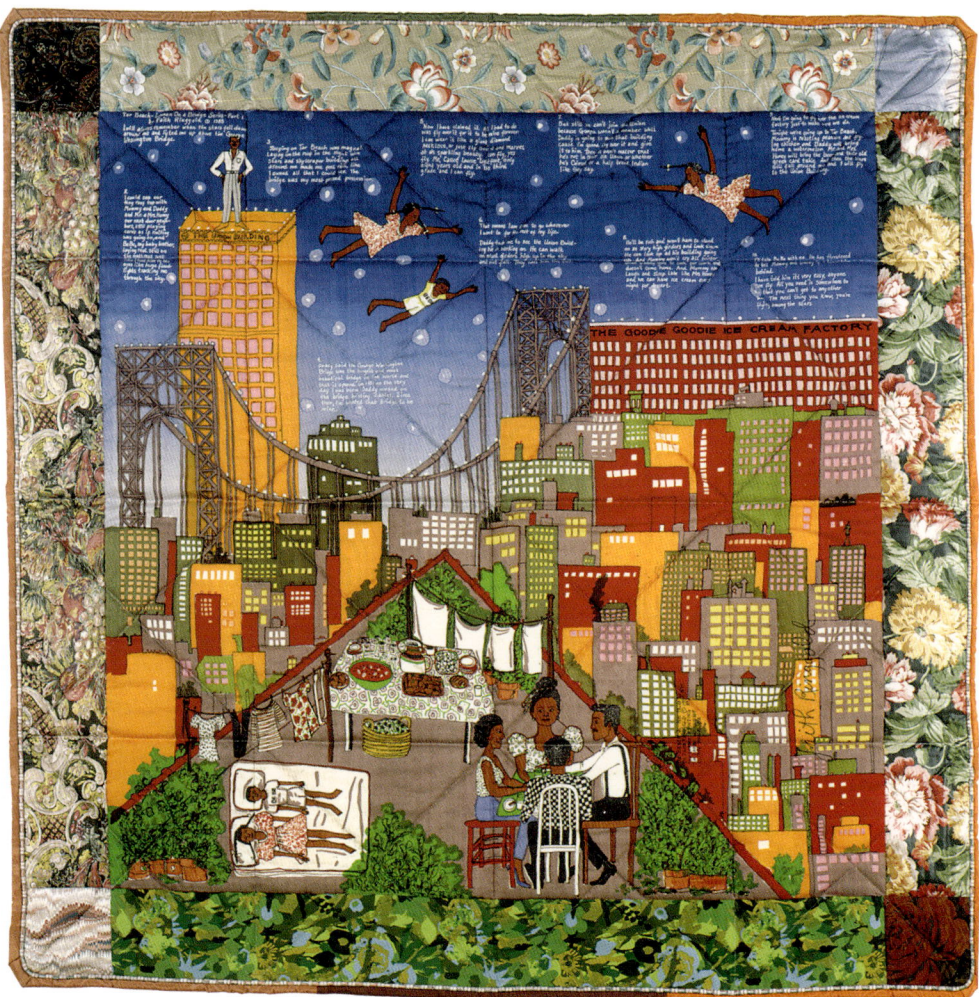

I'm dealing with the language of stereotypes.

— Lorna Simpson

Lorna Simpson ¦ American, born 1960 ¦ **Untitled** ¦ 1992 ¦ Framed Polaroid C-prints, plastic plaques ¦ 74 1/2 x 40 1/4 inches overall ¦ Museum Purchase, The Adolph D. and Wilkins C. Williams Fund, 93.9a–e

Simpson combines large-format Polaroid photographs with terse phrases meant to sensitize viewers to the misrepresentation and inaccuracy lurking in everyday words and images. Here, Simpson disrupts the usual relationship between observer and observed by turning her subject away from the camera. This raises a series of questions: Is the figure male or female? A corporate executive or a restaurant employee? Do the verbs (believe, possess, hold, keep, cling, faint, collapse, plunge, descend, fall) paired with the days of the week describe the figure's mental state? Simpson underscores the ambiguity of images and language to make us reexamine our understanding of racial and sexual identity.

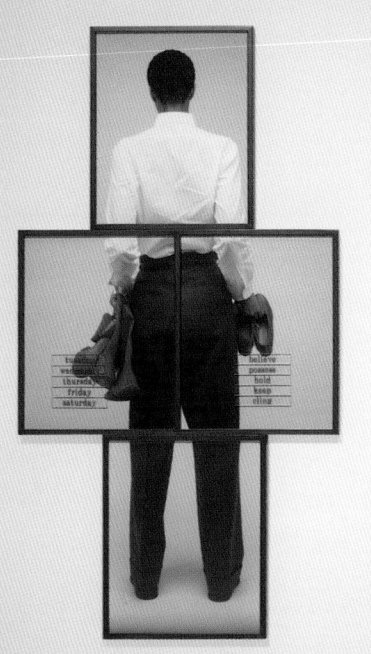
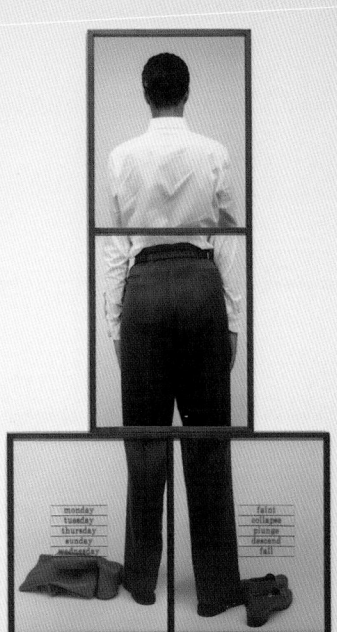

Memory and replica. . . . Photography is a system of saving memories. It's a time-machine, a way to preserve the memory. — Hiroshi Sugimoto

Hiroshi Sugimoto | Japanese, born 1948 | **Byrd, Richmond** | 1993 | Gelatin silver print | 20 x 24 inches | Gift of The Collectors' Circle of the Virginia Museum of Fine Arts, 96.93

Since the early 1970s, when Sugimoto left Japan for the United States, he has photographed a few subjects in closely related series: seascapes, wax-museum figures, natural-history-museum dioramas, and icons of modern architecture. In his approach to each group, Sugimoto seeks the fine line between the real and unreal, the visible and invisible. He captures this content using the dispassionate serial approach of a Conceptual artist. The viewpoint, lighting, and format remain fixed so that each work in a series functions as part of a larger idea.

Byrd, Richmond belongs to a series begun in 1975 of the empty interiors of pre–World War II movie theaters. The theater's ornate decor frames mysteriously glowing screens. Sugimoto gets this effect by leaving the shutter of his traditional box camera open during the entire movie, which turns the screen into a Minimalist rectangle of white light.

Although these vanishing Depression-era movie palaces (and, later, drive-ins) are the apparent subjects of the *Theater* series, pure light provides a deeper resonance: the open shutter suggests an eye whose unblinking stare yields a sublime vision.

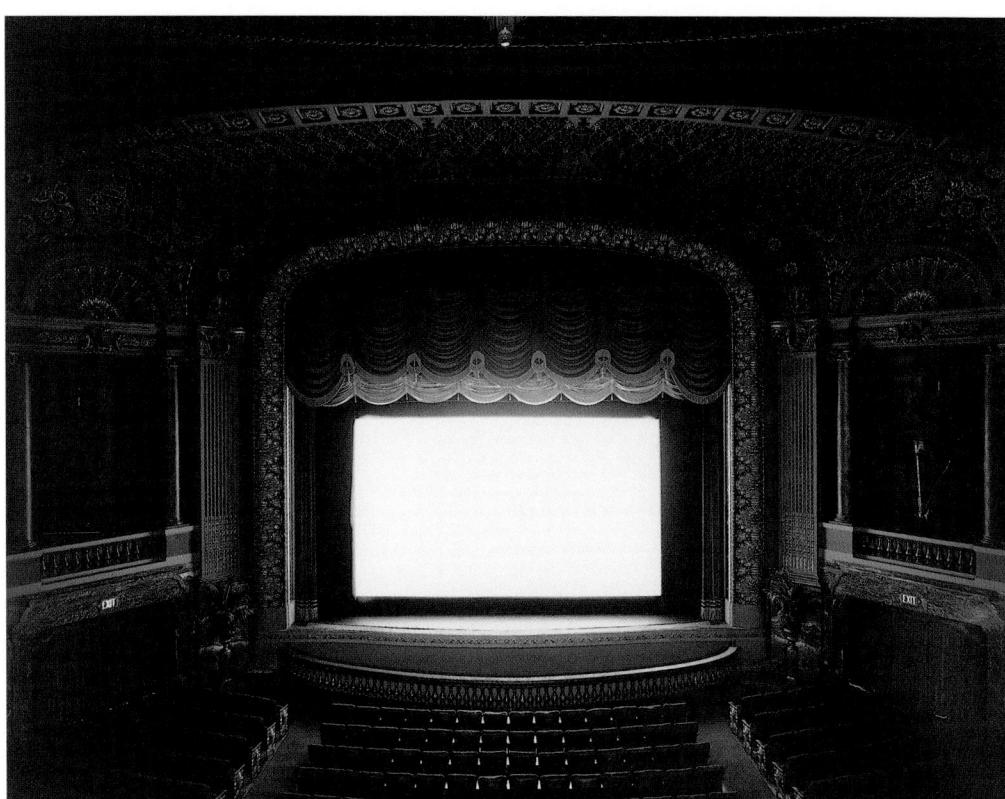

The more specific the interpretation suggested by a picture, the less happy I am with it. — Philip-Lorca diCorcia

Philip-Lorca diCorcia ⋮ American, born 1953 ⋮ **New York, 1997** ⋮ 1997 ⋮ Ektacolor print ⋮ 25 1/8 x 37 1/2 inches ⋮ Gift of the Massey Charitable Trust, 99.45

The *New York Times Magazine* commissioned diCorcia's *New York, 1997* for an article on Times Square. To create the photograph, diCorcia hid strobe lights above the sidewalk, placed his camera on a tripod, and stood aside to photograph the anonymous people who became his subjects.

The unsmiling passersby, a marquee for T. S. Eliot's *The Waste Land,* and the artificial light's shadowy effects make the picture seem a comment on the isolation and loneliness of contemporary urban life. DiCorcia's work combines aspects of "straight" photography, in which the image seems to capture a fleeting moment, and "art" photography, in which the image is understood as a fiction the artist created.

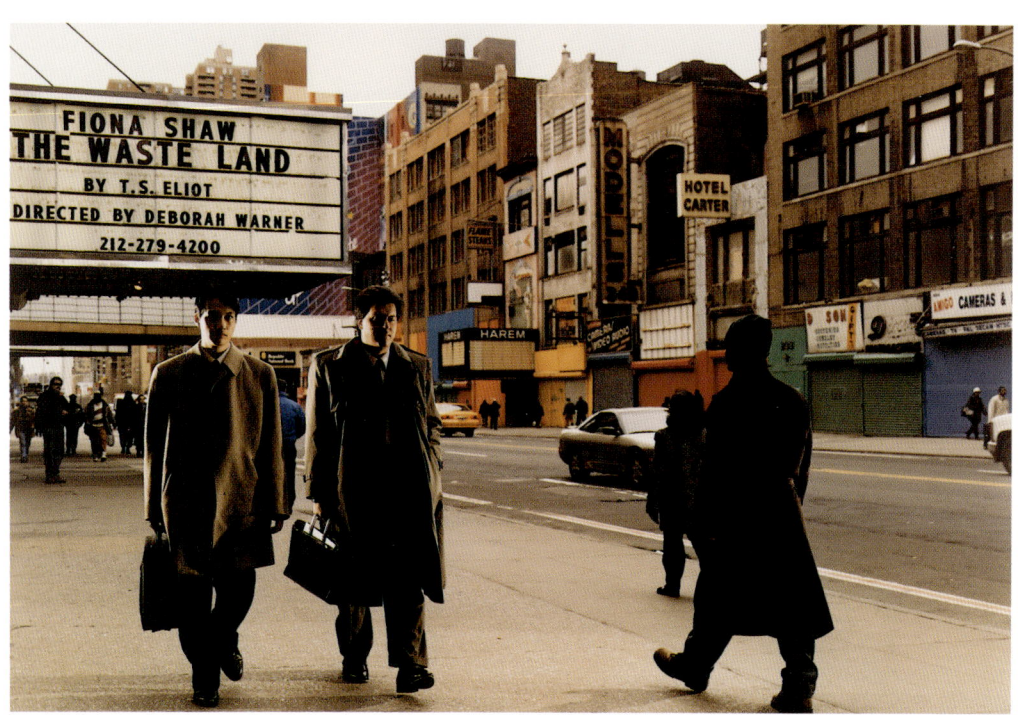

For me it is more interesting to try and find out something from the real than to throw something subjective in front of the audience. — Thomas Struth

Thomas Struth | German, born 1954 | **Monreale, Palermo** | 1998 | C-print | 73 ¼ x 91 ¼ inches | Gift of Marion Stroud-Swingle, 2000.78

Over the past twenty-five years, Struth has photographed various subjects in series, including deserted cityscapes, individual and group portraits, and museum-goers all over the world. *Monreale, Palermo,* shows a tour group at Monreale Cathedral outside of Palermo, Sicily, and extends Struth's museum series, which focuses on the outward forms of observation and contemplation.

Struth takes a "straight" approach to photography, using a large-format view camera on a tripod and working in available light. His unembellished images seem informal, as if he just happened to be standing in a particular spot observing. Yet the sharp focus, heightened clarity, and balanced lights and darks suggest the meticulous control required to produce these large, almost cinematic views.

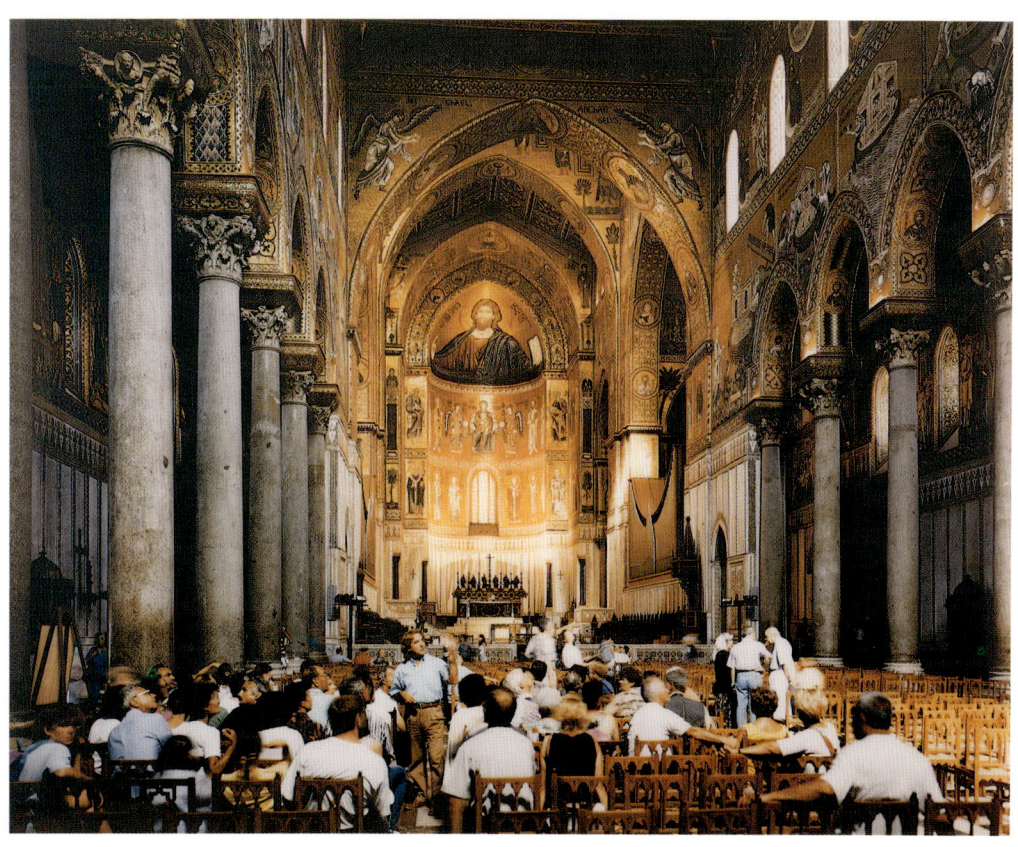

My prints and drawings are the result of trying to assess and define what surprises me in a sculpture, what I could not understand before a work was built.

— Richard Serra

Richard Serra | American, born 1939 | **D.T.E.** | 1999 | Etching | 59 ½ x 47 ¾ inches | Etching | Gift of Henrietta Near in memory of Pinkney Near (Museum Curator, 1954–1990), 2000.19

In the late 1960s, Serra's sculptures—composed of large lead or steel sheets—established him as a leading Post-Minimalist. Since the beginning of his career, Serra has also made drawings and prints. Serra's works on paper are unlike traditional sculptors' studies because he usually creates them after the sculpture is finished. They explore issues like weight and density in an entirely different medium.

D.T.E. ("double torqued ellipse") relates directly to Serra's highly acclaimed *Torqued Ellipses* (1996–1999), massive sculptures based on two ovals that overlap at an angle, creating a thick steel "skin" enclosing twisting, elliptical voids. In the prints from *Torqued Ellipses,* Serra used large-format etching to study these forms as if viewed from above. He translated the experience of the sculptures into printmaking through a labor-intensive process that pushed the medium to its limits, building up thick layers of molten paintstick and lithographic crayon that he pressed through an aluminum screen onto the copper plate with his feet. The plates required days of etching in an acid bath, and nearly three hours of inking. Printed on specially made paper, the dense surfaces of the prints echo Serra's sculptures.

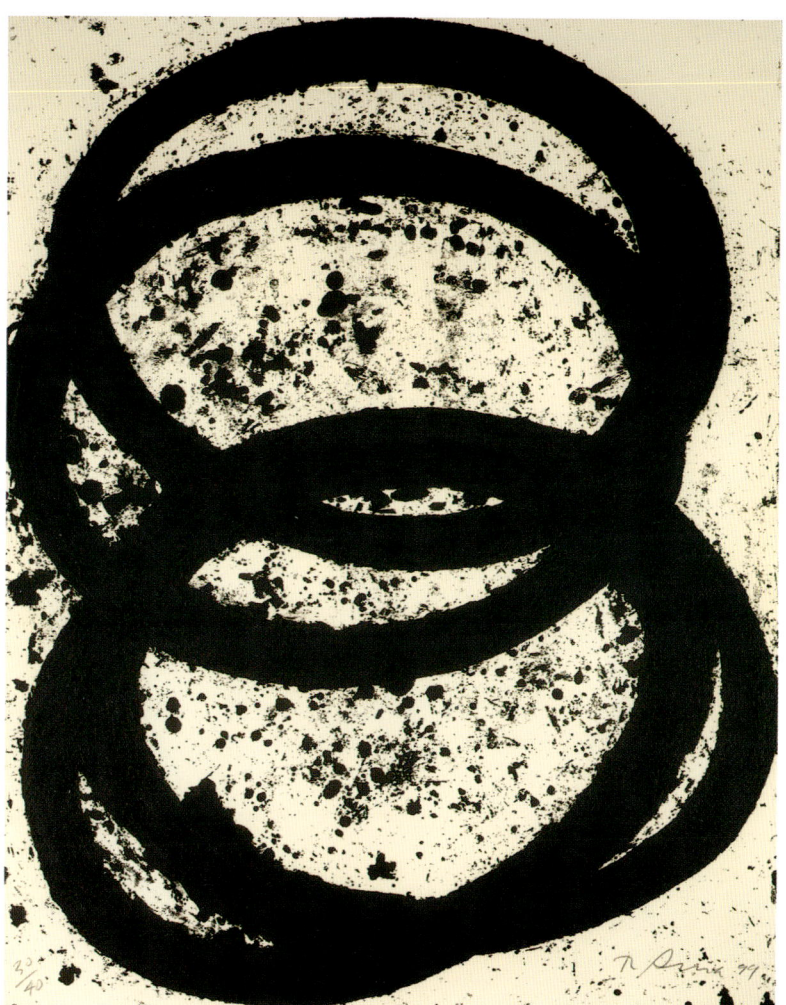

I have never tried to make illustrations of apartheid, but the drawings and the films are certainly spawned by, and feed off, the brutalized society left in its wake. I am interested in a political art . . . an art of ambiguity, contradiction, uncompleted gestures and uncertain endings . . . in which optimism is kept in check and nihilism kept at bay. —William Kentridge

William Kentridge | South African, born 1955 | **Walking Man** | 2000 | Linocut on rice paper | 99 3/8 x 40 1/8 inches | Museum Purchase, The Kathleen Boone Samuels Memorial Fund, 2000.105

Kentridge, perhaps the most widely exhibited contemporary South African artist, is known internationally for handmade animated films based on his charcoal drawings. Kentridge has also made prints since the beginning of his career. Although *Walking Man* is a linocut rather than a woodcut, its stark contrast and strong cuts and gouges recall Northern Renaissance and German Expressionist images.

Kentridge sets the striding figure in a barren industrial landscape that suggests the outskirts of his native Johannesburg. He offers few clues about the figure's race or social status, although the branches sprouting from the man's head and hands suggest transformation, perhaps reflecting the transitional state of South African society.

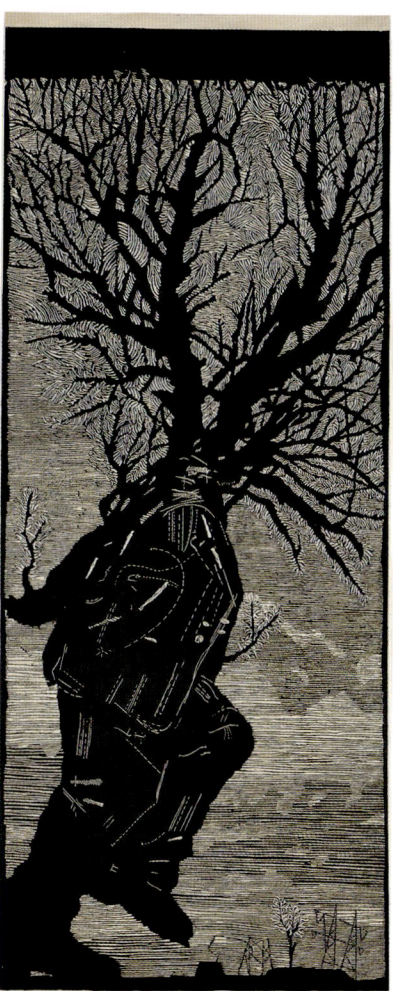

I'm very interested in . . . recognizing all of the layers of meaning that a very simple gesture can have, without feeling like I need to put closure around it being any one of those. — Ann Hamilton

Ann Hamilton ǀ American, born 1956 ǀ **commute 1** ǀ 2001 ǀ Iris print on watercolor paper ǀ 34 1/8 x 46 1/2 inches Gift of Page and Sandy Bond, Heyn and Sandy Kjerulf, and Henrietta Near, 2002.537

Hamilton works primarily in installation art, creating temporary structures that immerse viewers in visual, tactile, and auditory environments. She also makes sculptures, photographs, prints, and videos that build on her installations' themes: routine and primal activities such as speaking, eating, writing, and seeing.

commute 1 is an ink-jet print made from a photograph. It shows horsehair bristling from within the artist's mouth, transforming one sensory organ into another: the dark oral cavity reads also as an empty eye socket. This disruption of expectations creates a "state of between-ness" that Hamilton has termed her overall subject. In the process, the work represents one definition of the word "commute"—to change, or to exchange one thing for another—and conveys the visceral nature of Hamilton's installations.

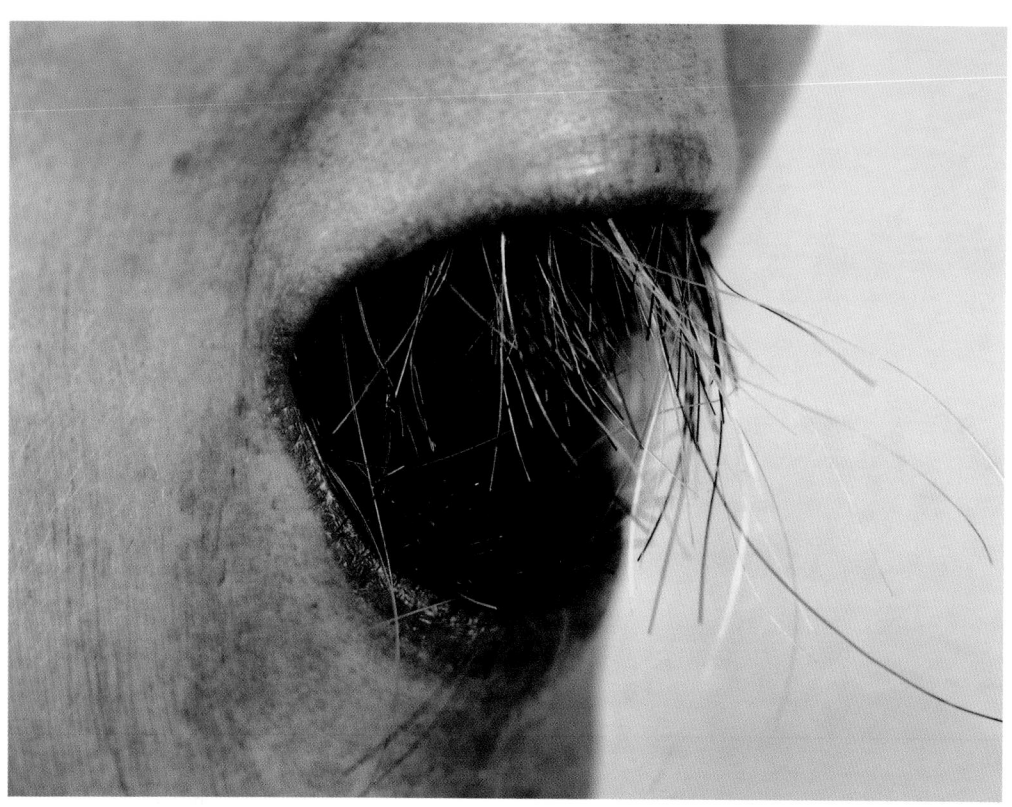

Our history of defeat and loss sets us apart from other Americans and because of it, we embrace the Proustian concept that the only true paradise is a lost paradise. —Sally Mann

Sally Mann ⎪ American, born 1951 ⎪ **Jessie #34** ⎪ 2004 ⎪ Gelatin silver print ⎪ 50 x 40 inches ⎪ Museum Purchase, The Arthur and Margaret Glasgow Fund, 2006.13

Mann's Southern identity has always fueled her art. In her painterly, gestural, and sometimes nearly abstract photographs of the Deep South, of Civil War battlefields, and of her immediate family in and around their Virginia home, Mann raises a deliberately regional perspective to universal significance. Here, the obsolete nineteenth-century photographic process that Mann uses—collodion wet plate— becomes alchemy, yielding an image at once timeless and overtly time-bound.

Despite the large scale of *Jessie #34* (Jessie is Mann's oldest daughter), the face exceeds the frame. Breakdowns of the image at the top and bottom, and vertical fissures on Jessie's cheek, emphasize the photograph's physical nature and also suggest time's ravages.

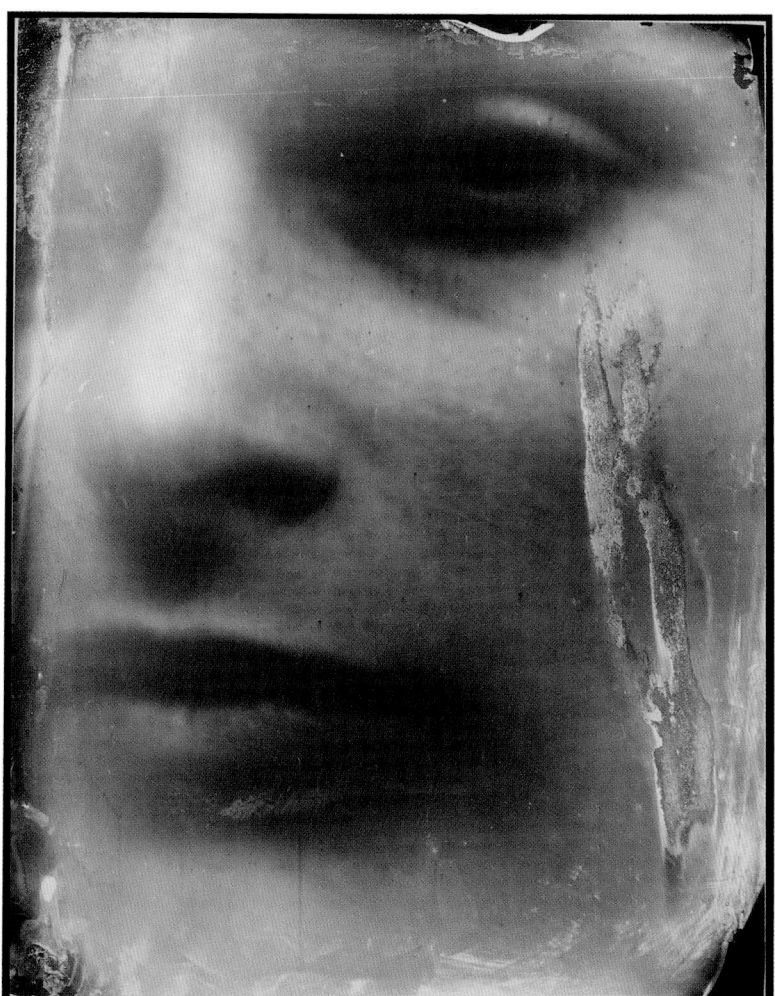

Artists Index

Image Credits

Every effort has been made to trace copyright holders; any errors or omissions are inadvertent and will be corrected in subsequent editions upon notification in writing to the publisher. Unless otherwise noted, all art is reproduced by permission of the artist or estate of the artist.

Photography Credits

Photo by Jan Kosmowski on page 147.

Photo provided by Eggleston Artistic Trust, courtesy Cheim and Read, on page 201.

Photos by Travis Fullerton on pages 87, 117, 127, 155, 185, and 231.

Photos by VMFA Staff on pages 3–7, 11–13, 21–23, 29, 33–35, 39, 43–47, 51, 61–65, 73–79, 119–121, 125, 129–131, 141–145, 151, 163, 191, 197–199, 203, 207–209, and 215.

All other photography by Katherine Wetzel.